Witness Against History

YOMI BRAESTER

Witness Against History

LITERATURE, FILM,

AND PUBLIC DISCOURSE

IN TWENTIETH-CENTURY

CHINA

Stanford University Press, Stanford, California   2003

Stanford University Press
Stanford, California
© 2003 by the Board of Trustees of the
Leland Stanford Junior University
Printed in the United States of America

Library of Congress Cataloging-in-Publication Data

Braester, Yomi
    Witness against history : literature, film, and public discourse in twentieth-century China / Yomi Braester.
        p. cm.
    Includes bibliographical references and index.
    ISBN 0-8047-4792-x (alk. paper).
        1. Chinese literature—20th century—History and criticism.   2. Motion pictures—China.   I. Title: Literature, film, and public discourse in twentieth-century China.   II. Title

PL2303.B73   2003
895.1'09005—dc21   2003004562
                                                                              CIP

This book is printed on acid-free, archival quality paper.

Original printing 2003
Last figure below indicates year of this printing:
12   11   10   09   08   07   06   05   04   03

Designed and typeset at Stanford University Press in 10/13 Minion

Acknowledgments

When I conceived the outline of this study, eight years ago, the link between Comparative Literature and China Studies was still tenuous, and in the process of writing, I had to come to terms with the fault lines between the two disciplines. It was therefore especially fortunate to find many scholars and friends who shared my conviction that the line drawn between literary analysis and China research is only a matter of academic convenience. Michael Holquist and Leo Ou-fan Lee advised me on the current project during its inception as a Ph.D. dissertation. In them and in David Der-wei Wang, I have found not only teachers and sources of inspiration but also dedicated mentors. I was also privileged to have many distinguished colleagues comment on parts of the manuscript at its various stages, among them Robert Ashworth, Jennifer Bean, Chris Berry, Marshall Brown, Tom Cerbu, Steven Day, Kirk Denton, Shoshana Felman, Andrea Goldman, Nicole Huang, Chris Hamm, Ted Huters, Charles Laughlin, Eugenia Lean, Sylvia Lin, John M. Liu, Chris Lupke, Meng Yue, Erik Sahlin, David Schaberg, Shih Shu-mei, Xiaobing Tang, Edna Tow, Sophie Volpp, Frederic Wakeman, Ban Wang, Wen-hsin Yeh, Paula Zamperini, John Zou, and anonymous readers of the manuscript and parts of it previously published as articles. I have truly cherished their help and concrete suggestions. My studies were assisted by generous grants from the China Times Cultural Foundation, the Pacific Cultural Foundation, the National Chinese Library Center for Chinese Studies (ROC), Yale University, the Center for Chinese Studies at UC–Berkeley, and the University of Georgia.

I thank Andrew Jones, Iris Wachs, and the staff at the Beijing Film Archives and the Chinese Taipei Film Archive for facilitating access to archival and other rare material. The publication of this book owes much to the encouragement and patience of Helen Tartar of Stanford University Press. I would also like to thank heartily Gossamer Kuik, my research assistant, and the Stanford University Press editors, Peter Dreyer, John Feneron, and Muriel Bell.

My gratitude to my parents, who brought me to the gates of knowledge, my many teachers who helped me walk through them, and my wife, Michelle

Liu, an attentive and reassuring reader, who has helped me at every stage of this project.

Parts of this book have been published previously. Part of Chapter 2 appeared as "Modern Identity and Karmic Retribution in Clara Law's *Reincarnations of Golden Lotus*," *Asian Cinema* 10, no. 1 (Fall 1998): 58–61; a version of Chapter 3 appeared as "Revolution and Revulsion: Ideology, Monstrosity and Phantasmagoria in Ma-Xu Weibang's Film *Song at Midnight*," *Modern Chinese Literature and Culture* 12, no. 1 (Spring 2000): 81–114; a version of Chapter 7 appeared in Chinese as "Taiwan rentong yu jiyi de weiji: Jiang hou de mitai gushi" (Taiwanese identity and the crisis of memory: Post-Chiang mystery), in *Shuxie Taiwan: Wenxueshi, houzhimin yu houxiandai* (Writing Taiwan: Literary history, postcolonialism, and postmodernism), ed. Zhou Yingxiong and Liu Jihui (Taipei: Maitian, 2000), pp. 233–52; and a version of Chapter 9 appeared as "Memory at a Standstill: 'Street-Smart History' in Jiang Wen's *In the Heat of the Sun*," *Screen* (Oxford University Press) 42, no. 4 (winter 2001): 350–62.

Contents

(3 pages of illustrations follow page 94)

Preface

"Texts are always written in ink. What is written in blood is still nothing more than traces of blood," Lu Xun writes,[1] reacting, like the other authors I examine in this book, against the belief that literature draws its authority from a purportedly direct contact with reality. The notion of "writing with one's blood" expresses the impulse to prove that the writer was present at the time and place where the things described happened, yet there is inevitably a gap between being a witness and bearing witness. For Lu Xun, the bloody display of affect amounts to affectation, the pretense that writing can reproduce reality. He warns that if writing tries to make a claim to reality by substituting blood for ink, the urgency of the text may give way to pathos; even worse, the words may be reduced to illegible blots. The power of writing, Lu Xun implies, stems precisely from the chasm between the text and what it represents, and draws on ambiguity and paradox. Words look sharper in ink, and only by using ink can they assert a distance from the blood-red traces of the real.

Ignoring Lu Xun's admonition, twentieth-century Chinese writers have often sanctified testimony as a direct link to reality. Little distinction has been made between authors wielding their pens and activists who have at times literally written letters and manifestos with fingers dipped in blood to show their conviction and devotion. I distinguish in this book, however, between two fundamentally dissimilar forms of testimony, which may be called bearing witness *for* history and witness *against* history. The first is evident in the words of those—party ideologues and social critics alike—who have spoken in the name of "history" to evoke a sense of events as tangible and purpose-driven. A famous example is the analogy, made in the 1988 TV series *Heshang* (River elegy), between the flow of the Yellow River and "the fate of history."[2] The author of reportage literature Liu Binyan, who proclaimed in 1986 that "human blood isn't rouge," further exemplifies those who emphasize the sense of unmediated reality that Lu Xun was trying to avoid.[3] The use of the figure of history in twentieth-century texts as a reference to the real, a practice Ann Anagnost refers to as "making history speak," has been well documented and persuasively analyzed.[4] I shall focus in this book on the other form of testimony, namely, bearing witness against history. A preponderance of authors have stated or implied that writing can neither reconstitute historical evidence nor demonstrate the significance of events within a larger historical order of things. Moreover, in claiming that writing is divorced from "history" (understood as the sign of reality, progress, and national destiny), the authors challenge their own capacity to bear witness. *Bearing witness against history perforce becomes bearing witness against testimony itself.*

This book rereads milestones in twentieth-century Chinese literature and cinema, as well as the narratives woven around them. The story of modern Chinese literature has often been told in terms of the emergence of texts that assert their historical mission to redeem the nation. At the time they were written, the works were often ascribed the role of tools for saving the Chinese people, which led later critics to neglect an equally important aspect of them, namely, that many of these texts question their own capacity to change the nation's fate. Instead of taking the authors' agendas at face value, I look at the textual dynamics that often belie the works' claims to historical agency. Rather than heralding national redemption and the coming of History, the texts I examine point out that historical consciousness cannot ensure the author's position as a witness, and that writing is part of a dysfunctional discourse. Many works, including those canonized for their faith in the power of the word and the image, have also implied their own limitations. The ostensible self-confidence with which writers and filmmakers have presented their art has often been a façade behind which they fashioned their work as a discourse in crisis. Beneath the utopian streak lies a programmatic critique and a dystopian drive.

In terms familiar to China scholars, I propose to rewrite some of the prevailing conceptions about the May Fourth movement and its legacy. The intellectual agenda of the late 1910s and early 1920s, named after the student demonstrations on May 4, 1919, called for a literary revolution that would change society and usher China into an age of enlightenment. Ever since the introduction of these terms, Chinese authors have had to situate their work in relation to this vision. Recently, excellent studies have shown that alongside May Fourth, other literary trends, commanding large readerships, addressed different aesthetic sensibilities. Leo Ou-fan Lee has emphasized the importance of "decadent literature," and David Der-wei Wang discerns "repressed modernities" pushed aside by May Fourth.[5] I suggest, however, that the resistance to the ideals associated with May Fourth came, not only from parallel literary drives, but also from inside the very works identified with the movement or paying tribute to it. The more upbeat platform proclaimed in prefaces and essays has often blinded critics to artists' implicit doubts and to the inner contradictions conveyed in literary texts.

That the works discussed here have consistently been placed within the accounts construed by programmatic manifestos demonstrates the need for a reading based on literary dynamics. The study of non-Western literature and film has largely tended toward an "area studies" approach, privileging paradigms taken from the social sciences. In focusing on production data, readers' reception of works, and literature as a reflection of national and transnational sociopolitical and economic trends, scholars have often neglected the inner resistance and conflicting messages within specific texts. Literature differs from other forms of discourse in its emphasis on the texture of the text. How things are said is just as important as what is said—if not more important. An emphasis on the literary nature of writing—which I define broadly to refer to a variety of texts, from fiction to drama and film, including both verbal and visual articulation—reveals ambiguities and undecided agendas.

Acknowledging the prevalence of the attitude I call writing against history has important implications for how we view modernity. The literary and filmic works at hand have often criticized narratives that see modernity as the realization of national, revolutionary, or other historical drives. Most conspicuously, they question the idea of the public sphere. Jürgen Habermas has famously argued that the rise of the modern bourgeoisie was accompanied by the emergence of a civil society based on a public domain of debate.[6] Yet the crisis of testimony in twentieth-century Chinese texts challenges the notion of a space of discussion that sustains critical witness. The witness against history reveals the concept of a beneficial public debate to be unfounded.

The idea that a space may materialize to provide an ideal conduit for debate has been conjured up by visionaries looking beyond the actual social conditions in twentieth-century China. Thinkers have been lured by the specter of a society that would contain mechanisms for unhindered and effective communication, and this conception has determined the logic of searching for a modern China and remembering its past. Chinese reformers, from those citing Rousseau in the first decades of the century to contemporary ones paying homage to Habermas, have looked for a model of interaction that would ensure the resilience of Chinese society. Meanwhile, many critics have been on the lookout for a civil society to validate universal models of social development paralleling Western patterns. The recent attempt of concerned scholars prompted by the events of spring 1989 to assess the chances of democracy in what might be interpreted as a nascent public sphere deserves special notice.[7]

Yet throughout the twentieth century, the exchange of ideas has been de-limited by the obstacles to expression that Michel Foucault invokes with the term "discursive practices," or, in short, "discourse." Public discourse has proved less conducive to social and political change than reformers and scholars had hoped. The upheavals that China has witnessed have rarely im-plemented ideas promoted through civic debate. I leave it for historians and social scientists to point out the material circumstances and specific mecha-nisms of interaction that short-circuited the connection between reformist thinking and political action. Neither do I aim at examining the validity in the Chinese context of the Habermasian model of developing a public sphere. I set out rather from a broad definition of public discourse, conducted mainly through print and mass media, and aimed at forming functional though nec-essarily imagined communities, and examine the literature that took part in that debate.

I focus on works by prominent authors, including many texts considered milestones in their genre. The novels and short stories have been widely anthologized and even translated into English (see the following Note on Translations). The films have all won critical acclaim and are often cited as representative of their period, even though not many have been distributed outside China. The texts and films reviewed cover the entire twentieth cen-tury, with emphasis on the mainland, but drawing also on works from Hong Kong and Taiwan. While I do not pretend to offer a comprehensive history of modern Chinese literature and film, the book's broad scope allows a re-evaluation of the ideological constructions that have overarched the twenti-eth century.

As a whole, the book traces the changing perception of the relationship between literature and history in various times and places in twentieth-century China. It is with some irony that I set out to write the history of a lit-erary corpus that questions historical narratives. Yet the texts consciously mark a tradition to be followed and establish their own history. As each work refers to its predecessors, modern Chinese fiction writes itself backward, reading new meanings into earlier pieces. This elective history has resisted official histories. The texts conjure up a version of "modern Chinese litera-ture" that questions the nature of their own modernity, Chineseness, and lit-erariness. These terms are left unstable and fragile, in need of constant justi-fication.

Note on Translations

To stress specific textual dynamics, I have as a rule used my own translations. Many of the texts, however, are available in English, and these are listed below in the order in which they are discussed.

Lu Xun, preface to *Outcry* and "Diary of a Madman":
—"Preface to *Call to Arms*" and "A Madman's Diary." In *Lu Xun: Selected Works*. Trans. Yang Xianyi and Gladys Yang, pp. 33–38; 39–51. Beijing: Foreign Languages Press, 1985.
—"Preface" and "Diary of a Madman." In *Diary of a Madman and Other Stories*. Trans. William A. Lyell, pp. 21–28; 29–41. Honolulu: University of Hawai'i Press, 1990.

Ouyang Yuqian, *Pan Jinlian*:
—Ou-yang Yü-Ch'ien. *P'an Chin-lien*. In *Twentieth-Century Chinese Drama: An Anthology*, ed. Edward Gunn, pp. 52–75. Bloomington: Indiana University Press, 1983.

Wei Minglun, *Pan Jinlian: The History of a Woman's Downfall*:
—*Pan Jinlian: The History of a Fallen Woman*. Trans. David Williams and Xiaoxia Williams. In *Theater and Society: An Anthology of Contemporary Chinese Drama*, ed. Haiping Yan, pp. 123–188. Armonk, N.Y.: M. E. Sharpe, 1998.

The Red Lantern:
—*The Red Lantern: A Modern Revolutionary Peking Opera*. Revised collectively by the China Peking Opera Troupe. May 1970 script. Peking: Foreign Languages Press, 1972.

Zhang Xianliang, *My Bodhi Tree*:
—*Grass Soup*. Trans. Martha Avery. Boston: David R. Godine, 1995.
—*My Bodhi Tree*. Trans. Martha Avery. London: Secker & Warburg, 1996.

Liu Daren, "Azaleas Cry Out Blood":
—Liu Ta-jen. "Azaleas Wept Blood." Trans. Nicholass Koss. In *Death in a Cornfield and Other Stories from Contemporary Taiwan*, ed. Ching-hsi Perng and Chiu-Kuei Wang, pp. 23–47. Hong Kong: Oxford University Press, 1994.

Chen Yingzhen, "Mountain Path":
—Chen Ying-chen. "Mountain Path." Trans. Nicholass Koss. In *Death in a Cornfield and Other Stories from Contemporary Taiwan*, ed. Ching-hsi Perng and Chiu-Kuei Wang, pp. 1–22. Hong Kong: Oxford University Press, 1994.

Yu Hua, "Past and Punishment":
—"The Past and the Punishments." In *The Past and the Punishments*, trans. Andrew F. Jones, pp. 114–31. Honolulu: University of Hawai'i Press, 1996.

Abbreviations

ACB Liu Daren. "Dujuan ti xue" (Azaleas cry out blood). In Liu Daren. *Dujuan ti xue*, pp. 153–92. Taipei: Yuanjing chubanshe, 1984.

HWD Wei Minglun. *Pan Jinlian—Yige nüren de chenlun shi* (Pan Jinlian: History of a woman's downfall). In *Pan Jinlian—Yige nüren de chenlun shi*, pp. 1–66. Harbin: Beifang wenyi chubanshe, 1987.

LXZPQJ Lu Xun. *Lu Xun zuopin quanji* (The complete works of Lu Xun). Taipei: Fengyun shidai, 1992.

MBT Zhang Xianliang. *Wo de putishu* (My bodhi tree). Beijing: Zuojia chubanshe, 1994.

MP Chen Yingzhen. "Shanlu" (Mountain path). In *Chen Yingzhen zuopin ji* (Collected works of Chen Yingzhen), 5: 37–66. Taipei: Renjian, 1988.

P&P Yu Hua. "Wangshi yu xingfa" (Past and punishment). In Yu Hua. *Xiaji taifeng* (Summer typhoon), pp. 41–64. Taipei: Yuanliu, 1993.

PJL Ouyang Yuqian. *Pan Jinlian*. In *Ouyang Yuqian quanji* (Complete works of Ouyang Yuqian), 1: 55–91. Shanghai: Shanghai wenyi chubanshe, 1990.

SHQZ Shi Nai'an and Luo Guanzhong (attributed). *Shuihu quanzhuan* (The complete *Water margin*). Taipei: Wannianqing shudian, 1971.

Witness Against History

Introduction

Critical Discourse in Twentieth-Century China

The concept of "bearing witness against history" is counterintuitive—the authority of testimony usually derives from the witness's knowledge of events and ability to convey their importance. How is it possible to contradict the course of events? Why should one testify against one's experience and thereby undermine one's own place in history? What are the implications of such acts for the collective ethos? To explore these questions, we must first define the uses of "testimony" and "history" and the relationship between the two terms in the critical and historical contexts.

A PARABLE

In *Longxieshu* (The dragon-blood tree, 1992), an autobiographical account of the Cultural Revolution, the film director Chen Kaige tells the following story:

After K was arrested, she was locked for the entire time in a military warehouse in the northern suburbs of Beijing. In her cell, in addition to a table and a bed, there was also a window. The window was nailed shut with large nails, and a newspaper was pasted on the outside of the glass pane. When the sunlight was good, the characters in the newspaper became very clear, like a slide, only the rays were weaker and yellower. The shadows of the trees outside would appear on the window according to the season of the year and the time of day. When she heard the sound of falling leaves, she would know fall had come. In the beginning, she would stand in front of the window and read with interest, surprised that the words were still news. At that time, she did not think about it. Afterwards, she would lie down on her bed and read the newspaper articles, entire paragraphs, including the punctuation marks, from memory. She read in a loud voice, at times jumping out of bed to corroborate and memorize again, until every character was correct. Once she suddenly stopped and thought about what she was doing and broke into a cold sweat. She wanted to forget the newspaper but eventually saw it in her dream. When she awoke in fright, she did not dare open her eyes, yet she could do nothing but open them. The place where the newspaper was constituted the only source of light. She felt that this was a verdict against her, that her crimes were written all over it.[1]

Although the passage describes a situation typical of China in 1971 and is probably grounded in facts, it is also a rich, compact parable about the relationship between written texts and the act of bearing witness to historical events. K, formerly a party member and a soldier, is no longer among those who set the wheels of history in motion. She ends up set apart from contemporary events and unable to engage in firsthand observation. Her only window on the outside world is an opaque, sealed hatch. Isolated from society for three years, K is restricted to a timeless existence in an enclosed cell, in a camera obscura that eventually reflects only her own thoughts and fears.

K attempts to make sense of the passing of time by looking at the silhouettes of trees on the newspaper, yet time is marked primarily by her changing attitude to the newspaper print. The longer she stays in the cell, the more the written word compels her to regard the newspaper as a meaningful message and to perceive the projected words as a communication from the world outside. The writing calls upon her to read the text and memorize it. It summons her to interpret the newspaper. Even when the text clearly fails to produce any relevant meaning, it still holds K under its spell. By its authority as the only source of light, the newspaper makes her accept the routine of incarceration, until the text comes to seem a verdict, which she starts to believe.

In the hermetic cell (notice how the description neglects to mention any door), the written word carries a false promise of communication. At first, K regards the newspaper as a window on the free world. Gradually she comes to see it as an obstacle, as the cruelest and most inhibiting of the devices that torture her. The newspaper stresses the impenetrability of the walls around her and etches itself on her mind as a mark of sequestration and a sign of persecution. The fact that the writing that comes to torture K takes the form of a newspaper is significant. A newspaper usually associates writing with timely knowledge and with the knowledge of time, but in this case, it is a flawed temporal index. Inasmuch as it does not change, its contents become dated and irrelevant. It is ironic that K is barred from society by a newspaper, the product of modern print culture that disseminates public information and creates a community of readers who share the same knowledge at the same time. Whereas the newspaper may be said to cast the shadows of time onto the present in written form, in K's case the paper projects an image of the meaningless debris of time.

The passage hints at K's fear that, rather than simply failing to communicate the passage of time, the newspaper may in fact convey the situation outside the cell only too well, announcing the arrest of time. Far-fetched as such an anxiety may seem, it should be borne in mind that Mao launched the Cultural Revolution with the explicit purpose of arresting the course of history, to keep the historical dialectic in a state of perpetual revolution. The unchanging newspaper text serves as a symbolic manifestation of history brought to a standstill. The figure of frozen time is further emphasized by the description of the cell as a camera obscura that produces a still image. (The resemblance to filmic technique and cinematic spectacle would not be ignored by the filmmaker Chen Kaige, who stresses that the newspaper resembles a slide.)

Confronted with the nonsensical nature of this motionless spectacle, K reappropriates the newspaper and internalizes it to produce a subjective meaning through mnemonic exercise. Memorizing the newspaper becomes a way of keeping in touch, of claiming a part in the world outside. In the absence of any eventful occurrence to be committed to memory, the memorization becomes a form of experience in itself. Memory too is divested of meaning— once the text has been perfectly memorized, reading is reduced to an orthographic drill. It is at this point that K comes to the nightmarish realization that by clinging to the newspaper, she has been losing touch with reality. The routine of memorization has driven her to a senseless existence, to obsessive repetition bordering on insanity. It is precisely as a timepiece, as a historical record, that the newspaper hampers K's consciousness of the present.

HISTORY AND ALLEGORY

K's story is emblematic of the texts explored in this book and an appropriate introduction to the strategies of reading through which I approach these texts. Read as a parable, the passage highlights the tension between writing and communicating a timely message. The tropes employed by Chen Kaige appear time and again in twentieth-century texts—the prisoner in a dark, sealed chamber, her loss of a sense of time, and the connection between memory and insanity. These themes question the writer's position as a witness to history and call for a definition of the terms of inquiry.

The first fickle term that needs clarification is "history." In daily use, "history" often denotes the past, tradition, or that which the present has cast behind it. "History" may refer to the written repository of events that have taken place, of what has truly happened. "History" can also mean the course of human civilization through time, perhaps even a progress guided by an immanent force. My argument, that modern Chinese literature has often borne witness against history, is informed by all of these meanings of "history" (which are also invoked by the equivalent Chinese word, *lishi*).

Perhaps the most unassuming definition of history is also the most difficult to reconcile with the objective of the present study. If history is the record of events and an index of reality, how can it be affected by fiction? Literature, one might argue, belongs to a separate realm and cannot challenge history. There are many possible responses to this reservation: some may raise doubts about the veracity of the records; others may cite the laxer historiographical standards prevailing in different times and places.[2] In this study, however, I pursue yet another aspect of the relationship between fact and fiction, namely, the fact that even nonfictional reports can be read allegorically. K's story, which is both an autobiographical narrative and a parable about writing, is a case in point.

The texts examined in this book refer to recorded events, some reported by first-person witnesses, yet I do not regard them as riddles that can be solved and explained away by using a historical key, in the form of reference either to specific events or even to factors that may have helped shape the texts—contemporary material conditions, the authors' social affiliations, or their mental makeup. It is important from the outset to dispel the notion that uncovering a text's factual, "historical" circumstances constitutes a privileged mode of reading. Even when the facts are uncontested, the literal meaning does not exclude simultaneous allegorical interpretations. In approaching Chen Kaige's account, for example, acknowledging the immediate historical reference only reinforces the parabolic reading. The text is never transparent, and neither do the facts speak for themselves. That "history" must be read as a parable is essential to understanding the works I address in this book. They tease the reader by evoking factual events and social reality, yet the historical specificity is belied by the texts' constant recourse to allegory. Moreover, the texts often anticipate that the less literal layer will be ignored and that they will be betrayed by readers scavenging for historical details. The reader must be attentive to these literary turns and resist the temptation of straightforward historicization.

K's story, for all its claim to be nonfiction, highlights the need for reading beyond the factual account. The passage itself foregrounds the theme of unearthing hidden signification—in the small chamber that comprises K's entire world, the shadows cast on the newspaper and the words printed on it become invested with allegorical meaning. She engages in a peculiar hermeneutic project, paying attention to every detail; in her state of experiential deprivation, she is drawn to interpretive excess. Moreover, Chen's narrative acquires a parabolic quality as it resonates with well-known literary texts. The depiction of the cell, nailed shut and hermetically sealed, bears a resemblance to a key text in modern Chinese fiction, namely, Lu Xun's parable of the iron chamber, discussed in Chapter 1. Chen's description of the shadows reaching into the dark cell reworks Plato's parable of the cave, which characterizes phenomena as shadows cast by an unseen source of light and urges humanity to face the ideas beyond appearances.[3] The parable at hand, however, is more of a Borges-like variation that blurs the borderline between reality and illusion. For K, both waking and dreaming become equally horrifying; the newspaper haunts her whether her eyes are open or shut. The passage stresses the unresolved paradox of K's existence, wavering forever between the illusion of being-in-time and a reality where time has stopped altogether.

The episode evokes the nightmarish stories of Franz Kafka, which had coincidentally been introduced to Chinese readership, together with the writings of Jorge Luis Borges, just before the publication of Chen Kaige's *The Dragon-blood Tree* (see Chapter 8). The protagonist's name, K, is also used by Kafka and bears a similar symbolic value. Like her namesake, the protagonist in Kafka's *The Trial*, K wakes up to face absurd accusations. Her logic proves inadequate in dealing with the uncanny world that closes in on her. K's name, abbreviated to a single Roman letter, stands as a firm sign of the allegorical dimension of her story. Chen explains the provenance of K's full name (chosen to commemorate the victory of the allied forces in North Africa in 1944),[4] but never discloses it. Instead, he comments abstractly on the name's revolutionary connotations. K's name, real as it may be, is marked with ideological significance from the start. The name gains further allegorical weight since, as in Kafka's case, the letter K could also be an oblique reference to the author's name.

The similarity between Chen Kaige's text and Kafka's stories should warn the reader against translating Chen's description into a direct historical reference. Sinology must not fall into the trap of what Milan Kundera derogatorily terms "Kafkology," the critical attempt to identify concrete allusions for parabolic metaphors.[5] Instead, K's story signals the excess of historical representation, overflowing with meanings to the point of paradoxically making testimony inadequate. A witness to real and painful events may find herself, like K, trying to make sense of fleeting shadows. She can never know for sure whether she is looking out of a window, observing a diaphanous screen, or facing an opaque barrier. We should allow for the paradox that in order to stay close to reality, the account may depart from the facts and take parabolic form. Like K herself, the reader remains suspended between the temptation to discern external events and the compelling urgency of subjective hallucinations. Literature, as an allegorical mode of interpretation, bears witness against history's claim to monopolize reality.

TRAUMA AND THE REPRESENTATION OF TIME

The problem raised by reading K's story as an allegory is stressed by the fact that the events described in the passage, as in the other works examined in this book, involve physical violence and mental torture. When the texts describe incarceration, executions, torture, famine, and massacre, they cannot be extricated from the immediate social and political circumstances. Hannah Arendt remarks that "the twentieth century . . . has become indeed, as Lenin predicted, a century of wars and revolutions, hence a century of that violence that is currently believed to be their common denominator."[6] China's twentieth century was markedly brutal, and its literary works are clearly rooted in that history of hard facts. How, then, can these same texts engage in a testimony against history? Is it not incumbent upon the critic to stress the incidents that have given these texts their urgency? Is it not that allegorical readings ignore, if not deny, the events, thereby becoming complicit with the revisionism that is already at large?

Political scientists and the testimony of the survivors of cataclysmic events alike privilege wars, revolutions, and famines as the punctuation of recorded history. This idea relies on the assumption that records of the past can be stored in a retrievable condition. Historians may immediately note the flaws of archives, but a more fundamental problem is that human memory resists straightforward recording of violent events. Testimony is hampered by the shocking and at the same time numbing effect of violence. On the one hand, violent narratives may point to the unmediated experience of what hurts most. Modern Chinese literature has often used bodily pain as evidence of the reality of the narrators' experience and the truthfulness of their stories.[7] On the other hand, violence can also denote the events' immunity to description. At the psychological and social levels, violence cannot be processed as an event with specific temporal parameters. Extreme events cannot be committed to memory, because they disintegrate one's psychological makeup, break down linguistic skills, and collapse social bonds. In this respect, violence accentuates and amplifies the discrepancy between history and its representation, between fact and fiction. By referring to violence, the works examined in this book foreground precisely the gap that makes the real inaccessible to words. They draw attention not only to the events but also to linguistic strategies for circumventing what has taken place.

Although I focus on violence of historical magnitude, the disrupting effects of violence do not include large-scale cataclysm alone. The theologian Emanuel Lévinas has gone as far as to state that one's very existence constitutes an act of violence. Lévinas contends that violence results from the painful realization that one necessarily exists in relation to others, and that there is only a blurry border between one's self and that which cannot be reduced to oneself. Violence, by this definition, is the challenge to the basic assumption that one is the same as oneself.[8] Infliction of physical pain and mental abuse are instances of violence because they point out how brittle one's identity is. The menace is not only posed to one's physical survival; far more harmful is the threat to one's identity with oneself, to the assumption that I am always I. This formulation explains why violence is always subjective and how it can be perceived as a menace to individual as well as collective identity. Violence also includes the experience of totalitarianism and bigotry, and even rapid changes in material culture and shifts of critical paradigms, since all of these challenge a fundamental sense of identity, dare one to think that the I and the other can be the same, and blur the boundaries of one's autonomous being in space and time.

Psychoanalysis is quick to note that when violence translates to mental trauma, it is repressed and becomes inaccessible to the victim, as well as to later records. In Freud's view, trauma is never perceived in real time. Often it is long after the originary event that the mental wound returns to haunt the mind and repeats itself in nightmares, hallucinations, and physical disorders.[9] Although trauma survivors may not be able to express the moment of violence—often they cannot even remember it—it perpetuates itself in disguised forms. The predicament of K, who rereads the same newspaper time and again, regardless of its diminishing relevance, each day anew, as if it were today's, illustrates such post-traumatic dislocation of her injury. Trauma exists only in displaced manifestations, in what may be called the psyche's parables of violence. In view of the traumatic distortion of time, it is precisely the pursuit of historical reality that undermines linear, "historical" time.

Traumatic effects are key to understanding the distance between history and representation, but not because they point to an originary event that explains the testimony that follows. On the contrary, the allusion to trauma reveals the unintelligibility of the past and, most important, the breakdown of narratives that would clarify the course of history and make sense of it. Cathy Caruth notes: "For history to be a history of trauma means . . . that a history can be grasped only in the very inaccessibility of its occurrence."[10] Moreover, while trauma is necessarily experienced by the individual, it is often perceived, not only as a rupture in personal time, but also as a blow that affects the history of the collective. Freud, in observing the consequences of World War I, noted the transformation of trauma into a social symptom. He comments on how war "tears up all bonds of community among the warring peoples and threatens to leave behind an embitterment that will make any renewal of these bonds impossible for a long time to come."[11] (Note Freud's own temporally dislocated voice, writing while the war is still raging, yet as if he had seen the end of the war.) The quick transition from personal suffering to historically irreparable damage to society is implied in the Chinese texts at hand too. They blur the line between personal trauma and collective crisis and emphasize the violence against social structures. The plots abound with breached understandings, legal transgressions, and dysfunctional communities, and through these themes, the texts question collective memory and historical narratives. "History" becomes no more than the collective articulation of trauma.

The temporal dislocation of testimony and its fundamental conflict with historical parameters comes to the fore when literature claims to have survived collective trauma. Theodor Adorno, writing in the wake of the Holocaust, famously claims that "[a]fter Auschwitz, it is no longer possible to write poems."[12] Adorno's statement is important precisely because it is evident that poems were in fact written during and after World War II. As Jean-François Lyotard comments, if the claim is to be read otherwise than as a burst of tasteless pathos, Adorno's words must be understood within a specific construction of experience and language. Lyotard points to the Hegelian underpinnings that qualify experience as an act of consciousness and that require self-awareness as a precondition to linguistic expression of that experience. If "Auschwitz" stands not only for a Nazi death camp but also for a negation of experience, it is because no verbal testimony, poetic or otherwise, can capture it.[13] These philosophical distinctions might seem foreign to a discussion of Chinese literature, yet I shall argue later that a post-traumatic dynamics have crucially informed the texts at hand. They have been construed as testimonies enunciated "after" the fact. In this sense, too, they bear witness against history—they are necessarily deferred, giving the lie to a view of history that seamlessly integrates violence into a coherent temporal narrative.

The texts I examine exemplify always belated testimonies, written after the event and around it, in parabolic form. The factual events are inaccessible to the present narrator and can be described only in terms of their aftermath. There is symbolic significance to the fact that many trends in twentieth-century Chinese literature are known by the violent events that preceded them. May Fourth literature (named after May 4, 1919) lasted into the 1920s; "resisting Japan" literature and film (about the 1937–45 war) had their heyday in the late 1940s and 1950s; the Cultural Revolution (1967–76) produced little literature at the time, but was described in hindsight by the scar literature of the 1980s; more recent trends are known as post-Chiang, post-Mao, and post-Deng (in Xiaobin Yang's coinage, the postmodern post-Mao-Deng).[14] Critical hindsight is compounded by a sense of temporal displacement.

EXPERIENCE AND HISTORICAL CONSCIOUSNESS

The texts at hand do not, however, limit themselves to representing trauma and providing evidence of the narrators' dislocation. It would be too simplistic to regard modern Chinese literature as a reaction to a series of traumas. Instead, the texts often use post-traumatic testimony as a hinge for reversing time and speaking against the grain of a predestined "history." In other words, rather than express the witness's helplessness in face of temporal displacement, testimony may force open questions relating to one's responsibility as an agent of history.

Psychoanalysts have noted with respect to the role of the witness that testimony is far from passive; it involves one's willful return to the moment of trauma, at the cost of repeating it. Jacques Lacan explores the process in his discussion of the dream of the burning child. Freud's *The Interpretation of Dreams* tells of a father who was sleeping in the room next to that in which lay the corpse of his recently deceased child, who whispered to him in a dream, "Father, don't you see I'm burning?" whereupon he woke up to find that a candle had in fact scorched the dead child's clothes. Lacan addresses the paradox of awakening, namely, that by leaving the dream, the father is forced to reexperience the traumatic loss of the child, who has just been revived in the dream. Yet the father chooses to wake up, because by acting of his own will, he asserts responsiveness to the needs of the child, whether dreamed or real. As Cathy Caruth observes, Lacan foregrounds the fact that the traumatic repetition becomes an ethical act, an act of testifying to having lost one's son and survived the trauma.[15] Only by treating the dead as part of the present and disregarding temporal parameters can one assert one's testimony.

A similar implicit recognition that displacement can be an empowering act is found in K's story. K is trapped between a violent reality and an abusive hallucination in the form of the newspaper, the sight of which drives her insane. Although opening her eyes forces K to see the newspaper that both symbolizes and augments her distress, she feels compelled to do so. K can choose to close her eyes and remain in the middle ground between dream and awakening, but she prefers to open her eyes and confront the nightmare of full awakening. Only by seeing can she bear witness to her condition. She puts herself back into the absurdity of her cell to testify to her displacement. That K opens her eyes reflects an ethical choice to remain aware of the present rather than deny her experience. As such, K's story may also illustrate the relationship between bearing witness and historical consciousness. Fashioning testimony as an ethical response to trauma depends on the premise that one's existence derives a moral dimension from being aware of one's experiences, of one's position as a witness—and yet, it is in bearing witness to one's own testimony that one acknowledges one's experience as fundamentally untestifiable.[16]

Herein lies an unresolved paradox—a witness *against* history cannot exist without paying tribute to the witness *for* history. Arguing against one's agency within a historical narrative must acknowledge the hope that such agency allows. Even if "history" is presented as an artificial way of organizing the past and an imperfect plan for the future, the witness against history cannot ignore the importance of human intent and will. The relationship between the two kinds of witness to history is dialectical. The responsibility of the witness consists in being aware of one's place in history, whether "history" denotes the process of humanity's self-realization or a critique of such a positive narrative.

What is at stake in bearing witness against history, then, is nothing less than the significance of human will in shaping the course of humankind and the meaning of modernity within that scheme. Conceiving history as an expression of human will and, more specifically, defining modernity in terms of humanity's consciousness of its place in history can be traced back to Immanuel Kant's 1784 essay "What Is Enlightenment?" ("Was ist Auf-klärung?").[17] Michel Foucault paraphrases Kant's quest thus: "[W]hat is our actuality: what is happening today? What is happening right now? And what is this *right now* we all are in which defines the moment at which I am writing?"[18] In this view, modernity entails a double recognition: first, that one's actions are determined by one's unique place in human evolution; second, that being aware of one's historical position privileges the present and allows one to direct the course of history. For the European *Aufklärer*, History—now often capitalized to distinguish the Enlightenment's understanding of the term from a mere parade of senseless events—constitutes the move-ment—and positive progress—toward humanity's "maturity" (to recall Kant's definition of the Enlightenment), spiritual freedom (the Hegelian grand narrative), or the resolution of material dialectics (Marxist redemp-tion). As Hayden White notes, history is inevitably "emplotted" and told by structuring time into end-driven narratives.[19] The Enlightenment's narratives of progress, however, created dubious metanarratives, which the witness against history calls into question.

REASON AND CRITIQUE

The Kantian view of modernity, modified by later thinkers, has led many to bask in the glory of humanity's progress and declare it the best possible scheme, the outcome of history's advance toward absolute Reason. This formulation has been made infamous by the chauvinism of Hegel's *Philoso-phy of History* and the racism of social Darwinism. On the other hand, it was also Kant's *Third Critique*, in discussing the sublime, that identified the lim-its of Reason. As Horkheimer and Adorno note, "[h]istorically, both the subjective and the objective aspects of Reason have been present from the outset."[20] It may be claimed that the counter-Enlightenment, with its oppo-sition to subjecting human values to universal laws, was inseparable from the original movement and used its values to add an important critical dimen-sion. It was, after all, the Enlightenment dynamics of inquiry that allowed thinkers to observe that social covenants cannot be imbued with intrinsic meaning. In questioning the social construction of historical patterns, bear-ing witness against history inquires into how truths are produced. It becomes akin with the Enlightenment and counter-Enlightenment and launches a "critique" in the sense elicited by Foucault: "the movement by which the subject gives himself the right to question truth on its effects of power and question power on its discourses of truth."[21]

One sign of the critique of Reason is the rethinking of violence. While the more optimistic among the *Aufklärer* envisioned the best of all possible worlds, in which violence would be eliminated, others acknowledged violence as an inevitable drive, a pathological and disruptive force that leads to a dysfunctional community. Twentieth-century Chinese literature abounds with references to mutilation, beheading, cannibalism, and other atrocities as indexes of modernity's failure to bring about humanity's redemption. In the context of bearing witness against history, reference to violence becomes not only a sign of the post-traumatic dislocation and silencing of experience but also the emblem of the false promise of History. In response to the claim that China has arrived at a historically privileged position, witness against history presents modernity as proof of the failure of narratives of progress.

Another aspect of the critique of Reason central to my study is the challenge to language as the vehicle of communication. As soon as the Enlightenment project was launched, the reason of language came into doubt, notably with the publication of Rousseau's *Essai sur l'origine des langues* (translated as *On the Origin of Language*) in 1781. Conceiving of language as a social cohesive would lead to opinions such as those of Habermas, who argues that in the public sphere, the exchange of opinions "serves the transmission and renewal of cultural knowledge."[22] This view, as Foucault and others have pointed out, is utopian and ignores the power relations that affect the circulation of purported truths.[23] Rather than operate in an open sphere, ideas are expressed within what Foucault calls "discourse," that is, a power structure that determines what can be enunciated in a specific setting. As Foucault argues, "discourse is not the majestically unfolding manifestation of a thinking, knowing, speaking subject, but, on the contrary ... a space of exteriority in which a network of distinct sites is deployed."[24] In this book, I use the term "public discourse" to refer to an imperfect space of debate, as a constant reminder that the Habermasian dream of public dialogue is curbed by the limits of discourse. The constraints of public discourse foreground that in a self-reflexive turn, bearing witness against history can ultimately become a critique of witnessing itself.

In its function as a challenge to language, bearing witness against history benefits from being expressed through literary texts rather than programmatic essays. Literature is well poised to advance a critique of linguistic utopia, not only because fiction foregrounds the shortcomings of writing as truthful representation, but also because the inevitable gap between author and readers stresses the opacity of the linguistic medium. "Allegory"—deriving from the Greek for "speaking differently in public"—demonstrates the need to displace speech in the public sphere. The use of allegory and parable is not only the outcome of the impossibility of addressing the historical facts directly; it is also an active strategy for indicating the distance between the real and its representation, or—to use Lu Xun's aforementioned metaphor—between blood and ink. Discursive practices have made it difficult for Chinese intellectuals to voice explicit critiques of the narrative of enlightenment, but literary texts have provided an extradiscursive space for portraying modernity as a condition of crisis.

To return for the last time to K's story, it should be noted that in addition to exemplifying the need to read factual accounts allegorically, the passage quoted is also a parable about giving testimony. More specifically, K's story demonstrates the witness's inability to assert her voice. *The Dragon-blood Tree* continues to describe K in her makeshift prison cell: "She started shouting incessantly in a shrill voice, cursing with rage, until the guard thought that she might have gone mad. When she tried to explain herself, the guard confidently concluded that she had indeed gone mad."[25]

At the heart of K's anxiety is her failure to convey her plight, her inability to shout out from her cell. Any appeal to reason only aggravates the situation. To cry out is mad, yet to rationalize is even more insane. Only she can see the writing on the wall, and no one will listen to her. Her loneliness and fears are those of a witness who cannot communicate the significance of her words to others. As a parable about authorship in modern China, K's story illustrates the despair of knowing the futility of one's testimony even before speaking out. The literary voices examined in this book are fraught with the paradox that speech amounts to speaking against one's reason. Witness against history employs paradox, open-ended narratives, absurd parables, unresolved moral dilemmas, unfinished confessions, and an excess of interpretation, because it mourns the testimonial voice that, together with historical consciousness, is realized and undermined at the same instant. When history becomes no more than the index of erased experience, writing remains the sign of a dysfunctional public discourse.

THE MAY FOURTH MOVEMENT AND THE

ENLIGHTENMENT MODEL OF PUBLIC DISCOURSE

So far I have defined the abstract notions and methodological concerns behind the witness against history. It is time to turn to the specific venues through which historical narratives and their critique were introduced to Chinese thought. The following description of the changing attitudes toward social debate and literary testimony in twentieth-century China provides also an overview of the book.

To trace the practice of bearing witness against history is to go against the grain of major trends in twentieth-century Chinese intellectual history. Since the late nineteenth century, Chinese thinkers had been eager to place China within the perceived historical drive toward a universal Enlightenment. Their utopian vision, fueled by the rhetoric of social Darwinism, saw modernity as the sign of historical redemption. May Fourth writers argued along Hegelian lines that the progress of scientific knowledge and social regulation could save future generations from natural disasters and man-made barbarism. The foundation of a Chinese nation-state in 1912, the mass movements of the 1910s and 1920s, the reunification of China under Mao in 1949, and the Cultural Revolution were all interpreted as the coming of History, the final maturation that would unite human will with an immanent historical drive. The sense that China has found its place in history was especially reassuring considering the strong bias in Kantian thought that identified the West with Reason and contrasted it with "the Orient."[26] Prasenjit Duara draws attention to the way in which striving for a Chinese nation-state framed historical consciousness as the instrument of the nation's survival. Grand narratives were construed in the name of the nation as the subject of history, to justify the brutality of dominant ideologies. The weight of such visions has led Duara to make a plea for "decoupling History and the nation."[27]

Other uncritical tenets of progress, such as the faith in open debate within a rational community, were expressed in equally unwavering terms. The issues of historical consciousness and public discourse were at the focus of the intellectual trends of the late 1910s and 1920s, including the "new thought tide" and the "literary revolution movement," loosely referred to as May Fourth.[28] May Fourth intellectuals expressed belief in scientific knowledge and open political debate, to the point of anthropomorphizing these ideals as "Mr. Science" and "Mr. Democracy." Following the European Enlightenment, May Fourth regarded the dissemination of knowledge as a major factor in the effort to transform social and political structures. The importance of public debate was first broached in Immanuel Kant's aforementioned essay "What Is Enlightenment?" which stated that "the public use of one's reason must always be free, and it alone can bring about enlightenment among men."[29] The belief in the importance of free debate led to the creation of physical meeting places for the exchange of ideas, such as salons and clubs, and, more important, conceptual spaces, such as newspaper columns. These spaces are well known in Habermas's formulation of the public sphere. Setting aside the specific social and institutional particularities of modern Europe addressed by Habermas, a similar idea of public debate emerges as a central concept in Chinese thought. In the first decade of the twentieth century, reformers used budding journalistic enterprises to spread their call for a public exchange of views. The Shanghai daily *Shibao* often called for nurturing "public opinion" (*yulun*) and "freedom of speech" (*yanlun ziyou*).[30] May Fourth thinkers—who saw themselves as part of a Chinese emancipation[31]—presented detailed programs for creating spaces for the dissemination of ideas, mainly through the periodicals *Xin qingnian* (New youth) and *Xin chao* (New tide). *Xin chao*'s founder Luo Jialun argued in 1919 that "freedom of thought does not consist of a single person sitting in a room and thinking what he likes. . . . Real freedom of thought . . . requires that all people be able to express their thoughts in full."[32]

As in other countries, the highly commercialized print culture gave an increasingly important role to literature in China. As Habermas notes in the European context, modern fiction and theater transformed the audience, formerly limited to aristocratic readers and spectators, into what became known as "the public."[33] The literary implications of public debate were not lost on May Fourth thinkers, as evidenced already in Hu Shi's influential essay "Wenxue gailiang chuyi" (My humble opinion on literary reform, 1917). The essay is often noted for its emphasis on writing in the modern spoken idiom, yet Hu's agenda is much broader in scope. He calls for a regeneration of Chinese writing based on the model of linguistic and literary reforms that made literature accessible to larger audiences and led to the creation of national literatures in Europe.[34]

Yet as recent studies have shown, promoting Enlightenment ideas, expressed with ostensible assurance, nevertheless contained the seeds of inner contradiction. Wang Hui, for example, discerns three major tensions in the May Fourth "enlightenment," namely, those between individual consciousness and national awakening, between humanism and the negation of the self, and between individual freedom and class liberation.[35] Although May Fourth thinkers touted their belief in humanity's enlightenment, alongside the confidence in human progress ran subcurrents that questioned the optimism of the mainstream. In literary circles, as C. T. Hsia points out, the patriotic "obsession with China" that harks back to May Fourth included "a vision of disgust if not despair."[36]

The development of literature under the aegis of May Fourth should be understood in the context of this critical stance toward the rational community. In a nutshell, the redemptive claims of the Enlightenment rested on the shaky assumption that the public sphere is a transparent medium of maximal conductivity, which transmits ideas in unadulterated form. Yet the effective interpretation of the conveyed message is hampered at various levels, from the fundamental inadequacy of language to cultural and ideological differences between author and readers. Even more problematic is the hypothesis that the public sphere functions as a filter that is conducive to the good of the community. Enlightenment thinkers implied that natural forces facilitate the endorsement of those ideas that are most beneficial for the collective. Once a worthy idea is introduced, its inherent good will persuade society and enlighten it. Kant's idea of the *sensus communis* identifies the sensibilities of the community with commonsense.[37] The emergence, from within May Fourth, of a literary discourse that challenged the possibility of communicating an effective and unambiguous message amounted to a critique of public debate.

Chinese reformers, witnessing social disintegration and powerlessness in the face of colonial aggression, were perhaps even more aware than their Western counterparts that public discourse was no panacea. Establishing the Republic of China in 1912 failed to provide a functional government embodying the will of the nation. May Fourth writers who had just adapted their thought to the Enlightenment's faith in humanity's progress started almost immediately to internalize the criticism of Enlightenment ideals voiced by some contemporary Westerners. Because of the simultaneous reception of ideas from different periods in Western thought, perceived by some as China's "belated modernity," thesis and antithesis were telescoped into a single intellectual movement.[38] The temporal conflation of ideological reception may account for the scholarly neglect of May Fourth's critique of the public sphere. To prove the existence of a strong resistance to the belief in open debate, I resort to rereading major literary works, starting with Lu Xun.

LU XUN'S CRITIQUE OF THE NOW

May Fourth thinkers are not noted for direct attacks on faith in Reason and public debate, but major authors alluded in their literary writings to the shortcomings of these ideals. I have chosen to start with Lu Xun (1881–1936) because his status as "the father of modern Chinese fiction" has often been cited in misleading ways. Lu Xun's writings have been used to argue that China's national literature, from its very inception, aimed at creating an engaged readership—in other words, a medium through which the writer could disseminate a redemptive social message. Yet I show that Lu Xun's case underlines the fact that the call for a new literature to save the nation was accompanied by doubts and self-irony. His well-known aversion to crowds acquires additional significance when viewed in conjunction with his views of public debate. Even in his column "Suigan lu" (Jottings), published in the May Fourth journal *New Youth*, Lu Xun finds fault with public debate because of the repulsive mass dynamics that dominate it. He denounces "collective chauvinism" and "patriotic chauvinism," attacks conservative nationalism, and argues in favor of individual creativity.[39]

Lu Xun's most virulent criticism of public debate is, however, presented in his fiction. As early as in his first collection, *Nahan* (Outcry, 1923), discussed in Chapter 1, Lu Xun describes the community not as an enlightened readership but as a lynch mob. He echoes both Freud's emphasis on individual and irrational drives and Marx's fear that social consciousness is numbed by commodification. Lu Xun demonstrates the necessity of visions of violence and torture and draws close to Dostoevsky's darkest visions. The very choice to convey his most poignant social criticism in literary form rather than in his many essays demonstrates Lu Xun's mistrust of the ostensible benefit of straightforward, well-reasoned argumentation. The community of readers, it is implied, does not vouch for an effective communication of ideas. By writing abstract parables and open-ended riddles, Lu Xun shows his preference for a medium that allows double meanings and paradoxes and thereby privileges subjective interpretation.

Of Lu Xun's paradoxes, perhaps the best known is the parable of the iron chamber, which describes the writer as trying to wake up his audience, only to witness their inevitable death. Many of Lu Xun's readers have glossed over the fact that the parable depicts the relations between author and readers as ineffective, violent, and self-righteous. It is precisely this neglected aspect, I argue, that accounts for the parable's seminal role in modern Chinese fiction. Lu Xun and other authors have often revisited it and rewritten it into their stories to emphasize the limits of public discourse and of their own writing in particular. The parable of the iron chamber in effect became a model for critical writing in twentieth-century China, a master trope reflected in the extensive body of Chinese literature that embraced what Albert Camus calls "the lyricism of the prison cell."[40]

Lu Xun's parable places twentieth-century Chinese literature in the context of European and Japanese debates about the rationality of public discourse. The metaphor of the iron chamber coincidentally resonates with Max Weber's description of modern economy as an "iron cage" that strips modern humanity of moral values and subjects the individual to bureaucratic regulation.[41] Lu Xun also explicitly raises the issue of China's place in world history, inasmuch as he presents the parable in conjunction with a passage describing the need for a readership with strong anational consciousness.

A close reading of these familiar texts does not support the widely accepted view of Lu Xun as an unwavering Enlightenment man. Rather than argue simply that the Chinese people must acquire historical consciousness and assume their place in the human progress toward a better society, Lu Xun points out that no immanent force governs the course of history. He warns that any attempt to arrogate a universal history in order to define China's destiny is doomed to fail. This point is well illustrated in Lu Xun's short story "Kuangren riji" (Diary of a madman, 1918). Although much celebrated, this is also one of the most misunderstood works in twentieth-century Chinese fiction and needs to be reevaluated. Playing on the themes of the parable of the iron chamber, the story gives voice to a man who believes that he is about to be eaten. Key to the plot is the Madman's loss of a sense of time and distortion of historical parameters. He overreads temporal experiences and brings disaster upon himself by looking for signs of historical redemption.

Lu Xun's argument should be understood, not as privileging the present moment, but rather as interrogating historical consciousness and criticizing historical narratives. While more programmatic May Fourth thinkers argued that armed with a consciousness of one's historical position, one acquires agency in shaping history—Li Dazhao, for example, called for emulation of the "veneration of the Now" that accounts for the Enlightenment's "activist view of history"—Lu Xun's literary writing takes a critical view.[42] "Diary of a Madman" stresses the dangers of historical consciousness. The protagonist's attempt to appropriate a historical identity ends up bearing witness only to the impossibility of pinning down one's temporal position and leaves him no recourse but to seek insanely to reinvent history. Historical consciousness leads the protagonist to a pursuit of immediate, messianic, and inevitably unattainable salvation. By extension, Lu Xun advances a version of public discourse and national revival that remains aware of its shortcomings.

THE DRAMATICS OF PUBLIC DISCOURSE

A very different form of declaring the limits of one's historical consciousness is found in twentieth-century rewritings of "historical," that is, premodern, novels. At the same time that Lu Xun often reworked texts from contemporary world literature (mainly from Russia and Japan), others rewrote earlier Chinese texts and declared themselves modern by distancing themselves from dated ideology. Yet the result is far from being an unmitigated celebration of modernity. The modern texts often end up reasserting the original plots. The texts foreground how the attempt to change the predetermined course of events is undone. At the allegorical level, the modern writers call their own motives into question. Like their protagonists, who suffer in vain for expressing modern views, twentieth-century authors who modify earlier texts fashion failure to change the plot's outcome as a punishment for their hubris in wanting to reinvent history, even if it is only literary history.

Chapter 2 explores how modern authors position themselves in relation to the limitations posed by premodern ideology. The introduction of historical consciousness as a trope that motivates the plot is already foreshadowed in Wu Jianren's *Xin Shitouji* (The new *Story of the Stone*, serialized 1905–8). Wu Jianren transports Jia Baoyu, the protagonist of the eighteenth-century novel *Honglou meng* (titled in English *The Dream of the Red Chamber*, and also known as *The Story of the Stone*), into the late nineteenth century. The novel's vitality draws on the comical dislocation of Baoyu into a time of technological novelty and political instability. Wu's protagonist undergoes a transformation from possessing the mental makeup of an eighteenth-century man to endorsing the utopian views of a modern Chinese reformer.

The full literary implications of historical consciousness were not explored, however, until the May Fourth period. Ouyang Yuqian (1889–1962), who broke away from the May Fourth mainstream in promoting a "national drama" (*guoju*), foregrounded the dilemmas of modernity in his 1926 play *Pan Jinlian*. Pan Jinlian is a character taken from the sixteenth-century novels *Shuihu zhuan* (The water margin) and *Jin Ping Mei*. As in the originary texts, the plot takes place in the twelfth century, but Ouyang brings Jinlian's character up to date and makes her express May Fourth ideals. The eponymous heroine denounces misogynist traits in Chinese society and pleads for women's right to free love. Yet the most important feature of the play, in my view, is its critique of public discourse. The portrayal of Pan Jinlian as a modern woman recasts her death as the result of her faith in the public sphere. It is precisely because she speaks out for the enlightened ideas of May Fourth that she is killed. Her fate demonstrates that free speech cannot assume the community's willingness to accept modern values. Airing one's opinions and submitting one's testimony might in fact provide the powers that be with the excuse to curtail individual freedom, and Pan Jinlian's enunciation of modern views leaves her exposed to the executioner's sword. A later rewriting by the same title, Wei Minglun's (b. 1942) Sichuan-style opera of 1986, further illustrates that the speaker is betrayed, not by "traditional" norms, but by the very limitations of literature's recourse to a purportedly benign public debate.

Fashioning public testimony as the reason for one's downfall may reflect the politics of the 1920s. With factions vying for power in a political vacuum, debates became more divided and acerbic. The dangers of revealing one's views would become apparent in the spring of 1927, when CCP (Chinese Communist Party) sympathizers were rounded up and gunned down by KMT (Nationalist Party) forces. Ouyang foreshadows such events in showing that Pan Jinlian's appeal to enlightened ideas, when tried in public and subjected to the dynamics of theatricality, becomes a transgressive act that invites harsh response. Through the dramatic genre, plays such as *Pan Jinlian* stress how the writer is at the center of a spectacle. Ouyang stages modern ideals for the public's judgment. It is of symbolic importance that *Pan Jinlian* culminates in a trial scene in which Pan Jinlian appeals to the audience's reason. Yet in addressing the spectators, she also puts herself at their mercy. The inner contradictions of modernity resurface in the tension between ideology and the poetics of spectacle in the 1920s and 1930s.

The limits that theatricality imposes on public discourse are even clearer in the case of Chinese cinema in the 1930s. Toward the end of *Tianming* (Daybreak, 1932), the revolutionary heroine Lingling (played by Li Lili) stands in front of a firing squad. When asked for a last wish, she says, with no apparent irony: "Wait until my smile looks best and fire only then, would you?" The episode is emblematic of the problem facing "left-wing" cinema on the eve of World War II—the transmission of the revolutionary message depends on violent spectacles such as execution scenes and on the appeal to visual pleasure. Lingling's request blurs the distinction between the revolutionary heroine's defiance of the guns and her willing submission to the aestheticizing camera.

Chinese cinema circles took part in the debates of the 1930s on the form of public discourse. The League of Left-Wing Artists set the tone in 1931 by calling for "making literature available to the masses" (*wenxue de dazhonghua*). Arguing in favor of art forms easily digested by the majority of readers, the League's policy marked the culmination of support for the public sphere. The intellectual atmosphere to a large extent vindicated the belief in the social message and rewrote the May Fourth agenda, in hindsight, as an unconditional faith in the dissemination of knowledge. Rewriting history was aided by the fact that many May Fourth thinkers had changed their views by then. Lu Xun, who had emphasized paradox in his earlier writings, now joined the League and saw little hope in "the third category," namely, authors who put their writerly skills before any ideological message.[43]

Engaged artists appreciated film for its appeal to a wide audience, and many cinematographers contributed by producing works with a clear socialist agenda. Yet as Lingling's last line in *Daybreak* indicates, the cinema of the 1930s barely covers up inner contradictions between the revolutionary message and its filmic representation. The power of the silver screen contested the audience's judgment and the role of mass media in producing a critical public debate. The tension between cinematic medium and social message is evident in Ma-Xu Weibang's (1905–61) film *Yeban gesheng* (Song at midnight, 1937), discussed in Chapter 3. The story line, which combines a revolutionary plot with a Hollywood-style horror film, develops through a dialectic of hiding and revelation. The hero cannot show himself in public and must use a proxy to convey his message. *Song at Midnight* gives the lie to the assumption that the audience is ready for the revolutionary ideology. Significantly, the protagonist is an opera singer, yet he chooses to appear as a masked shadow. The theatrical performance turns into a bloody spectacle, and the audience becomes a lynch mob. Although the revolutionary utopia is depicted in terms of total communication, Ma-Xu's hero is ousted from society, not to mention denied access to public discourse. As such, the film challenges the claim that art is the potent voice of coming social reform.

CODES OF SILENCE

Soon after the release of *Song at Midnight*, the outbreak of World War II put on hold the project of challenging utopian narratives and faith in public discourse in particular. Throughout the 1930s, left-wing literary circles demanded a literature that would respond to the Japanese aggression in the northeast. Authors with a clear message such as Zhou Yang and Xia Yan gained favor, while Ba Jin, Lu Xun, and others were denounced for voicing any skepticism. The urge for idealistic rather than self-critical writing became stronger with the Japanese invasion in 1937. Writers rallied behind the All-China Anti-Aggression Association of Literary Circles (Zhonghua quanguo wenyijie kangdi xiehui), established in 1938. The critique of enlightenment that had been part of the May Fourth project was now considered irrelevant, even dangerous, and was soon silenced.

In 1949, with the rise of the Communist Party to power, Maoist discourse became the only legitimate form of expression. The foundations were laid in Mao Zedong's "Talks at the Yan'an Literary Conference" ("Zai Yan'an wenyi zuotanhui shang de yanjiang," 1942). The Talks are usually discussed in terms of their prescriptive function in redefining literature as a propaganda tool. Yet even more devastating for literary opposition was Mao's denial of public discourse. Mao claimed complete identity between the author and the masses, and writers were required to be one with the proletariat. The Maoist emphasis on loyalty to the revolutionary cause as the primary aesthetic standard denied all recourse to ambivalent meaning. True to Marxist doctrine, Mao regarded literature as a reflection of society rather than as a form of negotiating with different perceptions of reality. The Talks not only outlaw undesirable forms of literature but also delegitimize the very pluralistic exchange of opinions as counterrevolutionary. Even though Mao traced a direct line between May Fourth and his call for a "cultural army" mobilized in the service of social reform, the Yan'an Talks contradicted the fundamental views of the earlier movement. By eliminating the space for debate, Mao instated the Party as the only organ regulating the transmission of ideology. It is in this light that one should understand Mao's attack on "people of petit bourgeois origin [who] use all kinds of methods, including literary and artistic methods, and stubbornly express themselves and propagate their views."[44] The recurrent campaigns against literary "poisonous weeds" were directed not only against specific works and authors but mainly against any challenge to the party's control over the ideological arena.

The hiatus in public debate under the aegis of Mao Zedong is described in Chapter 4, which illustrates the silencing effect of Maoist discourse on the cinema and drama of the 1950s and 1960s. In retrospect, Chinese films of the 1950s prepared the stage for the "model plays" that dominated aesthetics in the People's Republic of China (PRC) from 1964 to 1978. Taking their clue from the Yan'an talks, films such as *Yong bu xiaoshi de dianbo* (The undying transmission, 1958) and *Zi you hou lairen* (Where one falls, another rises, 1962, released 1963) describe the transmission of a revolutionary communication across enemy lines. The plots focus not on the meaning of the messages but on their successfully changing hands, implying that it is the party alone that determines the ideological message and holds the only means of decoding and interpreting it. The latter film was adapted into the first model play, *Hongdeng ji* (The red lantern, 1963). In line with the tight control of public discourse, the Cultural Revolution, which started in 1966 and continued in various forms until Mao's death in 1976, allowed almost no stage production other than the model plays. Mao delegitimized all exchange of opinions—even generals and politburo members who voiced criticism in closed circles were persecuted—and films held up a revolutionary discourse that was no more than a farce of public debate.

The silencing effect of Maoist discourse wore off gradually after Mao's death and the fall of the Gang of Four in 1976. The aftermath of the Cultural Revolution and subsequent struggle to rescue collective memory are discussed in a series of shorter chapters (5 through 9). At first, the Party allowed a small measure of debate, mainly to further its policy of purging "Gang of Four" elements. Perry Link gives a fascinating step-by-step account of the mechanisms for manipulating public access to literature in the post-Mao era.[45] Going with and against the current, writers and filmmakers used the new policy to bear witness to their experience during the Cultural Revolution and expand public discourse. The first, hesitant steps can be observed in the films of the early 1980s, discussed in Chapter 5. Both thematically and through cinematic language, films such as *Bashan yeyu* (Night rain in Bashan, 1980) and *Tianyunshan chuanqi* (The legend of Tianyunshan, 1980) proclaimed a break with Maoist aesthetics. Yet these pieces also reveal the wariness of intellectuals who had seen the public sphere trampled by the political authorities. The works of the director Yang Yanjin, *Ku'nao ren de xiao* (Bitter laughter, 1979) and *Xiao jie* (The alley), relegitimize subjective ideas but also relegate such opinions to a more private realm. It is only appropriate that Yang's first film pays tribute to Lu Xun and refers in its title to the earlier author's parable about the social dilemmas involved in expressing one's opinion.

Another problem facing authors in the 1980s was that the socialist realist style in which they had been trained did not equip them with a language to convey the shortcomings of public discourse. One of the first to break the distinction between factual testimony and fictional storytelling was Zhang Xianliang (b. 1936), to whom Chapter 6 is devoted. Zhang's sometimes naive style conceals a fundamental mistrust of taking history at face value. In an essay from the late 1990s, Zhang tells how in 1971, he destroyed the only photograph he had of his father, because it would have incriminated him as a capitalist.[46] The scene is emblematic of the difficulties of keeping a truthful record of history, especially during an age when visual culture is fetishized. True to the critical project of May Fourth, Zhang employs his writing to highlight the difficulties of conveying his experience in any "truthful" form. Bearing witness to "history" entails not only relating past events but also acknowledging how experience may sometimes remain suppressed and silenced.

Zhang addresses these silences in a particularly powerful manner in *Wo de putishu* (My bodhi tree, 1994), which rewrites and expands his labor reform camp diary from the 1960s. Here Zhang's voice is anchored neither in past circumstances nor in the narrative present, but rather emanates from the gap between trauma and testimony. As either victim or narrator, the author has no direct access to his experience. What is on the face of it Zhang's most factual and autobiographical account turns out to be a subtle parable about the discrepancy between being a witness and bearing witness. Realistic detail must also be read as an allegory of the deceptiveness of testimony. Zhang's first-person voice further foregrounds the author's limitations. The narrator doubts the veracity of his memories and even his sanity. Echoing Lu Xun's "Diary of a Madman," *My Bodhi Tree* is suspicious of the diary's accuracy and calls the author's judgment and the reader's reception alike into question. Although Zhang is associated with the "scar literature" of the late 1970s and early 1980s, which was based on faith in collective memory, his writings show how literature in the aftermath of the Cultural Revolution could at best convey experience in its negative form—forgetting, trauma, silence.

The plight of the witness who tries in vain to recover her voice after political oppression is echoed in Taiwan literature of the 1980s. After the death of Chiang Kai-shek (Jiang Jieshi) in 1975, and with the gradual relaxation of control over the public sphere, Taiwan writers could reevaluate the effects of KMT control of media and literature. The narrators, however, are often fashioned as surprised to find out that past events are as inaccessible as they were before. Against the euphoric belief that repressed sufferings may now be recounted, authors point out that the traumatic past has rendered their voices incapable of either bearing witness to the past or clarifying their present situation. The texts resist the hope that free expression would easily resume soon after the dictators' demise.

These themes are explored in the work of authors of different backgrounds such as Chen Yingzhen (b. 1937) and Liu Daren (b. 1939), whose works I examine in Chapter 7. These two writers can hardly represent the diverse literary scene in Taiwan; considering the rapid ascendance of Taiwanese "native soil literature" (*xiangtu wenxue*), Chen and Liu are exceptions in their declared affinity for the Mainland. Yet both authors have played important roles in shaping the voice of political dissent and post-Chiang fiction. Chen Yingzhen, Taiwan-born and a long-term political prisoner, describes how survivors of Chiang's "White Terror" try to speak out, only to find out that the testimony is always belated and displaced. Chen's stories from the 1980s focus on released prisoners' disheartening encounter with modern Taiwan. Liu Daren, of mainland origin and exiled by the KMT, lives and writes in the United States. His short story "Dujuan ti xue" (Azaleas cry out blood, 1984) depicts with particular poignancy the narrator's return to China in quest of concealed facts and repressed memories. The search for a vanished aunt brings to the surface the brutality and madness of the Cultural Revolution. Yet the narrator, as self-appointed detective, finds no conclusive answers in his search. Rather than unearthing objective history, he can only interpret the silences that surround past events.

Zhang Xianliang, Chen Yingzhen, and Liu Daren lay claim to the legacy of May Fourth. As they look at the intellectual and literary goals set by Lu Xun's generation from the vantage point of the post-Mao and post-Chiang era, they embrace engaged literature but foreground ironic awareness of the author's limitations. Grand collective narratives give way to personal, subjective memory, and history is fashioned, not as a detective story with a clear resolution, but as a mystery tale.

TESTIMONY AFTER THE END OF HISTORY

Already in his stories of the early 1980s, Chen Yingzhen notes that his generation is perceived as irrelevant. The changes in literary fashion were particularly swift, and by the late 1980s, the project of resituating oneself in relation to May Fourth was offset by other trends. Among the important factors that contributed to this change were the introduction of world literature in translation, from Kafka to Borges and Amichai, as well as the growing dependence on the market economy. Literature took radically new forms.

Of special interest is the prolific avant-garde fiction (*xianfeng xiaoshuo*) written in the PRC in the late 1980s. As Xudong Zhang shows, avant-garde fiction and the cinema associated with it responded to an intellectual agenda that sought to revisit May Fourth and called for establishing a functional public discourse. Pang Pu of the Chinese Academy of Social Sciences called for going "back to the unfinished manuscripts of May Fourth."[47] The idea of the public sphere came under scrutiny when younger scholars such as Gan Yang introduced new terms from Western sociology, including "the minimal state" and "civil society."[48] Yet the philosophical endeavor resulted, in Xudong Zhang's words, in a "mirage of the coming into being of a Chinese 'public culture' or a Chinese 'public sphere'"[49] and was conspicuously at odds with political reality.

Avant-garde fiction boldly experimented with new forms, often constructing absurd situations and engaging in metafiction. These stylistic hallmarks mark a sharp break from Maoist literary practices, from which the authors were seeking to free themselves. Ironically, the young authors of avant-garde fiction had been taught to regard May Fourth works as the precursors of Maoist prose and therefore saw their writing as a reaction against May Fourth. In fact, they followed in Lu Xun's footsteps in writing narratives that resist historical reference and call for reading history as a parable.

The debt to Lu Xun can be observed in an early work of avant-garde fiction, namely, Liu Suola's (b. 1955) "Zuihou yizhi zhizhu" (The last spider, 1986). Written from the viewpoint of a spider living alone in a deserted prison cell, the story adds both a historical dimension and a touch of playfulness. The spider tells of the cell's last inmate, a high-ranking prisoner during the Cultural Revolution who went insane and died; the parable of the iron chamber and "Diary of a Madman" are placed in a Maoist setting. Yet with her characteristic sense of humor, Liu Suola takes what Camus called "the lyricism of the prison cell" to an absurd level. The last witness is a disillusioned spider contemptuous of its own survival—"the world's last spider, the smartest and most stupid, the loneliest and most pitiful."[50] An unwilling witness, it tells its story in a Becketian monologue in order to forget.

Chapter 8 addresses the work of one of the main representatives of avant-garde fiction, Yu Hua (b. 1960). Yu's compact parables often describe extreme forms of violence, interlaced with the absurd. "Wangshi yu xingfa" (Past and punishment, 1989) tells of two men's quest for an aesthetic death. In fact, the characters describe various forms of torture. The interaction between the two men emphasizes an inner contradiction—aesthetic death is the ultimate form of experience, yet at the same time, death is an ultimately inexpressible experience that no witness can survive. Insofar as Yu Hua signals what his translator, Andrew Jones, calls the "crisis of representation,"[51] it is because of the paradox also pointed out in Liu Suola's story, namely, that for testimony to take place, the last survivor cannot be one and the same as the last witness.

More specifically, "Past and Punishment" deals with the vulnerability of historical testimony. Temporal reference becomes increasingly nonlinear—the protagonist moves in time, from 1990 to 1954 and then to 1965. He loses his foothold in time and eventually finds redemption in transcending history. While the declared goal of Chinese writers has been to resituate China within world history and thereby achieve national salvation, Yu Hua's fiction stresses the ahistorical dimension of utopia. "Past and Punishment" in fact reiterates the message of Lu Xun's "Diary of a Madman": "history" is the sign of recurrent crisis, and the author fails to recover and redeem historical experience.

The failure of memory is also a central trope in the work of Yu Hua's contemporary Wang Shuo (b. 1958), who has come to represent the literary mood of the 1990s. Embracing the erstwhile derogatory labeling of his style as "hooligan literature" (*pizi wenxue*), Wang offers a lighthearted and playful rethinking of historical narratives. In Chapter 9, I turn to one of the many films based on Wang's texts, Jiang Wen's (b. 1963) *Yangguang canlan de rizi* (English title *In the Heat of the Sun*, 1995). In a brilliant cinematic gesture, the narrative comes to a halt as the narrator rethinks his testimony and admits his inability to construct a coherent account. Spoofing Maospeak and revolutionary cinema, Jiang's film shows memory to be tainted by Maoist rhetoric and by filmic images. *In the Heat of the Sun* comes to terms with revolutionary history by remaking it into farce. While demonstrating how historical events became ingrained in collective memory, the film also points to the breakdown of memory and testimony.

The persistent concern with the limits of public discourse and collective memory, from the May Fourth movement to the postsocialist era, calls for revisiting seminal works of twentieth-century Chinese fiction, drama, and film. They should be read, not only as part of an intellectual history, but primarily as literary pieces that rely on complex textual dynamics.

PART ONE

May Fourth and Its Discontents

1

Dreaming a Cure for History

The Resistance to
Historical Consciousness
Within the May Fourth Movement

In 1933, in the midst of the quest for social reform in China, Lu Xun (the pen name of Zhou Shuren, 1881–1936) made a jarring statement:

Some dream that "everyone will have food to eat," some dream of "a classless society," some dream of "a utopian world." Yet very few dream of what precedes building such a society: class struggle, white terror, air raids, torturing to death, chili extract forced down one's nose, electric shocks. . . . As long as one has not dreamed of these things, a good society will not be coming. . . . It will ultimately be a dream, an ungrounded dream.[1]

The images of violence evoked by Lu Xun correspond with his contemporary reality but are hardly the stuff dreams are made of. For the preceding ninety years, China had known the brutality of the opium wars, hunger, rebellions, and warlord strife. In the early 1930s, the situation was aggravated when Japan invaded China's northeastern provinces. Yet Lu Xun is scathing with regard to the hope of anything better in the short run. How are we to understand the fact that Lu Xun presents both terror and utopia as dreams? What is the difference between dreams that signal the coming of social well-being and the dreams that Lu Xun repudiates as ungrounded? Why does he place the dream of terror at the foundation of utopia?

The dream trope is key to understanding Lu Xun's views on how history is experienced. It is indicative of his ambivalence about his position as a witness to events of historical significance that many of his essays—notably those in the collection *Yecao* (Wild grass, 1927)—begin with "I dreamed that. . . ." Likewise, for Lu Xun, awakening is not a symbol of enlightenment but rather a trope for the witness's self-delusion. Lu Xun's vision of the writer as a portender of dreams brings together Freudian and Marxist thought in surprising ways and is akin to ideas expounded by his contemporaries Franz Kafka and Walter Benjamin. For Lu Xun, the experience of reading and writing is linked to dream and trauma, and the role of literature is not to awaken the reader but rather to create a dialectic that transcends simplistic utopian revelations. Lu Xun not only criticizes historical consciousness as the ultimate unfounded dream but also challenges the author as one who only sees a mirage that poses as history.

Through exploring Lu Xun's complex and often counterintuitive use of the dream metaphor, I hope to foreground some neglected and misunderstood aspects of an author often referred to as the figurehead of modern Chinese literature. A master of the short story and the essay, as well as an accomplished poet, Lu Xun has been a venerated father-figure to writers and artists since the 1920s. As a contributor to major journals associated with the May Fourth movement and translator of many literary and philosophical writings, he earned a reputation as the leading intellectual of his generation. Yet misconceptions were easily formed when Lu Xun was portrayed as a thinker representative of his times. May Fourth faced the need to define the newly established Chinese nation-state as the representative of a common national legacy and a legitimate sovereign power in the family of nations. Subsequently, Lu Xun was popularly conceived of as pushing for the awakening of a modern Chinese literature, aware of its place in history and devoted to shaping the historical consciousness of the Chinese people. Yet Lu Xun betrays deep-rooted doubts about historical consciousness, and his fiction casts doubt on the possibility of bearing historical witness.

My discussion is burdened by the legacy of Lu Xun studies, a field that has arguably provided the most prolific examination of a single modern Chinese author.[2] I must therefore explain the need for the present reading of some of Lu Xun's best-known and most-discussed texts. Lu Xun studies have often revealed an ideological bias, which may be traced back as far as the uneasy relation between Lu Xun and his less political brother Zhou Zuoren, on the one hand, and between the author and the League of Left-Wing Writers, on the other. Mao's endorsement of Lu Xun as the model revolutionary writer, the idolization of Lu Xun in Cultural Revolution rhetoric, and the debate between Jaroslav Průšek and C. T. Hsia in the 1970s about his ideological ambivalence have further politicized Lu Xun studies.[3] In the late 1980s, criticism took an important turn, spurred mainly by two parallel developments. The first occurred with the publication of Leo Ou-fan Lee's *Voices from the Iron House* (1987), which shifted the emphasis to Lu Xun's literary qualities. A number of inspired readings followed, notably Marston Anderson's analysis of the discursive uses of Lu Xun's realism in *Limits of Realism* (1990) and David Der-wei Wang's essay "Lu Xun, Shen Congwen and Decapitation," originally written in 1990, on the symbolic value of decapitation in Lu Xun's essays.[4] The following decade saw a revival of Lu Xun studies that paid meticulous attention to Lu Xun's literary technique and was often well informed by postcolonial and poststructuralist theory.[5] The second factor that transformed Lu Xun studies had its origins in the reevaluation of the May Fourth movement in the post-Maoist PRC. As early as 1981, voices had started calling for a "scientific" study of Lu Xun that would take him off the (Maoist) pedestal;[6] in the same year, Liu Zaifu published a book-length study in which he resituated Lu Xun, not as a harbinger of communist ideology, but rather in the context of nonconformist thinkers like Nietzsche.[7] The agenda behind such studies becomes clearer in the work of Wang Hui, whose books on Lu Xun date back to his 1988 dissertation for the Chinese Academy of Social Sciences.[8] Like other thinkers in the Academy in the late 1980s, Wang was concerned with rereading the May Fourth movement as an unfinished and later misrepresented project of introducing Enlightenment ideals to China. Wang was outspoken about the need to de-Maoify Lu Xun studies.[9] Yet although Wang Hui acknowledges the inner contradictions in May Fourth in general and in Lu Xun's thought in particular, the approach is clearly that of an intellectual historian who aims at sketching a coherent system of thought. Wang and later critics attribute the inconsistencies in Lu Xun's writings to contradictions in his psychological makeup.[10] Later studies have been more nuanced—Li Tuo, for example, pays close attention to Lu Xun's linguistic turns and stresses the need for a similar revolution in language in contemporary fiction.[11] Yet many continue to imply a discernible "Lu Xun thought" that ostensibly fits perfectly with contemporary intellectual trends and presents a clear philosophical system.

The reading I offer here diverges from what has been expected following Wang Hui's plea to understand Lu Xun "historically." Despite my debt to the trends mentioned above, and although my argument places the author in the context of May Fourth, those looking for an intellectual history of Lu Xun and his generation will be disappointed. My method of closely reading short passages emphasizes the intratextual nature of Lu Xun's parables yet challenges the view of him as an author with an integrated system of thought. Instead, I see Lu Xun as a manipulator of symbols, always ready to destabilize his references and build another layer of the maze he has drawn with his words. I subscribe to Leo Ou-fan Lee's emphasis on Lu Xun's technique, which Lee characterizes as "symbolic narrative."[12]

I focus on Lu Xun's collection of short stories *Nahan* (Outcry, 1923), in particular its preface and "Kuangren riji" (Diary of a madman, originally published in 1918), because these well-known texts can dispel central misconceptions about Lu Xun. Many readers consider the preface to *Outcry* to be preeminently autobiographical, believe that it calls for national salvation, and remember "Diary of a Madman" as equating Confucianism with cannibalism. A careful reading questions these and other widely accepted assumptions. Neither does Lu Xun indulge wholeheartedly in national allegory. In fact, *Outcry* invites the reader to reconsider the claim that the author is called upon to communicate a moral lesson to the nation. Lu Xun doubts not only the power of writing to bring about historical consciousness but even the author's qualifications as a witness to history.

AUTOBIOGRAPHY AND ALLEGORY

If Lu Xun is known as an autobiographical writer who stresses his own experience, it is because of essays such as the preface to *Outcry*, which leads the reader to believe in the narrator's presence and participation in historical events. Acting in retrospect as the introduction to Lu Xun's entire oeuvre, this preface describes the author's utopian dreams and their shattering. He describes how he "had an ideal dream," to study medicine in Japan and return to China to treat its people. The passage, possibly Lu Xun's most renowned piece, is famous for setting a clear nationalist tone: although it is his father's death, the result of a misdiagnosis, that motivates the young man to become a physician, he also looks forward to becoming a military doctor, "promoting the Chinese people's faith in reforms" (LXZPQJ, 1: iii). Lu Xun's hopeful dream sees his father's death as the reaffirmation of a larger mission. Regarding the Chinese nation as a community of patients, he sets out to cure not only his immediate kin but all his fellow countrymen. The nationalist tone becomes more emphatic in the following passage, which has since become emblematic of Lu Xun's call for a literature promoting national consciousness. The preface describes how, in 1906, while studying medicine in Sendai in Japan, the young Lu Xun goes through a transforming experience. He is shown a slide of a Chinese man being executed during the Russian-Japanese War of 1904–5. Not only his Japanese fellow students but even the Chinese bystanders in the photograph watch cheerfully as their fellow countryman about to die, Lu Xun observes (LXZPQJ, 1: iii), and he desires to change the mentality of the Chinese people by promoting the new literary movement. The passage portrays literature as a cure for the pernicious lack of a national consciousness; moreover, the young Lu Xun resolves that writing must take an active role in reaching out to a national audience and awakening its members to their fatal condition. His decision to abandon the study of medicine for literature is tantamount to his literary Hippocratic oath.

At first, the slide scene seems to profess the healing power of literature and the author's historical agency. A closer reading reveals, however, that even in this seminal passage, Lu Xun undermines the credibility of his position as a witness. In transposing the specific autobiographical events to the national scale and fashioning his literary beginning as anticipating and forming a national literature, Lu Xun ignores the parameters of his personal experience. It is ironic, although typical of national ideologies, that he lays claim to historical consciousness while censoring his biography, superimposing a national reading on his life, and writing over his past. Just as the writer's pen substitutes for the physician's scalpel, the author-to-be sacrifices his former identity. He doctors the dates, truncates details, and sketches a vague time frame. One wonders why it took Lu Xun six months to leave Sendai after seeing the slide. Likewise, having set his mind on promoting literature, why didn't he start writing extensively until twelve years later?[13]

One may dismiss these discrepancies as insignificant compared to the conviction expressed in the passage, but I argue that the autobiographical reference must not be understood literally but rather at the allegorical level. The barely noticeable slip from fact to allegory allows the author to portray the slide scene as a personally traumatic event and at the same time to construe the preface itself as recreating that scene, transposed to the national level, when the passage exposes a national readership to a shock corresponding to the young Lu Xun's purported experience. Readers would presumably react similarly to the young Lu Xun and be shocked into acquiring a historical consciousness. In the slide scene, the narrator experiences a sordid vision of brutality and indifference that induces him to turn his back on his dream of becoming a physician; Lu Xun's narrative fashions the author's writing as a response to the episode. According to this account, Lu Xun's writing begins with his reaction to decapitation, which Michel Foucault calls "the zero degree of torture."[14] Before starting to write, he undergoes torture, if only vicariously through the dreamlike spectacle in the dark room where the slide is projected. One should bear in mind that Lu Xun was familiar with Freud's conception of trauma through the writings of Kuriyagawa Hakuson (1880–1923), whose *Kumon no shōchō* (Signs of anxiety) he translated. In accordance with Kuriyagawa's emphasis on trauma as the source of artistic creativity, Lu Xun fashions his shock at violence as the inception of writing. He becomes an author by transforming and sublimating his trauma. Likewise, the preface itself is construed as a text that will shock the readers; the experience of reading is presented as a moment of violent rupture that will awaken Lu Xun's audience.

This use of autobiographical narrative as an allegory for the relationship between the writer and his readership has been noted by David Der-wei Wang, who argues that the beheaded body recalls the disintegration of the body politic and establishes terror and trauma as the foundation of modern Chinese literature.[15] By masking allegory in the form of a factual account, Lu Xun is able to forge a new historical awareness for his readers, who are expected to imitate the process by which the violent image makes the narrator give up his dreams.[16] Lu Xun's depiction of his own conversion into a writer and of the audience's transformation into a national readership hinges on a dynamics of substituting one form of dream for another, utopia for trauma.

THE ILLUSION OF HISTORICAL PRESENCE

Lu Xun uses the account of the slide scene to assert his role in bearing witness to the nation, only to undermine the historicity of the event revealed through the visual image. The author places the entire burden of his conversion to writing and the nation's awakening to historical consciousness on a single moment, that of viewing the execution slide at Sendai. The preface to *Outcry* doctors the visual data and manipulates the narrative to instate the young Lu Xun as the only witness to the historical event. Instead of dwelling on the photograph, the preface stresses the circumstances in which it was viewed by the young Lu Xun, who fashions the rays of light on the wall before him as the revelation of a quasi-theological truth. Symbolically, in his ignorance, the young man is enveloped by darkness, and the moment of awakening becomes a literal enlightenment. The distance between the recorded event and the classroom situation is further diminished inasmuch as the narrator refers to the execution scene as if it happened in his presence. Regarding the photograph as an incontrovertible record of reality, Lu Xun presents himself as a firsthand witness, having come "face to face" with the people involved. The narrative gives the impression that the young Lu Xun does not merely stand in front of the slide but rather faces the historical event itself. Conveniently, the image in question is a slide, projected on a screen, so that the opaque surface that separates the scene of the execution from the room in which the young Lu Xun stands becomes invisible. The author is able to recount the incident as if he had been physically present at the scene of execution. He can claim to look history in the eye.

The slide provides the author with unmediated access to the past, laid out before him as an object of investigation. Lu Xun explains that prior to projecting the execution slide, his teacher at Sendai had shown photographs of bacteria. Like the bacteria cultures, presumably taken from an infected body, the execution scene becomes a pathological specimen, a blowup of a disease in need of diagnosis. The photographic record enables Lu Xun to assume the role of a hands-on forensic coroner. In doing so, he takes up a long-standing concern of photography—Susan Sontag remarks how soon after its invention photography adopted "a moralized ideal of truth-telling, adapted from nineteenth-century literary models and from the (then) new profession of independent journalism. Like the post-romantic novelist and the reporter, the photographer was supposed to unmask hypocrisy and combat ignorance."[17] Lu Xun comes as close as possible to being an eyewitness to the crime.

The correspondence between Lu Xun's experience as a firsthand witness and the national transformation he seeks to promote through his writing has led many readers to ignore more insidious layers of the preface. Yet the author's position as a witness is also undermined by the photograph. To some extent, any photograph, especially one portraying a person who has already passed away, signals the distance between the viewer and the recorded event. Roland Barthes notes that photographs are closely connected with death, as "a figuration of the motionless and made-up face beneath which we see the dead."[18] Lu Xun also remarks on the instinctive association between photography and violence: "[Photographic] portraits of the torso were generally taboo, for they resembled [people executed by] being chopped through at the waist."[19] In particular, the slide mentioned in the preface is directly linked to the morbidity of the bacterial culture and the mortality of the man awaiting imminent execution. As such, the image connotes, not the presence of the historical moment, but rather its irretrievable existence in the past. Lu Xun addresses an image that he cannot recuperate, having seen it only for a few seconds, a full sixteen years before writing about it. The reference to the image stresses the inaccessibility of the event to narrator and readers alike.

Moreover, the specific way in which the image is presented disarms its visual force to emphasize Lu Xun's role as narrator. In fact, the author's testimony derives its power from the fact that the text bars access to the image. What may at first be taken for focusing on the graphic violence turns out to foreground the witness. The passage shifts the reader's attention from the condemned at the center of the spectacle to the audience—first those watching the execution, then the young Lu Xun himself. The disinterest in the condemned is noteworthy, considering that images that correspond to Lu Xun's general description contain riveting details that anticipate the execution: the bared nape of the condemned; the raised blade; the eyes of the executioner's aide, fixed on his own hand pulling back the long queue of the man to be beheaded.[20] Yet Lu Xun diverts the reader's attention from the center to the outer ring of the spectators,[21] whom he blames for their lack of involvement as witnesses.

Lu Xun's manipulation of this scene, omitting and supplementing the factual account at will, has often been noted. Rey Chow, for example, remarks that it is hard to justify the description of the execution audience as apathetic. Although the crowd may have been forced to watch, Lu Xun's description comports with his interest in portraying the nation as numb and in need of awakening.[22] Indeed, Lu Xun would later admit that the audience's reaction in such cases had more to do with the attraction to bloody spectacles than with lack of national sentiments (LXZPQJ, 4: 94). Nor is Lu Xun a naive reader of images—elsewhere he remarks on the cultural parameters of photographic conventions and notes that looking unaffectedly at the camera was accepted practice in China (although even then he reads it as an allegory of the submissiveness of the Chinese people: LXZPQJ, 17: 97–101). Lu Xun disregards the context that may have influenced the photograph to stress the passivity of the crowd in contrast to his own active witnessing.

To emphasize that the crowd is self-absorbed and lacks self-consciousness, the narrative effaces visual hints of the camera's intervention. The images known to us from contemporary executions show that the people are keenly aware that they are the object of another spectacle, namely, the photograph. The cumbersome equipment of the time was especially likely to draw attention to the photographer. Some stop watching the execution and turn to look at the camera. They face it frontally and pose for it, comporting with the conventions of ceremonial photography. Rather than being passive participants, they acknowledge their role in the staged spectacle.

Lu Xun overlooks the theatricality inherent in the photograph, however, and employs what may be called a "reflective" interpretation. The reflective reading regards the projected slide not as a window through which one gazes into a virtual space but rather as an impenetrable, mirrorlike surface. Rather than assert himself as an observer, the young Lu Xun looks at the slide only to see himself and the classroom in Sendai. In the context of the budding Japanese colonization of China, the overseas student is especially aware of the other students' gazes directed at him and experiences what Franz Fanon calls the "third-person consciousness" of the colonized.[23] In the Chinese student's mind, the spectacle of the execution is replicated in his own position among Japanese nationalists. It is as if his classmates too stopped looking at the slide and turned their eyes to him, the victim in the midst of a mirrored spectacle. The three spectacles—the execution scene, the classroom slide show, and Lu Xun's self-inspection—converge their focus on the young student.

Lu Xun's account of the slide scene stops at this point. The two crowds, one purportedly unaware of the camera, the other seemingly turning away from the slide to the overseas student, are suspended in time before the impact of the sword—and before the metaphorical blow to China's national consciousness. The effect is twofold—on the one hand, the visual terror is played down. The crowd, Elias Canetti explains, "lives for its discharge" in violent spectacle,[24] and Lu Xun's description arrests that catharsis. On the other hand, in the absence of an eruption, the crowd is frozen in its place, awaiting Lu Xun's testimony, which reinstates the narrator as the one who frees the crowd and instills national consciousness into it.

There are important implications to the fact that the slide is made known to the readers only through Lu Xun's verbal description. The exact image has remained unidentified, although Ōta Susumu's discovery in 1983 seems especially plausible.[25] As Rey Chow points out, the absence of the image has made critics "seek tirelessly to unsee this image *as image* by rewriting it into *literary history*."[26] Yet I disagree with Chow's conclusion that Lu Xun's reference is primarily visual and cinematic. As I have argued, Lu Xun fashions himself as present at the execution scene; he is not a voyeur, as Chow would have it, but rather an active witness. Furthermore, Lu Xun presents the image only to repress it. While one is tempted to concur with Susan Sontag that "now all art aspires to the condition of photography,"[27] Lu Xun's narrative overrides the image. The scholarly response—some have gone on a wild-goose chase to find the original slide, while others have ignored the visual reference altogether—attests to how Lu Xun's text invites a critical blindness to the author's manipulative description of the photograph.

In the absence of the slide, Lu Xun can present himself as the only witness able to reconstitute the historical event and its significance. Lu Xun narrates against the image, for his words take precedence over the photograph (unlike journalistic captions, for example, which subordinate the word to the image). In fact, if we are to rely on the photograph discovered by Ōta, Lu Xun takes his clue not from the image but rather from the appended verbal commentary about the crowd's reaction, which states that "present at the spectacle were also soldiers, who were laughing." The preface further invests the slide scene with a clear message. Susan Sontag remarks that "[w]ithout a politics, photographs of the slaughter-bench of history will most likely be experienced as, simply, unreal."[28] Lu Xun politicizes the image by marginalizing the visual content and introducing a national message.

The photograph conveys ambivalent meanings, signaling Lu Xun's position as an eyewitness to history but also implying an unbridgeable gap between him and the event. If Lu Xun averts the reader's attention from the fact that he has seen no more than a quick still image, it is because it is convenient for him to bring time to a standstill and impose his own narrative of how history is perceived. In subsequent passages, Lu Xun more explicitly pursues the problematic position of the author as a failed witness.

THE CRUELTY OF WRITING

The preface to *Outcry* further prepares the ground for Lu Xun's vision of bearing witness by condemning writing as the failure to forget. The first lines of the preface present the following ironic remark:

When I was young, I too had many dreams, most of which I later forgot, but I do not regret this. So-called memories are supposed to be able to make one happy, but at times they can make one lonesome and entangle the mind in bygone times of loneliness. There is no sense in that. On the contrary, I suffer from not being able to forget everything altogether. That part that I cannot completely forget has now become the source for *Outcry*. (LXZPQJ, 1: i)

One is tempted to picture Lu Xun, known for writing into the night,[29] trying in vain to divest himself of lingering memories before finding refuge in a dreamless sleep. From the outset of his published oeuvre, Lu Xun presents a bleak image of writing. Calling for the abolition of dreams, Lu Xun begins by addressing his fears, working through his dreams, and coming to terms with his writing. He recounts how he had rejected the mission of becoming an author. According to the preface, in 1918, a friend came over and asked him to contribute to the newly established magazine *Xin qingnian* (New youth).

At first Lu Xun refused, producing a parable to explain his decision:

Imagine an indestructible iron chamber without a single window. Many people are inside, sound asleep, and they will all soon die of suffocation. However, they will die in their sleep and will not feel the pain of death. If you start shouting now and wake a few lighter sleepers, you'll make this unfortunate minority suffer the agony of dying without hope of rescue. Do you think your behavior would be excusable? (LXZPQJ, 1: vi)

Regardless of this episode, Lu Xun submitted his short story "Diary of a Madman" to *Xin qingnian* in 1918. Within the economy of the parable, however, the narrator makes no concession to hope and describes a Kafkaesque, nightmarish situation, where awakening fails to bring redemption. Lu Xun likens the relation between the author and his readers to that between the shouter and the sleeping people inside the iron chamber. The account does not clarify whether the shouter himself is inside the chamber, one of the people doomed to die, or outside, an uninvolved witness. In either case, an impenetrable obstacle prevents communication between the two parties, so that the shouter—the author—has to make an effort to address the prisoners, a readership that can hardly make out his words. The author cannot get his message across, and even if the readers heard clearly and understood what he was conveying to them, they would still face their death helplessly. The chamber guarantees the author a captive audience, but the structure also functions as a barrier to expression and renders all interaction even morally unjustifiable. The readers are at the mercy of the writer, who decides whether to remain silent or sound a warning that would only cause them more pain. Writing might become no moral act of bearing witness but rather merely voyeuristic cruelty, calling upon the prisoners in the iron chamber to witness their own slow death. No solution is given to the problem posed by the parable, which states that the author's ethical obligation to his readers is rather *not* to contact them.

A similar point is made in Lu Xun's description of his father's deathbed in "Fuqin de bing" (Father's illness, 1926):

For a long time even I had to strain myself to hear my father's breath, and no one could help him. At times the idea would flash into my mind, "Let him breathe his last soon . . .," and immediately I would feel that it was improper to think this way, that I was committing a crime. Yet at the same time, I also felt that this way of thinking was right, that I loved my father very much. Even now I still think so. . . .

"Call him!" said Mrs. Yan. "Your father is at his last gasp. Call him quickly!"

"Father! Father!" I started calling.

"Louder! He cannot hear. Call him, quickly!"

"Father! Father!"

His face, which had calmed down, suddenly became tense. He opened his eyes slightly as if he felt something bitter and painful.

"Shout! Shout! Quick!"

"Father!!!"

"What is it? . . . Don't shout . . . Don't . . .," he said in a low voice. Then once more he started gasping frantically for breath. After a while, he recovered his earlier calm.

"Father!!!"

I kept calling him until he breathed his last. I can still hear my voice at that time. And each time I hear it, I feel that this was the greatest wrong I have done to my father. (LXZPQJ, 4: 72–3)

The episode clearly resonates with the parable of the iron chamber and draws an analogy between Lu Xun's rapport with his dying father and his attitude toward his readership.[30] In both cases, the shouter knows that calling can only prolong the listener's painful death, yet an inner moral imperative (represented in the autobiographical passage by Mrs. Yan) compels him to continue shouting regardless of the consequences. It is hard to resist reading the autobiographical details as a key to Lu Xun's psychological motives. One may conjecture that Lu Xun regards his fiction metaphorically as a way to revive his father, or at least to make amends for his past helplessness. In this light, Lu Xun's doubts about writing may owe something to the recollection of his futile calling to his father. Yet even without the psychological background, the autobiographical passage reaffirms the parable of the iron chamber. The narrator's voice continues to warn against facile identification of awakening with curing, and against regarding writing as bringing about the readers' redemption.

DREAMING THE CURE

Lu Xun's parables push the inner contradictions to the point where readers might dismiss the paradox altogether. After all, hasn't Lu Xun transcended his doubts and proceeded to become a prolific writer? Why should one read intricate machinations into the narrative to conclude that the author would evoke a photograph only to neutralize its visual effect? Could Lu Xun have been so cunning as to expect his readers to see through these manipulations and thereby present his narrative as an exemplary failure of historical testimony? Before further investigation, one should keep in mind Lu Xun's admiration for Dostoevsky, whose work he describes as follows:

Dostoevsky locates the characters in his own works in exceedingly unendurable, hopeless, and implausible circumstances, putting them in a position where they can do nothing. He uses mental torture to send them on the road to crime, idiocy, drinking, and suicide. . . . Yet in the laboratory of this "high-minded realist" the entire human soul is processed. From mental torture, he also sends them on the road to introspection, amendment, repentance, and resurrection; until this too becomes the road to suicide. Thus at first it is difficult to decide whether he is "cruel" or not, yet for those who like things tepid or cool, he does not portend any mercy. (LXZPQJ, 20: 140)

These words may apply to Lu Xun himself, relentlessly promoting a vision according to which enlightenment and awakening are suicidal. Lu Xun, like Dostoevsky, may be called a realist,[31] but his realism has little to do with self-affirmation.

The Lu Xun scholar Qian Liqun calls attention to how Lu Xun sums up the situation described in the preface: "Although I have my convictions, I cannot blot out hope, because hope is located in the future, and my evidence to the contrary could not refute [the visitor's assertion] that hope may still exist. So eventually I promised him a piece and wrote it" (LXZPQJ, 1: 6). Qian explains the "double negation and doubt" involved in the passage. First, Lu Xun's experience gives rise to a conviction that despairs of the "dream of Enlightenment" and negates hope. Second, recognizing the limitations of personal experience, Lu Xun is willing to set his reservations aside. Yet doubting his own experience is yet another form of negation of hope and enlightenment. Qian also points to Lu Xun's words in a letter to his wife, Xu Guangping—"Only darkness and nothingness are real existence"—and to a line by the Hungarian poet Sándor Petöfi that Lu Xun often quoted: "Despair is unfounded, just like hope."[32]

Lu Xun presents the parable of the iron chamber, like the slide scene, in an autobiographical context. Yet the real-life references are consistently dislocated to the allegorical level. For example, a footnote in his *Collected Works* identifies the friend who visited Lu Xun as Qian Xuantong, co-editor of *Xin qingnian* (LXZPQJ, 1: iv). Lu Xun, however, calls the friend Jin Xinyi, the name of a fictional character in a story by Lin Qinnan that purportedly satirizes Qian. Qian may be said to visit Lu Xun in his literary avatar. Parabolic references such as this one consistently belie Lu Xun's realistic account. Rather than being an exposé of the events that led to Lu Xun's career, the parable is an allegorical manifesto, the author's literary "apology," a defense of his poetics.

Lu Xun's parable puts readers in a position similar to that of the prisoners in the iron chamber. An airtight logic of the absurd prevents readers from asking not only how the prisoners come to find themselves in a sealed chamber but also why they should die. Mirroring the hermetic chamber, the preface locks readers into a paradoxical situation. The same contradictions faced by the author, who shouts against his own judgment, apply to the readers. One might presume that the prisoners in the iron chamber, like the character in Dostoevsky's parable about the man who wakes up in a coffin,[33] would continue struggling, even though they recognize the futility of doing so. Similarly, the readers read on, but not to find relief or redemption.[34]

The interchangeable position of the writer and the readers as helpless witnesses to their destruction is made clearer in the short story "Diary of a Madman," first published in *Xin qingnian*. Purportedly the empirical proof that Lu Xun could not bring himself to believe in his own bleak parable and stop writing, the plot presents a variation on the iron chamber theme. The text consists of a man's testimony to his suspicions that his fellow villagers wish to kill and eat him. At first, he assumes the role of the shouter who tries to save those in the dark. He vows to explain to the villagers that they might eventually become the victims of their own cannibalism, but they lock him up in a dark room. The would-be savior thus becomes the victim.[35] "Diary of a Madman" is largely about writing—the Madman's main occupation through the story consists of writing his diary—and as such the short story demonstrates that writer and readers share the same fate. One might be prone to identify with the plight of the Madman, whose words are unheeded. Yet the villagers too are in danger, as they will find no cure for cannibalism.

Like the parable of the iron chamber, "Diary of a Madman" pushes the paradox to the point where one might mistake the absurd for the senseless. Lu Xun does not, however, simply dismiss the concept of historical awakening. To understand how he envisions meaning in his parables, we should rather return to his call for his readers to dream of terror, quoted at the beginning of this chapter. Lu Xun consistently proposes dreams as the solution. In his speech, "Nala zouhou zenyang" (And what after Nora leaves home? 1923), he also states that "the most painful thing in life is to wake up from a dream and find no way out. . . . To my mind, if we can find no way out, what we need is precisely dreams" (LXZPQJ, 6: 177). Combining such statements with the parable of the iron chamber, the writer is presented with the task of communicating with the readers without waking them up, through dreams. The shout to which Lu Xun objects may function as a speech-act—that is, convey a verbal meaning and at the same time shock the listeners and sound an alarm. By contrast, a better form of communication would only announce the danger from within the dream. The shouter would appear in the prisoners' dream to tell them that they are asleep, that they have dreamed themselves into false safety (a situation reminiscent of Freud's dream of the burning child, mentioned in the Introduction to this book). Lu Xun's formulation insinuates that literature may serve as a dream-within-a-dream, leaving the choice of awakening to the readers' own judgment.

This situation does not solve the paradox but rather introduces another, namely, that if the writer appears in the readers' dream, his existence as an author depends on the readers' continued sleep. Once the dream is interrupted, the shouter and his message disappear. Even if they did not die by suffocation, the awakened prisoners would not remember being shouted at. Insofar as the dream constitutes the repository of memory and seed of testimony, the awakening becomes an obstacle to the dreamers' act of witnessing. Writing carries with it the menace that the readers' awakening will erase their memory of the dream, that their enlightenment may achieve the very opposite of consciousness. The ultimate paradox is that for Lu Xun, writing becomes a shout against awakening.

Lu Xun joins a lineage of thinkers who have defined the promises of history in the paradoxical terms of dreaming. The Enlightenment has created a myth that identifies modernity as a moment of awakening. Marx states that one must "make the world aware of its own consciousness, . . . arousing it from its dream of itself."[36] Lu Xun comes even closer to Freud—although in "Listening to Dreams," Lu Xun criticizes Freudian interpretation, like many modernists, he rejects psychoanalysis only to incorporate its tropes. Freud saw more than wordplay in the association between trauma (Greek for "wound") and *Traum* (German for "dream"), and his *Die Traumdeutung* (The interpretation of dreams, 1900) is based on the paradoxical thesis that heightened awareness is achieved by awakening *to* rather than *from* one's dreams. As Carolyn Brown demonstrates, Lu Xun draws an implicit analogy between himself and his readership, on the one hand, and the psychoanalyst and his patient, on the other.[37] Lu Xun finds that society must awaken to its wounds, to the violence of history, and that such awakening is achieved by working through one's personal and collective dreams.

Lu Xun brings together dreaming and terror, thereby questioning the claim that scientific progress entitles each and every person to freedom from physical and social maladies.[38] Conceiving of literature as a higher order of medicine comports with Marx's view of his ideology as an awakening that counters a social form of anesthesia, an antidote to religion, fashioned as the drugging "opium of the people."[39] Yet Lu Xun does not partake in the Marxist quest for a reality and a history distinct from dream and illusion. As Wang Hui notes, Lu Xun's vision of history differs from Marx's in that Lu Xun regards material progress as contingent upon human will.[40] Lu Xun's parables are, however, more than mistrustful of those who hope for the immanent coming of History. Instead of entrusting conscious will with the course of history, Lu Xun favors dreaming as a form of awareness that does not claim direct access to history, in either image or word.

UNWRITING HISTORY

Lu Xun confronts the issue of historical consciousness in more explicit terms in "Diary of a Madman." Usually noted for its condemnation of Chinese tradition, this short story should be acknowledged as an eloquent parable about the problems facing the witness to events of historical significance. The Madman serves as an allegory for the writer who finds himself disjointed in time, dislocated through trauma, and disenfranchised from an experience to testify to.

The short story contains two direct references to history. The first appears when the Madman, plagued by insomnia, leafs through a history book and finds the words "Eat people!" written in red characters, hidden between the lines. The Madman also finds the phrase, "Benevolence Righteousness Morality" "written aslant on every page" (LXZPQJ, 1: 4). The cannibalistic message and the Confucian adage alike are clearly figments of the Madman's obsessive imagination, as they appear out of nowhere, written all over the pages in irregular script. For reasons that I shall address later, readers have often referred to the text as a Confucian classic with hidden cannibalistic undertones,[41] yet Lu Xun's story clearly sets up both cannibalism and Confucianism as challenges to the historical text. From the Madman's point of view, history is constantly cannibalized by primitive drives and forces of tradition that exclude alternative, possibly more enlightened, narratives.

Another, more seditious form of historical reference pervades Lu Xun's text in the absence of dates. The Madman finds that "this history"—note how he refers to the book simply as a "history," as if he confronted the immanent entity of History—surprisingly "did not have years" (LXZPQJ, 1: 4). Insofar as the Madman reads the history book in quest of temporal parameters to pin down his experience, the book fails to provide him with such standards. On the other hand, the Madman's attempts at penmanship establish an equally problematic relation between writing and time. He writes a diary, a genre that emphasizes the text's reliance on the temporal dimension. The diary at hand, however, echoes the history book in bearing no dates. The undated entries emphasize how the diary as a genre parcels time and cuts the text in pieces. Whether out of defiance or helplessness, the Madman writes a personal time outside historical contingencies.

The full implications of the undated entries on the writer's position as a historical agent are borne by the story's namesake, Nikolai Gogol's *Zapiski sumashedshego* (Diary of a madman, 1835). Gogol's madman, Poprishchin, dates his diary entries with increasing nonsensicalness, including "A day without date."[42] Critics have ignored this important connection to the point of dismissing Lu Xun's title's homage to Gogol as irrelevant.[43] Yet separate studies of Lu Xun and Gogol have each discerned their respective concern with perceived historical dislocation, resulting from their respective countries' marginal positions in a purportedly universal history. Michael Holquist states that Gogol's Poprishchin is "out of joint with the irresistible sweep of history" because "[a]ccepting Western chronology as normative forced Russians to condemn the incongruities between their own past and that of 'the others.'"[44] Xiaobing Tang places Lu Xun's Madman in the context of Chinese thinkers' anxiety in the face of imported discourses of modernity.[45]

Lu Xun follows Gogol not only in regard to the erratic diary dating but also by incorporating other details that demonstrate the protagonist's historical dislocation. Poprishchin writes "between day and night";[46] Lu Xun's Madman "discovers" the red writing while suffering from insomnia—in other words, during displaced awakening. Poprishchin is a "titular councilor," a councilor in title only; Lu Xun's Madman is reported to have assumed the position of an official-in-waiting (*houbu*; LXZPQJ, 1: 15), a rank in the imperial civil service that often served to defer duty indefinitely. Moreover, although the story takes place in the late 1910s, the Madman answers to a title abolished back in 1911. Even more telling is the Madman's statement that by his discovery of the red inscription "eat people," he has finally caught up with China's four-thousand-year history: "I have lived through four thousand years of cannibalism. . . . now it's clear" (LXZPQJ, 1: 14). The hallucinatory declaration, delivered with pathos, that he has found his place in history resonates with Poprishchin's sudden gesture of identifying himself as none other than the new king of Spain.[47] As Holquist notes, Gogol's madman chooses this identity precisely because at the time, rivalries delayed the succession to the Spanish throne, which was left empty. Poprishchin situates himself at the center of a historical crisis of legitimacy.[48] The comic scene in which Poprishchin finds the answer to the mystery within himself, that he is the missing king, is echoed in the Madman's "realization" that he too is a cannibal. Both madmen speak from highly suspect positions and root their testimony in the historically absurd.

Lu Xun's story foregrounds the Madman's failure to situate himself in history as a parable about the crisis of writing. The history text is cannibalized before his own eyes, and the diary's chronology crumbles to pieces. The Madman echoes Poprishchin's misappropriation of writing, as described in Gogol's story:

I have discovered that China and Spain are the same thing and it's only ignorance that makes people take them for two separate countries. I advise anybody who doubts it to take a piece of paper and write the word "Spain" and they'll see for themselves that it comes out "China."[49]

Gogol displaces the Russian allegory farther and farther away, first to Spain and then to China, as if prophesying the transmigration of his madman, self-declared king of Spain, into a Chinese character. Already for Gogol, China is the ultimate sign of historical dislocation and testimonial paradox. Furthermore, Poprishchin's absurd proof that Spain turns into China underscores the fickleness of writing. The writer's belief that readers will interpret his words correctly is based on illusion. Gogol and Lu Xun each promoted a literature of national redemption, yet their stories reflect a deep-rooted suspicion of writing, as their respective protagonists prove to be lunatics rather than purveyors of historical progress.

In two instances, historical dating resurges from outside the diary's text and forces itself upon the Madman's words. The first date appears at the end of a short prologue, composed by the Madman's friend who edits the diary and brings it to print.[50] After explaining that the Madman has already recovered from his "persecution madness" and left to assume his position as official-in-waiting, the friend dates his prologue "April 12, Year Seven," that is, 1918 in the Republican year count. The Republican calendar, instated after the revolution of 1911 to replace the dynastic count, calls forth a particular vision of history. Revolutions have often used new calendars to highlight their historical significance, as if historical time had started anew. The French Revolution and the Meiji Restoration in Japan each restructured the calendrical year, in 1793 and 1868 respectively, as an example of the reshaping of

history; the Taiping rebellion, believing that its leader was the Messiah, in-
stituted a new year count in 1851 to signal post-Messianic time; one may also
recall Gogol's madman, who as self-appointed king of Spain heads an entry
with "1st Date."[51] The friend's prologue, which dismisses the Madman's diary
as insane rant, presents an alternative truth and a distinct historical vision,
one that regards the current political state of affairs as the coming of history
into its own. The Madman's undated entries, on the other hand, symbolically reject the pattern in which history keeps devouring earlier histories.

The second date is found, strictly speaking, outside the text of "Diary of a
Madman." At the end, Lu Xun appends the date "April 1918," abiding by the
Gregorian calendar that he habitually used in dating his writings (and his
own diary). The two chronological indexes that bracket the Madman's diary
signal the inevitable resurgence of history. Yet even as Lu Xun dates the story
and acknowledges the temporal dimension of writing, the Madman's diary
demonstrates the danger that the writer might lose his last chance to inscribe
time and fail to testify to his place in history.

THE WITNESS AS SUSPECT

The Madman's diary in Lu Xun's story and the events it records also allude
in more indirect ways to the writer's failure to construct a testimony rooted
in time. Even disregarding the fact that the Madman leaves the entries undated, the diary form would not, by definition, require a coherent narrative.
Diary fragments are written in a continuous present tense that is ignorant of
the future. Rather than building up toward a final resolution, each entry provides an arbitrary closure. (The derailed narrative linearity is already foreshadowed in the prologue, where the friend explains that he made a detour
in order to visit the Madman's village.) The Madman, on the other hand,
projects a future goal, namely, the exposure of the cannibalistic conspiracy,
and reaches his conclusion at the very beginning. In a parody on the typical
detective novel, Lu Xun's short story specifies the perpetrators, their motives,
the victim, and the method of murder from the start. What remains to be examined is whether the crime of cannibalism has occurred at all. "Diary of a
Madman" turns out to be a peculiar detective story that asks, "Is there a
crime in this story?" It is not a *whodunit* but an *ifdunit*.

Within the parameters of fiction, the reader of Lu Xun's story must decide
whether to believe the Madman's accusations or the version presented in the
friend's prologue. The dilemma has long been at the center of Lu Xun stud-

ies, and is well summarized by Theodore Huters: the reader faces the choice of either reading the text without taking into account the framework provided by the prologue or regarding the prologue as a sign of the Madman's lack of authority and the weakness of his authorial voice.[52] The Madman adds little credibility to his claims by hurtling his imagination at the most harmful outcome. He sees blood-red characters ooze from between the lines and reads all clues as anticipating his coming cannibalization. (The Madman describes the characters "eat people" as "bright red and fresh," using a nonstandard form for the word *zhanxin* that omits the "mountain" radical, so that the writing is literally "bright red and new as decapitation"; with each of the Madman's fresh readings and new interpretations, more gory meanings resurface.) He gives in to hermeneutic excess and even suspects that he has unwittingly eaten his own sister. Like Sophocles' Oedipus, he seeks the source of violence that contaminates the community only to end up convinced that he himself is the transgressor of the most inviolable taboo, in this case, internecine cannibalism. He exhibits the hubris of bearing witness at all costs, even if it entails acknowledging a crime that he may never have committed. Intended to exonerate the Madman, his confession only further incriminates him. Counter to the psychoanalytical view that the patient's act of talking has an intrinsic therapeutic value, the diary makes the Madman's speech sink deeper into unreason.[53] His words serve only to ascertain his insanity—which is precisely how they are put to use by the villagers who incarcerate him and by the friend who introduces the diary as evidence that its writer is mad. On the other hand, unlikely as the Madman's account may sound, it constitutes a deposition that may disqualify the prologue. Since the Madman claims that all the villagers and even his family are accomplices to the crime, one must be suspicious of the explanation provided by the self-proclaimed friend. The Madman has purportedly assumed an official post elsewhere, but his disappearance leaves a trace of doubt. Why is the key witness unable to endorse his testimony? Has he perhaps been incarcerated in an asylum, or even killed and eaten? The conundrum hinges on our evaluation of the mechanism of bearing witness.

At first, the friend's version seems reliable. He stresses his own detective work, verifying the ink color and handwriting to ascertain that the entries were written at different times. He finds no traces of forgery and concludes that it was the Madman who (presumably after recovering) inscribed the booklet with the title "Diary of a Madman." According to this account, the Madman himself disqualifies his testimony as the words of a mentally unstable person. Yet the self-proclaimed friend takes much liberty with the Madman's text. He exercises full editorial and publishing rights, without consulting the author, whom he discredits as disorganized and incoherent. Perhaps most dubious is the friend's reference to the Madman only as "Mr. so-and-so." As Lu Xun notes elsewhere, this anonymous reference ostensibly protects the person under discussion but might also be an underhanded way of casting doubt on that person's reputation.[54] The author of the prologue echoes the fictional editor in Dostoevsky's *Zapiski iz mertvogo doma* (Notes from the house of the dead), who rescues an abandoned, slightly incoherent manuscript and offers it for the public's judgment. He comments how the notes are "interrupted by another narrative, some strange, terrible reminiscences scribbled down in irregular, convulsive handwriting."[55] Doubts linger about the Madman's friend's purported objectivity and innocence.

What is at stake, however, is not simply the question raised by Lu Xun scholars of whether the Madman is indeed insane and therefore unreliable. The underlying dilemma is that of authenticating the witness and establishing the qualifications for bearing witness. The friend's prologue and the Madman's diary cancel each other out, disqualifying both witnesses. The unsolved *ifdunit* remains suspended between the two texts, one written by a dubious author and the other added by a suspect editor.

Most damning to the Madman's testimony is not his supposed insanity but rather his inability to tie the text down to a stable chronological index. Apart from the historical dislocation shared by the Madman and Gogol's Poprishchin, Lu Xun's protagonist shows other symptoms of temporal displacement that do damage to his position as witness. From the very first sentences of his diary, the Madman writes into a temporally disoriented and history-less present: "This evening, very good moonlight. It's already more than thirty years that I haven't seen it" (LXZPQJ, 1: 1). The moon's hiding denotes a cosmic failure to keep time, echoed in turn by the diary's chronological deficiency. The Madman's confinement further suspends time: "The sun doesn't come out, nor does the door open" (LXZPQJ, 1: 13). It is, of course, not the sun but the Madman himself who cannot come out of the room in which he is locked up, but he identifies his incarceration with the arrest of time itself. He writes of his confinement, "Day after day, it's two meals" (LXZPQJ, 1: 13). In the dark room, food is the Madman's only indicator of time, and conversely, the deprivation of time becomes a sign of the villagers' depraved eating habits. The description also comes close to imagining time itself as being devoured, as if the days were served as meals. Although the Chinese for "diary" is literally "a record of days" or "a record of the sun," the Madman's text does not testify to the sun's movement or to the passing of days but only to hallucinations in the dark about the cannibalistic destruction of time.

At this point, we may recall the connection between temporal dislocation and trauma, discussed in the Introduction to this book. The Madman's condition may be understood in terms of a post-traumatic incapacity to come to terms with the past. Such an interpretation is supported by Lu Xun's interest, reserved as it may be, in psychoanalysis. The Madman's constant overreadings, unfailingly making the most sinister and abject conjectures, are in line with Kuriyagawa Hakuson's Freudian view of hysteria—as a result of a traumatic event, the memory of which is repressed and stored in the individual preconscious and even in the collective unconscious, the Madman's insanity is an escape from earlier experience.[56] His writing wishes to dream away his past and history itself.

That the Madman's hallucinations echo the traumas of modern China is further supported by Lu Xun's homage to Leonid Andreyev's *Krasny smekh* (The red laugh, 1905), which he speaks of as a major influence on "Diary of a Madman" (LXZPQJ, 18: 30), and which focuses on the neurotic consequences of traumatic historical events. Andreyev's novel is narrated by a Russian officer in the Russian-Japanese war. The narrator survives the gory battles only to go to pieces after life has returned to normal. In his madness, Andreyev's narrator starts to see everywhere "the red laugh," the mien of the dead, blood gushing from their mouths: "It was in the sky, it was in the sun, and soon it was going to overspread the whole earth—that red laugh!"[57] Similarly, the paranoia of Lu Xun's Madman expresses itself in finding cannibalism wherever he looks. Past trauma taints all experience, until murder, terror, and unreason dominate and distort all testimony. If, in Lu Xun's words, Andreyev's story conveys the message that "Reason is a fiction,"[58] "Diary of a Madman" asks how one retains one's sanity and delivers a viable testimony in the face of unreason. The Madman observes that the cannibal's "talk is all poison, his smiles are all daggers" (LXZPQJ, 1: 4)—yet his own imagination is mutilated, his writing poisoned. In the diary, time becomes a sign of the disaster of reason, after which there can be no reliable witness. For the Madman, to ground writing in history is to reiterate past violence and allow trauma to resurface in his testimony. He prefers to confess to a crime of which he may not be guilty rather than subject his testimony to historical year counts and the rule of time.

BETRAYED WITNESS

Lu Xun's parables are important, not only as an indication of the author's views on the threat to the testimonial voice, but also because they have come, in retrospect, as well as through the author's foresight, to represent twentieth-century Chinese literature. As Theodore Huters argues, "Diary of a Madman" is a "key meta-narrative in the subsequent development of modern Chinese fiction," owing, among other features, to "the narrator's ultimate failure to communicate with anything other than his own feverish mind."[59] Before turning to later texts, it is therefore important to review how Lu Xun's witness has been distorted and misunderstood. In view of the intense critical attention to "Diary of a Madman," simple neglect or ideological bias can hardly explain why readers have consistently overlooked the text's pervasive concern with the failure of historical consciousness. To understand why the story has been known simply as a condemnation of premodern Chinese society, disregarding Lu Xun's logic of the absurd, one must recognize in it a yet more surreptitious form of allegory. Apart from using the Madman to illustrate the condition of the modern writer, Lu Xun makes "Diary of a Madman" itself into a metaphor of the misunderstanding that awaits historical testimony. In the same way that the preface to *Outcry* invites a critical blindness to the specific dynamics of the slide scene, in "Diary of a Madman," Lu Xun defiantly launches a text that facilitates misreading and ensures that the story will remain a cause of readers' unease, an unsolved riddle at the center of modern Chinese literature.

"Diary of a Madman" shows foresight in portraying the Madman as aware of the futility of his efforts—like the prisoners in the iron chamber were they to wake up—but nevertheless trying to write his way out. His horror increases as he comes to believe that he is writing on borrowed time and will not survive to tell his story. His only hope lies in the diary, which becomes a letter that might remain undelivered, a will that risks being betrayed. The story shows the Madman's fears to be well grounded, as his testimony is dismissed as insane and the friend compromises the diary by editing and censoring it. Lu Xun's fears that modern Chinese readers would be as unforgiving have also been vindicated by subsequent interpretations of "Diary of a Madman." Programmatic ideologues have offered rigid readings to fit their own views of history. As early as November 1919, eighteen months after the publication of "Diary of a Madman," Wu Yu's essay "Chiren yu lijiao" (Cannibalism and Confucianism) concluded from the story that "Cannibalism is about Confucianism, Confucianism is about cannibalism!"[60] The essay contributed to establishing Lu Xun's reputation, but at the same time, it pinned down the story's significance to a simple and direct message. To support his secularist agenda, Wu Yu equates Confucianism and cannibalism, ignoring the role of the history book in which the Confucian and cannibalistic phrases appear. He reserves no ironic distance and takes the Madman's revelation at face value. Ever since, critics have turned a blind eye to the inner contradictions in Lu Xun's text. PRC critics in particular have regularly asserted that the cannibalism in "Diary of a Madman" stands for the cruelty in "feudalistic" China. These critics felt compelled to determine whether the Madman was "a real madman or a false madman,"[61] as if his words contained either absolute truth or the ultimate fallacy that demonstrates truth-in-reverse. It is only recently that scholars reacting against such interpretative paradigms have foregrounded the paradoxes in "Diary of a Madman."[62] Arguably the most damaging interpretation, however, was advanced by Lu Xun himself. As James Reeves Pusey argues, Lu Xun's writings of the 1930s encouraged misrepresentations of his early views by people close to him, such as Qu Qiubai and Xu Guangping.[63] In 1935, Lu Xun added in his notes: "the meaning of 'Diary of a Madman' lies in exposing the harm of the family system and Confucianism" (LXZPQJ, 18: 30). The author's stress on the presumably absolute meaning of the text compromises the complexity of "Diary of a Madman." Lu Xun's later notes comport with changes in the author's views in the 1930s, but they need concern only those looking for a single, synthetic vision of Lu Xun's thought.[64]

Lu Xun's voice was further betrayed when the apocalyptic metaphors of "Diary of a Madman" materialized, after the fact, in concrete events. After the massacre of protesting students on March 18, 1926, Lu Xun wrote: "I never cringed from ascribing to the Chinese the most evil intentions, yet this time a few things came from beyond the pale of my imagination" (LXZPQJ, 9: 116). "Diary of a Madman" was mobilized to symbolize modern China's "self-cannibalization." For example, in his memoirs of the Cultural Revolution, Ji Xianlin compares the cruelty of the "struggle sessions" to the Madman's description of the self-righteous cannibals.[65] The last sentence in "Diary of a Madman," "Save the children ..." (LXZPQJ, 1: 15)—originally warning that the village children might turn into cannibals—would be reread as anticipating bloody clashes with students, from May 4, 1919 to June 4, 1989. History has provided its observers with gruesome details that reason could not have foreseen, turning Lu Xun's paradoxical parable into uncontested reality.

Twentieth-century events have elevated "Diary of a Madman" to the level of prophecy, but they have also vindicated Lu Xun's foresight that reading historical reference into his texts would result in distorting them as literary works. The Madman's monomaniac interpretation parodies the critical obsession with seeing modern Chinese literature as bearing witness for history. As the next chapter will show, writers who sought to bear witness against history time and again had to address the danger that their testimony would be construed as a positive force, conveying clear, upbeat messages. Lu Xun's Madman foreshadows the dangers of public discourse in twentieth-century China and is emblematic of how, in Kafka's century, historical cataclysms have forced themselves on literary interpretation and turned the texts into betrayed testaments.

2

Rewriting Tradition,
Misreading History

Twentieth-Century (Sub)versions
of Pan Jinlian's Story

Although Lu Xun's Madman is arguably the best-known fictional character to have voiced May Fourth doubts about public discourse, other texts also probed its implications. What would happen if a modern character literally took the witness stand and testified to her position in history? Who would judge her, and on what grounds? Could she avoid the Madman's tragedy and carve out a space in which to testify?

During the 1920s, those who contemplated these questions faced increasingly difficult challenges. They hoped that literature might be able to change the course of the nation's history, yet inasmuch as they endorsed the Enlightenment call for historical consciousness, they also inherited a paradox that rose from the European movement's ideology, namely, that locating one's unique position within a historical continuum entails a repudiation of the past and an empowering of the present moment. Consequently, May Fourth writers were ambivalent about their heritage.

This chapter addresses the crisis of testimony that arose from the uneasy cohabitation of nationalism and rupture with tradition. While writers in the 1920s condemned the social values promoted in earlier literature, they also sought a literature that would affirm China's "national character" and turned to premodern texts for that purpose.[1] As in other national movements, the invention of a "national literature" involved writing new texts to support the claim to a distinct modern identity, along with reevaluating the premodern canon to establish a common, timeless heritage across political discontinuities. Writers who produced new works to dispel China's perceived backward position in world literature simultaneously declared their debt to the rich corpus of premodern Chinese literature.

In examining the twentieth-century forging of historical consciousness through the reworking of premodern texts, I focus here in particular on dramatic rewritings of Pan Jinlian's story in chapters 23–26 of *Shuihu zhuan* (The water margin), attributed to Shi Nai'an and Luo Guanzhong (henceforth SHQZ).[2] The rewriting of this well-known text, which probably dates from the early sixteenth century, typifies the contradictions inherent in modern historical consciousness. On the one hand, the revision allowed the playwrights to assert stylistic innovation and ideological divergence from their predecessors and stress the idiosyncrasy of the modern. On the other hand, relying on an older text acknowledged its continued relevance. In fact, modifying novels such as *The Water Margin* to bring them up to date echoed a long tradition of rewriting, starting with the adaptation of material from Yuan drama into the novel, through the late sixteenth-century elaboration of the four chapters in *The Water Margin* into a full 120-chapter novel, *Jin Ping Mei* (known in English as *Golden Lotus*), and ending with numerous operatic renditions in the nineteenth century. Grafting modernist ideology onto literary tradition resulted in intratextual tensions and in an admission—albeit reluctant and implicit—of the modern subject's limited ability to change the course of history.

Three twentieth-century versions stand out, namely, Ouyang Yuqian's 1926 play *Pan Jinlian* (henceforth PJL),[3] Wei Minglun's 1986 "Sichuan-Style Opera of the Absurd" *Pan Jinlian—Yige nüren de chenlun shi* (Pan Jinlian: the history of a woman's downfall; henceforth HWD),[4] and the 1989 Hong Kong film *Pan Jinlian zhi qianshi jinsheng* (Past and present incarnations of Pan Jinlian; English title *Reincarnations of Golden Lotus*). While the two later pieces provide useful comparison, the main focus of this chapter is Ouyang's piece, which elicits the concerns of the late 1920s. Many other rewritings of the same plot were published over the course of the twentieth century,[5] but these three versions in particular share important traits. They foreground the modern author's license to change earlier literary plots and social values but at the same time stress that that this license does not amount to the writer's ability to change the course of history. The works remark in self-referential manner on their own failure to reverse time and reconstruct the past. They demonstrate how historical consciousness might often be accompanied by a resistance to modernity.

The encounter between May Fourth writers, who held to Enlightenment ideals, and literary texts based on the Buddhist notion of enlightenment, is therefore of special interest. Nirvana manifests itself, in Borges's words, in that "our acts no longer cast shadows,"[6] but Chinese thinkers of the late 1910s and the 1920s were committed to casting their shadows on history. Yet insofar as writers envisioned modernity as a redemptive moment, their texts acknowledge that the past continues to overshadow the present.

Ouyang Yuqian's *Pan Jinlian* reworks *The Water Margin* and adds a proto-feminist twist to the plot, which takes place in the twelfth century. As told in the sixteenth-century novel, Wu Song meets his elder brother's beautiful wife, Pan Jinlian, who tries in vain to seduce the righteous brother-in-law. Later, when Wu Song is out of town, Pan engages in an illicit affair with the affluent dandy Ximen Qing. The two poison Pan's husband, and when Wu Song returns, he avenges his brother's death by killing both of them.

The Water Margin sides unmistakably with Wu Song, in line with the novel's notoriously misogynistic tone. The narrator has scant sympathy for Pan Jinlian and passes clear judgment on her: "unlike [her husband], she was always good [at flirting]; most of all she liked having men on the side" (SHQZ, p. 356). Later commentators find little fault with the novel's attitude. The seventeenth-century critic Jin Shengtan, whose abridged and annotated version of *The Water Margin* became the standard edition, singles out the episode for special praise: "not to read *The Water Margin* is not to know the beauty of the world; to read *The Water Margin* and not to read 'conducting the ceremony for the dead' [chapter 26, in which Wu Song kills Pan Jinlian] is not to know the beauty of *The Water Margin*." Jin also commends Wu Song as the ultimate hero, who personifies the virtues of all the other characters in the novel put together.[7]

Despite Jin Shengtan's efforts to equate *The Water Margin* with the Confucian classics,[8] the literati looked down upon such novels. It was not until the May Fourth movement emphasized the importance of premodern vernacular fiction that the novel was given canonical status. The important critic Hu Shi (1891–1962), for example, included *The Water Margin* in his recommendations for the high school curriculum.[9] In his correspondence, Hu noted that the novel should be studied despite Wu Song's behavior, which would be considered immoral by "Western" standards.[10] Hu Shi also argued with Lu Xun over the work's compatibility with the values of modern China. Thus even before a single word of *The Water Margin* was rewritten, May Fourth commentaries had already resituated it within the debate on modernity.

Meanwhile, the grounds for professing the May Fourth social agenda in theater were prepared by a vital movement for new drama. Already in 1907, social reform and Western-style drama (*huaju*) were associated with each other in productions staged by Chinese overseas students in Tokyo, such as *Chahuanü* (The camellia woman) and *Heinu xutian lu* (The black slave's sigh to heaven), adapted from *La dame aux camélias* and *Uncle Tom's Cabin* respectively. The literary reforms associated with May Fourth were launched through drama, with Hu Shi's 1917 play *Zhongshen dashi* (The greatest event in life) and his introduction of "Ibsenism" in 1918.

One of the most prominent figures in the new drama movement was the actor, translator, theoretician, playwright, and later opera singer and filmmaker Ouyang Yuqian (1889–1962), who took part in staging *The Black Slave's Sigh to Heaven* and other milestone productions. Like many other dramatists in the early 1920s, Ouyang was troubled by the fact that the new theater did not appeal to large audiences. Faith in the communicability of modern plays was shattered by incidents such as the box-office failure and vocal rejection of the 1920 Shanghai production of George Bernard Shaw's *Mrs. Warren's Profession* (translated as *Hua Nainai zhi zhiye*), despite the fact that the piece won critical acclaim as "the first Western realist drama touching on Chinese society."[11] Ouyang, who played a lead role in the fateful *Mrs. Warren*, subsequently integrated more action, pathos, and traditional acting style into his plays. While a programmatic debate was taking place between mainstream, "Ibsenist" May Fourth thinkers, on the one hand, and proponents of "national drama" (*guoju*), who looked for a theater that would express a Chinese "national character," on the other,[12] Ouyang demonstrated the arbitrariness of the division by combining the two forms in his plays. Central among the new pieces was *Pan Jinlian*, written as a Western-style drama but staged in 1927 by the Southern Society (Nanguo she) as a Chinese opera, with Ouyang himself cross-dressed in the title role.[13] The play was among the first successful attempts to combine traditional form and contemporary content, a trend that would culminate in the "model plays" of the Cultural Revolution (see Chapter 4).

Pan Jinlian targets the traditional view of Pan Jinlian as the paradigm of the evil adulterous woman. The play presents an alternative view, empathizing with the title protagonist, portraying her as a wronged woman, and stressing the injustice done to her throughout her life. In *The Water Margin*, Pan Jinlian is first a maid in the household of the rich Zhang Dahu, and because she resists Zhang's approaches, he marries her off to Wu Song's brother, a man notorious for his ugliness. In his preface to the play, Ouyang highlights the earlier abuse of Pan Jinlian, explaining that she was in no position to resist Ximen Qing's advances. Had she been able to marry Wu Song, she would not have resorted to crime, but in the historical circumstances of the twelfth century, "the natural course of events led to her final murder."[14]

Pan Jinlian advocates woman's freedom to choose her love, even over her lawful husband, supporting the May Fourth criticism that patriarchal values present women with an impossible choice. As Lu Xun pointed out in "Wo zhi jielie guan" (My views on chastity, 1918), in terms of traditional values, an unchaste wife deserves to die, and a wronged woman can best prove her chastity by killing herself.[15] In his preface to *Pan Jinlian*, Ouyang also denounces the catch in the premodern view of adultery: "According to old customs, there is nothing notable about a man seducing a woman, committing adultery with another man's wife or concubines; but if a woman commits adultery, her husband can kill her at will, and it does not count as a felony in the eyes of the law."[16] *Pan Jinlian* sets out to challenge this attitude. Together with other plays by Ouyang, notably *Pofu* (The shrew, 1922) and *Huijia yihou* (After returning home, 1924), the play should be counted among the "new woman plays" inspired by Hu Shi's translation of Ibsen's *Et dukkehjem* (*A Doll's House*).[17] The new woman pieces presented women taking control over their lives, declaring and enacting their freedom. Significantly, the Southern Society staged *Pan Jinlian* following productions of *A Doll's House* and Oscar Wilde's *Salomé*, which like *Pan Jinlian* climaxes in a scene where the woman protagonist is presented with the head of the man she desired and is then killed. Ouyang expands the relevant scene in Pan Jinlian's story to foreground the injustice done to the woman.

HEAD OR HEART?

Ouyang's most significant divergence from the content and spirit of *The Water Margin* consists in adding a scene in which Pan Jinlian explains her point of view and tells Wu Song that she loves him. In *The Water Margin*, Wu Song demands that Pan Jinlian confess to her crime, at which point the novel simply says that Pan Jinlian "recounted each matter . . . telling it all from beginning to end" (SHQZ, p. 416).[18] The text silences Pan Jinlian by omitting her words from the narrative, summing up her confession cursorily and in indirect speech. The reader may infer that the woman's deposition fully corroborates the novel's description and reaffirms Wu Song's judgment. Pan Jinlian's discourse is subjected to the male viewpoint that condemns her without reservation. Ouyang's play, on the other hand, gives Pan

Jinlian her own voice. She admits her crime but claims that she has been wronged by the men in her life. What is intended to be her self-incriminating confession turns into an accusation targeting the patriarchal system, including Wu Song himself.

Pan Jinlian's detailed statement comes in the fifth and last act of Ouyang's play:

PAN JINLIAN: [. . .] Yes, I committed adultery, but I committed adultery because with him it wasn't true, mutual love. [. . .]

WU SONG: [. . .] I'll kill you right now!

PAN JINLIAN: Everyone has to die. [. . .] If I can die at the hands of the man I love, then I'll die willingly! Brother, do you want my head, or do you want my heart?

WU SONG: I want to cut out your heart!

PAN JINLIAN: Oh, if you want my heart, that's excellent! I've given you my heart long ago; it was here, but you didn't take it! Brother, come take a look! (rips open her clothes) A snow-white breast; inside there is a red, warm, true heart. Take it! (the neighbors look with astonishment as Wu Song excitedly pulls Pan Jinlian toward him in one yank; she lies half-fallen on the ground)

WU SONG: Who permitted you to talk this much? Today I'm only going to avenge my brother! To tell you the truth, I've already killed this Ximen Qing. (takes a cloth bundle from his orderly and throws it down in front of Jinlian. A man's head rolls out) A woman like you—my brother would not like to see you even in the underworld! You follow Ximen Qing! (raises the knife)

PAN JINLIAN: (raises both hands) Oh, you killed Ximen Qing! I can see I had a good eye! But, brother, you really hurt me when you tell me to go with Ximen Qing. If in this life I can't be together with you, in my next incarnation I'll turn into an ox and flay my skin to make your boots! I'll turn into a silkworm and spin your clothes! If you kill me, I'll still love you! (spreads her arms as if to embrace Wu Song and looks at him passionately)

WU SONG: (Steps back, grasps Pan Jinlian's right hand with his left, his eyes wide open) You love? Me . . . I . . . (Wu Song thrusts his knife and Jinlian falls. Wu Song stares at the corpse; all present are dumbstruck, too.)

(curtain) (PJL, pp. 90–91)

In order to introduce her viewpoint, Pan Jinlian brings the plot to a temporary halt just before she is murdered (cf. Lu Xun's emphasis on the moment preceding the execution in the slide scene discussed in Chapter 1). The heroine rejects the patriarchal silencing effect described in another context by Hélène Cixous: if women "don't actually lose their heads by the sword, *they only keep them on condition that they lose them*—lose them, that is, to complete silence."[19] Pan Jinlian's statement of love displays a logic foreign to Wu Song's and reverses his view at each turn of the dialogue. Yet although

Pan Jinlian and Wu Song speak on parallel tracks of mutual unintelligibility, they manifest their respective wills through the same act, Pan Jinlian's death. Wu Song takes vengeance, while Pan Jinlian regards her death as proof of her love.

The two interlocutors' different interpretations of the choice Pan Jinlian presents to Wu Song, her head or her heart, articulate their respective views. For Pan Jinlian, head and heart are mutually exclusive. The heart stands for Wu Song's acceptance of her love, whereas the head symbolizes his uncompromising animosity and wish to behead her. For Wu Song, on the other hand, head and heart are one and the same. For him, both decapitation and gouging out the heart constitute proof that justice has been done. In *The Water Margin*, the avenger presents the heads of Ximen Qing and Pan Jinlian, together with the latter's heart and inner organs, on his dead brother's altar. Having killed Pan Jinlian, Wu Song pursues Ximen Qing and confronts him with the woman's blood-dripping head in his left and a dagger in his right. Ouyang reverses the plot, so that Wu Song shows Ximen Qing's head to Pan Jinlian, stressing the brother-in-law's resolve to behead Pan Jinlian.

Pan Jinlian's differentiation between head and heart introduces modern categories foreign to Wu Song's mind. Pan Jinlian's Nora-like character represents modern, Enlightenment views that Wu Song, mired in a twelfth-century mentality, could not share or even comprehend. While the female protagonist distinguishes between being condemned to part with her head and the implications of her "heart's" emotions, Wu Song refuses to allow matters of the heart to interfere with legalistic considerations. Pan Jinlian distinguishes between lust, which may warrant capital punishment, and love, which in her mind justifies adultery. She considers her tryst with Ximen Qing as morally untenable, "because with him it wasn't true, mutual love," but believes her offense to be mitigated by the fact that she turned to Ximen only after her true love, Wu Song, had rejected her.

Pan Jinlian's language invokes a distinctly modern ethics of passion. In premodern Chinese fiction, the "heart" (*xin*) is not a symbol of love, and the word "love" (*ai*) does not have the Platonic connotation that sets it apart from carnal desire.[20] Both *The Water Margin* and *Jin Ping Mei* describe the lascivious encounter between Pan Jinlian and Ximen Qing in terms of *ai*, which may be translated in this context as "lust." The earlier novel explains that once Pan Jinlian, who was used to having affairs behind her husband's back, laid eyes on Ximen Qing, "her heart harbored a lust" (*xin'ai*) for him (SHQZ, p. 377). *Jin Ping Mei* focuses on the man's reactions to Pan Jinlian's looks, which were "lusted after [*ai*] by thousands and coveted [*tan*] by tens of thousands."[21] On the other hand, Ouyang's heroine's celebration of the purity of love is rooted in Nora's world and in the rhetoric that allows Ibsen's protagonist to justify breaking her marriage by telling Helmer, "You have never loved me. You only thought it amusing to be in love with me. . . . I no longer love you" (in Hu Shi's translation: "wo rujin bu ai ni le").[22] Pan Jinlian's use of "love" refutes her characterization in earlier texts as a woman motivated by lust and redeems her punishment as a vindication of love rather than submission to patriarchal law. Ouyang's play presents a distinct feminine voice, which intervenes in the dynamics of modernity and changes them by introducing a new view of the concept of love.

Ouyang's play modifies the definition of the terms of discourse and thereby changes irrevocably what can be said about love and how it can be talked about. It is precisely by placing the word "love" in the dialogue, without providing a definition, that Ouyang forces the audience to infer the word's new connotations. The term can then generate a debate that reformulates gender and testimony.

THE LETTER OF THE LAW

If Ouyang sides with Pan Jinlian's view, why does not the play change her fate and allow her to walk away, like Ibsen's Nora or Hu Shi's Yamei, as a free woman? Clearly, it is hard to exonerate Pan Jinlian altogether—she is, after all, a murderer.[23] Ouyang may have thought of Pan Jinlian as a case to illustrate his point that "those who drive history forward are often not those who succeed but those who fail."[24] As such, the protagonist would bear witness to historical progress even as she herself is relegated to the vanquished. At another allegorical level, however, Pan Jinlian's death symbolizes the power not only of male domination but also of the premodern text. Although she can address the audience and explain her motives, Pan Jinlian fails to change her fate, first and foremost because she cannot modify the narrative dynamics of the original plot. The literary past continues to cast its shadow and sentences her to die again, demonstrating the limits of textual rewriting to testify to and argue for her modernity.

Moreover, being aware of the importance of her testimony, Pan Jinlian is an author-figure in her own right (which is stressed by the fact that Ouyang himself played the role in the play's premiere). Armed with a modern sensibility, she embodies the condition of twentieth-century Chinese writers and demonstrates how historical consciousness can be her nemesis. Even as modernity is presented as rewriting traditional values, the modern author cannot modify the historical narratives that prevent her and her readership from changing their fate. In this context, the poignancy of Ouyang's plot lies precisely in the heroine's indefensible position, pleading against her irrevocably foretold and even justified death. Pan Jinlian's moral shortcomings become a literary device, a pretext for placing her in a helpless situation. Her demise is predetermined and overdetermined by several narrative elements in the plot of *The Water Margin*, which she challenges in vain. To fully understand how the premodern text trips up Pan Jinlian, we must examine how Ouyang engages the textual dynamics of *The Water Margin*.

Pan Jinlian's story relies on the legal conventions of the twelfth century. *The Water Margin* describes Wu Song as a righteous, law-abiding man who takes the law into his own hands only after the influential Ximen Qing has barred the case from being heard by the magistrate. Even then, he slays Pan Jinlian, not as a spontaneous act of revenge, but within a meticulous imitation of legal procedure. Since Wu Song cannot appeal to the appropriate judicial authority, he turns his encounter with Pan Jinlian into a makeshift court, where he himself sits as judge—a civil position vaguely equivalent to his military rank.[25] He faces a problem known to contemporary courts, namely, that perpetration of or complicity in premeditated homicide was punishable by beheading, yet the law stipulated that the accused could be put to death only after specific measures had been taken. The accused were required to confess and to confirm the written court proceedings by signing them. This stipulation was a major obstacle for judges who wanted to impose the death penalty. Almost as a rule, they used torture until they obtained the incriminating confession.[26] In terms of the legal code, Wu Song provides Pan Jinlian with a fair trial. He assembles neighbors as witnesses and assigns one of them to take down Pan Jinlian's deposition. Only after extracting the incriminating confession and having the witnesses sign the record does Wu Song kill Pan Jinlian.

Yet while in *The Water Margin*, Pan Jinlian is frightened into confessing her crime, Ouyang's heroine tells the story willingly, thereby providing Wu Song with legal grounds for executing her and facilitating his task. She chooses to testify, and it is precisely because she speaks out that her words can be used against her, especially when the confession is committed to writing. Ouyang's text shows clearly that Pan Jinlian is aware of the fatal consequences of her confession, telling Wu Song, "I'm staking my life in speaking to you" (PJL, p. 369). Pan Jinlian can only invoke love as an extralegal argument; insofar as the letter of the law is concerned, she can be the author of her own story only at the cost of her life. The slip from confession to testimony introduces a new power structure. Speech empowers both the woman protagonist and her persecutor within their respective constructs of "head" or "heart." Both patriarchal values and resistance to them rely on ritual reiteration of the motivation of the accused and her public submission to the legal code.

A DEATH FORETOLD

Pan Jinlian's fate is sealed, however, not only by the legal dynamics but also by narrative structure. *The Water Margin* calls for a closure that necessitates the woman's death. Chapters 23–26 of the novel stand on their own as an autonomous, well-wrought episode, structured in a meticulous pattern so that each and every phrase drives the plot to its inevitable end. Arguably more than any other part of *The Water Margin*, the narrative displays fine dramatic suspense.[27] In the scene of Pan Jinlian's seduction by Ximen Qing, for example, the plot progresses through a pattern of condition and response. After spotting Pan Jinlian, Ximen Qing asks for help from Mrs. Wang, a local teahouse proprietor. In a colorful exchange of banter, Mrs. Wang starts by setting five conditions: the seducer must be good-looking, possess "the large goods of a donkey," and have money, patience, and leisure in abundance (SHQZ, p. 371). Only after Ximen Qing responds in detail to prove that he answers the description in full does Mrs. Wang present her plan of ten gradual stages to seduce Pan Jinlian. The latter responds favorably to each of the advances, after which she and Ximen Qing consummate their passion. Mrs. Wang acts both as procuress and as the moderator of the narrative, setting the sequence of events that Ximen Qing and Pan Jinlian must repeat and act out. The plot is laid out already before it takes place, and the protagonists are left only with the task of following the script. The episode resembles a detective story, where the crime is retraced step by step, and indeed the plot builds toward Wu Song's final detective work, in which he reconstructs the murder by uncovering the scheme detail by detail, recovering material evidence piece by piece and making the witnesses retell the events testimony by testimony.

The tit-for-tat dialogues are part of a larger structure that calls for an appropriate measure for each challenge. The episode that begins with Pan Jin-

lian's murder of her husband must end with her own violent death. *The Water Margin* subscribes to a common literary device that shaped the expectations of readers of premodern Chinese fiction, namely, the scheme of retribution (*bao*). This structure loosely employs the Buddhist idea of karma,
which involves a complex calculus compensating for past conduct; good and
evil deeds committed earlier, sometimes in a former incarnation, constitute a
form of favor or debt that must be returned either in this life or a future one.
Premodern fiction and drama often portray karma as determining the narrative's origin and closure, as the protagonist commits an act that calls for re-
taliation or compensation.[28] The retributive causality calls for Pan Jinlian's
death, as evidenced by Wu Song's speech in front of his dead brother's altar.
Wu Song addresses his slain brother and tells him that his soul has been set
free to transmigrate now that his murder has been avenged (SHQZ, p. 418).
Meting justice allows for closure, and Wu Song's mourning rituals, which
include offering the adulterers' heads at the altar, bring the story to its resolution. The retribution plot is elaborated and enhanced in the novel *Jin Ping
Mei.*[29]

Already in *The Water Margin*, Pan Jinlian fails to recognize the signs that
forebode her death and misidentifies Wu Song's motivation. In a passage curiously incongruous with her image of voluptuous femininity, Pan Jinlian
imagines herself as a stout fighter on a par with Wu Song and tells her
brother-in-law: "Although I don't wear a turban, I am a manly hero . . . I can
lift a man with one fist" (SHQZ, p. 365). Ouyang Yuqian reproduces this retort verbatim in his play to emphasize Pan Jinlian's free spirit.[30] *The Water
Margin* punishes Pan Jinlian for her brazenness and portrays it as a misreading of Wu Song's commitment to fight against all manifestations of desire.
Significantly, Wu Song is introduced into the novel when he kills a ferocious
tiger, leaving it as limp as an "embroidered bag" (SHQZ, p. 347). Whether
read in Freudian terms (as symbolic of a limp phallus) or as a Buddhist allusion (realizing that one's human form is no more than a "skin bag"), the episode demonstrates Wu Song's ability to subdue desire (another tiger appears
in the novel's first chapter, where it clearly stands for a man's impure desires). Pan Jinlian mistakes Wu Song's prowess and finds him attractive because he has killed the tiger: "She thought to herself, ' . . . Considering that
Wu Song could even knock down a tiger, he must have vigor, and they also
say he isn't married'" (SHQZ, p. 357). She misidentifies his "vigor" (*qili*) with
sexual potency, but ironically Wu Song has just proven himself immune to

desire. When Pan Jinlian taunts Wu Song, "you can beat a tiger to death. . . . If you and I could be together, wouldn't it be a perfect match?" (SHQZ, p. 370), her role model fails to appreciate her gesture and kills her.

Regarding herself as Wu Song's match and in accord with the narrative symmetry, Pan Jinlian proceeds to imitate Wu Song's feat of killing the tiger by murdering her husband. *The Water Margin* describes how she administers poison, then squats on her victim and smothers him, in terms reminiscent of Wu Song's weighing down the tiger and choking it. When the tiger dies at Wu Song's hands, "fresh blood gushes forth from the tiger's eyes, mouth and ears" (SHQZ, p. 347). These words, typically used to describe human death by poisoning, foreshadow the condition of Pan Jinlian's murdered husband, "blood oozing from his seven orifices" (SHQZ, p. 399). Retribution catches up with Pan Jinlian, however, and comporting with the requirement of measure for measure, Wu Song kills the woman in a way that recalls the tiger scene yet again. Jin Shengtan comments on the odd similarity between the deaths of Pan Jinlian and the tiger, although one is delicate and one fierce: "How come Wu Song mustered all his force to kill the tiger, and also mustered all his force to kill the woman? I read this passage until I choked, my eyes popped out, and I didn't look human any longer."[31] Jin Shengtan (who playfully portrays himself, the reader, as the next victim in line) concludes that both episodes demonstrate Wu Song's lionlike valor. In killing the adulterers, Wu Song reenacts the vanquishing of desire, this time personified by Pan Jinlian and her paramour. Insofar as Wu Song's encounters with the tiger and with Pan Jinlian constitute a preparation for his later task as a righteous brigand, Pan Jinlian's death signals the successful completion of his formation. Legal conventions, retribution narratives and repudiations of desire dominate the *Water Margin* story and combine to seal the woman's fate.

The interdependence between moral issues and narrative structure in premodern fiction, linked through the notion of retribution, forces Pan Jinlian's story into the mold of a moral play. Both *The Water Margin* and *Jin Ping Mei* mitigate these dynamics by introducing bawdy dialogue, yet the plots continue to drive toward the inevitable moment of judgment. The weight of the premodern texts on writers who sought to revitalize Chinese drama, such as Ouyang Yuqian, cannot be overstated. Any deviation from the established conventions—and any repetition of the conventions within a new setting—therefore constitutes a significant statement about the text's meaning.

MODERNITY AND TRAGEDY

Ouyang Yuqian sends Pan Jinlian, as it were, to die at the hands of the old patriarchal law and traditional narrative dynamics. Yet the deeper irony lies in the difference between Pan Jinlian's respective deaths. In Ouyang's play, she is no longer a culpable adulteress but rather a modern woman, a Chinese Nora willing to defend her love and argue for her desire. With Scheherazade-like defiance, she opposes the narrative that would kill her and is ready to tell her story until her anticipated execution is called off. She rejects the dynamics of retribution in favor of the triumph of love. In promising to reward Wu Song in a future reincarnation, saying, "I'll turn into an ox and flay my skin to make your boots," she is asserting that her love transcends karma; she anticipates a lovers' reunion, and makes no reference to retribution. In Ouyang's play, Pan Jinlian dies tragically for her modern views.

Substituting tragic drama for the retribution narrative reflects an influential call for remolding Chinese literature in the form of tragedy. In 1904, Wang Guowei (1877–1927) published his "*Honglou meng* pinglun" (Critique of *The Dream of the Red Chamber*), in which he promoted tragedy as the only literary genre that could provide Chinese readers with an existential remedy. Drawing mainly on Schopenhauer, Wang explained that life is based on a desire that can never be satisfied, so that all living beings are inevitably doomed to suffering. Tragedy demonstrates the need to reconcile oneself to this suffering by relinquishing desire. Wang found fault with premodern literature for providing few examples of tragedy and implicitly called for modern literature to emphasize the tragic genre.[32] In a long survey of new dramatic theory published shortly after *Pan Jinlian*, Ouyang Yuqian displays knowledge not only of Wang Guowei's writings but also of Western theories of tragedy from Aristotle to Nietzsche. Ouyang emphasizes the mission of rewriting premodern plays and likens his *Pan Jinlian* to Western dramatic reinterpretations, significantly citing tragic paradigms—*Oedipus Rex* and *Hamlet*.[33] Following the example of Wang Guowei's reading of the classical novel *Honglou meng* (Dream of the red chamber, ca. 1791), which disregards the novel's prominent retribution scheme and fashions it as a tragic plot,[34] Ouyang Yuqian modified chapters 15–16 of *The Dream of the Red Chamber* into the tragic drama *Mantou an* (Wheat-cake priory, 1916), explaining that the episode "necessarily had to end in tragedy."[35] Likewise, he portrays Pan Jinlian as a tragic figure who fails to acknowledge desire as a paradoxical longing for what cannot be achieved. Having overcome the retribution scheme, the modern Pan Jinlian must still die, this time because the text defines its modernity through the dynamics of tragedy.

Pan Jinlian's demise as a modern woman compounds the other allegorical readings of her death. The heroine's fate turns into a metaphor for the struggle between May Fourth ideals and traditional values; the juxtaposition of love story and retribution narrative becomes a comment on the conflict between modern and premodern literary approaches, and her tragic struggle signals the obstacles to literary modernity. The ultimate tragedy of Pan Jinlian's death is that she expires as a martyr for the inherently unsatisfiable desire to redefine history.

THE HISTORICAL CONSCIOUSNESS OF FICTIONAL CHARACTERS

Pan Jinlian's tragedy hinges on the tension between *The Water Margin*'s traditional worldview and the twentieth-century ideas professed by Ouyang's heroine. Implicit in this tension is the assumption that the ideological gap that sets Pan Jinlian apart from the twelfth-century social reality and the sixteenth-century narrative structure is a *historical* one. The source of her malaise is the perceived divide between the "modern" and the "premodern." Pan Jinlian shows awareness of her unique position in history and implicitly denounces earlier social and narrative codes as incompatible not only with her views but also with the course of history.

Pan Jinlian marks the reassessment of the historiographical use of literature, which consists of endowing fictional characters with a historical consciousness. While Hu Shi's Yamei, like Ibsen's Nora, simply stands for a woman who has endorsed contemporary modern values, Ouyang's characters share the same stage but represent two incompatible ideological timelines, unconstrained by the narrated time. Whereas Wu Song is shown mired in tradition, Pan Jinlian ejects herself from twelfth-century values and assumes a modern set of beliefs. Ouyang thus stresses the rupture between the modern and what must be defined by contrast as the premodern.

Ouyang foregrounds a change that had started taking place earlier in the century. Arguably, the first clear signs of anxiety about the historical agency of fictional characters are to be found in Wu Jianren's (1866–1910) *Xin Shitou ji* (The new *Story of the Stone*, serialized 1905–8). Shortly before composing this novel, Wu wrote his *Liangjin yanyi* (Romance of the two Jin dynasties, 1907) and stressed the difficulty in writing a "historical novel" (*lishi xiaoshuo*) that would retain "the true mien of history."[36] In *The New Story of the Stone*, however, Wu presents a historical satire. Jia Baoyu, who stands at the focus of Cao Xueqin's eighteenth-century plot, finds himself in turn-of-the-century China. Jia Baoyu's extrahistorical status makes him a convenient mouthpiece for Wu's criticism of the social ailments of the late Qing. The protagonist voices anti-colonial resistance, sides with abolishing foot binding,[37] and is eventually transported to the utopian "Civilized Realm" (*wenming jingjie*), which is explored through the second half of the novel.

The scope of the present study cannot do justice to the complex view of history in *The New Story of the Stone*, yet one episode deserves special attention. At first, Baoyu does not find his bearings in the new territory and fails to realize that he suffers not from spatial disorientation but rather from temporal dislocation. When he introduces himself, people laugh at him for taking himself for a fictional character: "Did you read *The Dream of the Red Chamber* until you lost your mind?"[38] Baoyu's dislocation is complete when his character is plagiarized, as it were, by factual history—tea-house customers associate Jia Baoyu's name, not with the novel, but with Shanghai's courtesan houses. Only in chapter 6 does Jia Baoyu understand that he has traveled in time and that those whom he knew have long been dead. The realization that his world has ceased to exist, that "no wonder . . . people of this time are talking as if I were [part of] a story,"[39] is a moment of historical awakening. Baoyu attains historical consciousness, and his dreamed "Civilized Realm" represents a new world order in which China will overcome its perceived historical backwardness.

Ouyang Yuqian's rewriting of *The Water Margin*, eighteen years after *The New Story of the Stone*, brings into sharper focus the historical consciousness of fictional characters. The choice of text is fortuitous, since *The Water Margin* has been linked with the representation of personal character ever since Jin Shengtan's seventeenth-century commentary. Jin trimmed the novel, citing as one of his reasons the fact that the longer version portrayed the character of the brigands' leader, Song Jiang, in an excessively positive light.[40] David Rolston convincingly argues that Ming novels and commentaries such as *The Water Margin* represent a literary shift of attention from event to character, resulting in livelier, multidimensional, and even ambiguous personae.[41] Yet while characters' morality was emphasized, historical criteria were at best ignored. Wang Jide (d. 1623) went as far as to claim that paying attention to anachronisms in Yuan drama was the sign of a vulgar reader.[42] Implicit challenges to the conception that fictional characters inhabit a timeless realm seem to appear for the first time in early twentieth-century Chinese texts. Responding to a social Darwinist view of history, fiction writers contrasted traditional and contemporary society by rewriting premodern novels. The works created, in David Wang's words, new "time-and-space zones."[43] These works dwelt, however, mostly on the novelty of the material culture, and with the exception of *The New Story of the Stone*, they do not seem to attribute ideological difference to historical parameters.

Ouyang Yuqian's writings may be the first to fully recognize the characters' historically determined makeup. Ouyang devoted many essays to the "relation between history and historical drama" and used the term "historical drama" (*lishi ju* or *lishi xi*, referring to any kind of costume drama) in a way that clearly suggested adherence to a historically realistic setting. He required that such plays "reflect the spirit of the period," and that "when writing about historical personages ... one has to write about them so that their philosophical opinions, attitude to life, and social relations comport with the period of those personages and do not violate history."[44] Although Ouyang stated that "historical drama is drama, not history" and argued elsewhere that the playwright does not share the historian's task of elaborating on historical events and personages, he nevertheless demanded that history not be misrepresented.[45]

Ouyang's *Pan Jinlian* openly transgresses the standards of historical realism set by the playwright himself. Unlike Wu Jianren's Jia Baoyu, who travels to the future and simply illustrates the discursive gap between past and present, Ouyang's heroine is fashioned as a woman with twentieth-century sensibilities projected back in time to assert her modernity. Unlike fictional interventions in the form of sequels (such as *The New Story of the Stone*), *Pan Jinlian* repeats the original plot with subtle though insidious modifications.

Ouyang creates distinct chronotopes, or literary time zones, that denote Chinese tradition and modernity, only to disrupt this division. By forcing the two temporal dimensions—personified by Wu Song and Pan Jinlian—into the same space, the play stresses the contradictions inherent in professing modernity. Pan Jinlian can never be a Nora—and not only because, as Lu Xun had argued two years before Ouyang wrote his play, Nora herself might not find a way out of patriarchal exploitation after leaving home.[46] Insofar as Pan Jinlian's testimony is emblematic of modern Chinese writers' bearing witness to history, her doomed deposition reflects the writers' failure to find redemption in historical consciousness and underlines the breakdown of coherent historical time. In fact, it is precisely her newfound awareness of and resistance to the past that contribute to her demise. Rereading herself as Nora necessarily entails misreading herself as Nora.

Pan Jinlian's failure to change the plot stands for the modern writer's limitations when she faces the forces of social and literary history. Intervening in the dynamics and ideological messages of earlier texts cannot modify the past, of course, but only comment on the present. Yet Ouyang employs the intratextual gap between premodern and modern texts to elicit intertextual tensions, to the point where the protagonist's—and author's—claim to a privileged "modernity" implodes.

HISTORY AS THE ABSURD

The themes of historical dislocation and the limits of modern authorship are taken up in Wei Minglun's (b. 1942) opera of 1986, *Pan Jinlian: The History of a Woman's Downfall*. Wei pays explicit tribute to Ouyang Yuqian's reevaluation of Pan Jinlian,[47] reacts to the reception of *The Water Margin* through the twentieth century, and reflects the specific concerns of the 1980s. Through revisiting *The Water Margin* and Ouyang's *Pan Jinlian*, Wei comments again on the burden of literary history, the limitations of the May Fourth "Enlightenment," and the inner contradictions in bearing witness to modernity.

Choosing to rewrite Pan Jinlian's story in the 1980s reflects the need to revise, not only the premodern verdict on Pan Jinlian, but also the Maoist politics of reading. Ouyang's play did not suit Maoist aesthetics and, as Wei notes, was criticized in the 1960s.[48] Even *The Water Margin* was subjected to political criticism under Mao. It had long been hailed in the PRC as one of the few premodern novels sympathetic to the lower classes; as a character in Wei's play tells Shi Nai'an: "You, Sir, wrote *The Water Margin* and extolled the Liangshan [outlaws], and are worthy of being called spokesman of the peasantry's revolt" (HWD, p. 6). In 1975, however, *The Water Margin* was embroiled in the campaign indirectly targeting Zhou Enlai, and it was subsequently labeled "capitulationist."[49] Wei explains: "In my childhood I 'read it in veneration [*jingdu*],' at my prime I 'read it in repudiation [*gongdu*].'"[50]

The mid 1980s saw a reappraisal of the intellectual agenda of the twentieth century, and some thinkers called for "going back to the unfinished manuscripts of May Fourth."[51] Despite contradictory signals from the political apparatus, writers plunged into prolific production of texts that presented an alternative to Maoist lingo and aesthetics. Wei Minglun's play shares the characteristics of his contemporary "avant-garde fiction" (*xianfeng xiaoshuo*), such as including playful metafictional interventions and citing Franz Kafka and Gabriel García Márquez as influences (for a discussion of avant-garde fiction, see Chapter 8). Wei Minglun stands out, however, in turning to Chinese opera. Like Ouyang Yuqian before him, Wei paradoxically used the traditional form to launch a rejuvenation of drama. As Xiaomei Chen notes, the immense popularity of Wei's play, notwithstanding criticism of its "unhealthy" subject matter, was indebted to a sense of crisis in Chinese drama.[52] Wei's choice of Sichuan opera, a less common provincial variety of Chinese opera,[53] skirts both the revolutionary romanticism of Maoist "model plays" (*yangbanxi*), which were carefully groomed to suit Beijing operatic conventions (see Chapter 4), and the somber Chekhovian drama favored by playwrights and scriptwriters in the early 1980s (see Chapter 5).[54] Notably, 1986 also saw another milestone production of experimental Chinese opera, namely, the staging of *Macbeth* in *kunqu* style, entitled *Xie shou ji* (Story of the bloody hands).[55]

The politically motivated rise and fall of *The Water Margin* and Ouyang's *Pan Jinlian* made the plot especially appropriate for Wei Minglun as a vehicle for expressing his concerns. In a parodic extravaganza, the play ridicules historiographical concerns even in its stage directions, which declare it to be "cross-dynastic, trans-period, making no temporal distinctions" (*kuachao yuedai, bufen shijian*; HWD, p. 1). The basic premises of the piece are similar to those of Ouyang's play, depicting Pan Jinlian as a victim of traditional society. Wei's opera starts with Pan Jinlian's execution, after which two characters, "a modern woman" and "an ancient literatus," enter and debate Pan Jinlian's virtue. The two turn out to be Lü Shasha, a path-breaking investigative reporter in the popular novel, adapted into film, *Huayuanjie wuhao* (5 Huayuan St., 1984), and Shi Nai'an, to whom *The Water Margin* is attributed. Lü Shasha calls for reexamining Pan Jinlian's case, although—she adds, echoing Ouyang Yuqian—reversing the verdict would be too simplistic (HWD, p. 7).[56] The following scenes retell Pan Jinlian's story, and Shasha brings forth witnesses to argue Pan's case. Pan Jinlian meets her author Shi Nai'an, historical figures such as Empress Wu Zetian (r. 690–705), and fictional characters such as Jia Baoyu and Tolstoy's Anna Karenina on stage. This pastiche derives its parodic force from ignoring the difference between historical and fictional characters. True to the opera's self-description as "trans-period," the piece brings together characters from different works, written in different periods and about different periods.

Moreover, Wei Minglun dispenses with the unity of time and action.

Commentaries on *The Water Margin* are staged next to the original plot and at times break into it, confronting the characters with personae from outside the novel. In a piece written to complement the play, Wei Minglun describes a convention of writers, including Shi Nai'an, Ouyang Yuqian, Eugène Ionesco, and a self-referential Wei Minglun.[57] Although aiming at a more playful effect than Ouyang Yuqian, Wei Minglun follows the earlier playwright in straddling temporal boundaries and transgressing historical realism.

At the center of Pan Jinlian's encounter with extratextual characters is the question of whether her fate should be changed to fit modern norms. It is on this account that Anna Karenina is summoned to testify. The Russian woman urges her to follow her example and commit suicide. Anna points at the arsenic that Ximen Qing gave to Pan Jinlian and sings:

> Please follow me and lie on those icy railway tracks,
>
> . . .
>
> I died —
> I purified my soul, I transcended my sorrows.
> This is the only way out for a woman.
> This is God's set path for the weak.
> Quickly swallow the arsenic,
> The god of death is calling . . . (HWD, pp. 59–60)

Although Pan Jinlian ignores the advice and instead administers the arsenic to her husband, Anna's appearance draws a parallel between Pan Jinlian and the heroines of novels about adultery, such as Emma Bovary and Anna Karenina, who put an end to their lives.[58] More than Nora, Wei's Pan Jinlian is Emma's and Anna's equal, bold enough to declare her disgust with an incapable husband and seek refuge in the arms of another man. Yet the example of Anna Karenina only serves to demonstrate that, as Wei Minglun's Anna states, the social circumstances make death "the only way out for a woman."[59] Pan Jinlian's fate resonates with the way in which Flaubert and Tolstoy portray Emma Bovary and Anna Karenina (as well as their husbands) as victims of their misguided belief in modern values. Emma Bovary fails to distinguish between historical reality and fictionalized romance; in search of a timeless present, she imitates the novels she reads in life. As Anne Green notes, Emma Bovary ends up perceiving history only in a fragmented, self-nullifying form.[60] Anna Karenina expresses her faith that society will treat her reasonably, yet construes her love affair as a counterforce to temporal experience. Her nemesis comes symbolically in the form of trains, emblems

of mechanical punctuality; the train becomes the vehicle of historical violence, the juggernaut of time that literally crushes her. As I have argued, Pan
Jinlian's similarly misled belief in modernity also accounts for the demise of
Ouyang Yuqian's protagonist. Wei Minglun's Pan Jinlian faces the same
danger.

Against Anna's pessimistic view, Pan Jinlian is presented with more encouraging examples from contemporary China. Lü Shasha says, "I come
from a bright society . . . the new generation of the eighties" and repudiates
Shi Nai'an's "traditional prejudice" (HWD, pp. 5, 7). Shasha also consults a
PRC judge, who opines that Pan Jinlian would have led a fortunate life today,
thanks to modern marital legislation (HWD, p. 55). The metafictional character Wei Minglun also states: "The conclusion is: the tragedy of history
cannot be reenacted, . . . mankind progresses and society develops!"[61] The
contemporary characters, notably led by the author's stage persona, profess
their faith in modernity.

Yet the PRC judge, despite her positive assessment, also explains that literary characters such as Pan Jinlian lie outside her jurisdiction and that the
problem is rooted in the classics (HWD, pp. 54–56). At the opera's end,
when Wu Song expresses his intent to disembowel Pan Jinlian, and she, as in
Ouyang's play, defiantly welcomes his gesture, causing him to waver, the
modern judge reappears to sum up the arguments in the case. At this moment, however, the events are decided, not by modern characters, but rather
by the premodern text, or more precisely by the premodern author. Shi
Nai'an appears on stage and roars: "This book is not concerned with the affairs of later generations; Wu Song—act, kill!" (HWD, p. 65), at which
command, Wu Song proceeds to stab Pan Jinlian to death. Pan Jinlian is
sentenced to death, not by Wu Song's mock court and the traditional social
values he stands for, but by a literary tribunal of fictional characters, in which
Shi Nai'an overrules Lü Shasha's objections.

Wei Minglun takes up the issues raised by Ouyang Yuqian and spells
them out more clearly. Whereas Ouyang takes liberties with the plot to
challenge the advantages of historical consciousness, Wei Minglun's self-
acclaimed "transdynastic, supranational 'absurd' style"[62] transports Pan Jinlian into a fantasy world where purportedly historical events are subjected to
an Alice-in-Wonderland logic, with Shi Nai'an as a single-minded tyrant
ready to lop off Pan's head. Wei acknowledges that "the tragedy of history
cannot be reenacted." To extend his metaphor, what Ouyang once wrote as a
tragedy is now rewritten as parody. Pan Jinlian's "history" (as the subtitle

calls her story) has already occurred as a tragedy and must repeat itself as a farce.

The tragic, absurd resolution of Wei's opera points to the limitations of bearing witness to history. To recall Schopenhauer's words, tragedy fails when put to the test of reality: "[O]ur life must contain all the woes of tragedy, and yet we cannot even assert the dignity of tragic characters, but, in the broad detail of life, are inevitably the foolish characters of a comedy."[63] Wei Minglun implies that the modern witness should be prepared that once she takes the stand, her tragic fate will turn into parody.

THE KARMA OF MISREADING HISTORY

Three years after Wei's opera, Li Bihua (Cantonese: Lee Bik Wah) came up with her own irreverent treatment of Pan Jinlian's story in the novel *Reincarnations of Golden Lotus*, which was soon made into a film by Clara Law (Cantonese: Law Cheuk-yiu), one of Hong Kong's leading "second wave" directors. Li, a prolific and popular novelist and scriptwriter best known for her contribution to the film *Bawang bieji* (Farewell my concubine, 1992), has shown consistent preoccupation with the theme of transporting premodern plots to the setting of present-day China and Hong Kong.

The protagonist of Li's script is Shan Yulian, a woman born in the PRC around 1950. She is raped by Zhang, a Party cadre, who subsequently banishes her to the countryside. She falls in love with Wu Long, a fellow member of her brigade, but he is forced to join her accusers when she is denounced as a counterrevolutionary. In order to escape further abuse, she marries the ugly Hong Kong merchant Wu Ruda and emigrates to the British colony. Wu Ruda's chauffeur turns out to be none other than Wu Long, who is torn between his love for Yulian and his loyalty to Wu Ruda, whom he regards as an elder brother. Rejected, Yulian lets herself be seduced by a fashion designer, Simon (whose name sounds similar to the Cantonese pronunciation of Ximen, Sai Moon). Wu Ruda takes an overdose of aphrodisiac supplied by Simon and falls unconscious. Believing that his boss is dead, Wu Long takes revenge on the fashion designer and kills him. Meanwhile, Yulian has found a copy of *Jin Ping Mei*. Reading it, she experiences a series of flashbacks that link the premodern novel to her own experience. Yulian realizes that her life has so far repeated the *Jin Ping Mei* plot, and that she is Pan Jinlian's reincarnation. Having just killed Simon, Wu Long chases Yulian, who, fearing that he intends to kill her the way Wu Song killed Pan Jinlian, runs him over with her car.[64] With his last gasp, Wu Long tells her that he loves her. Only then does she realize that her present life is not meant to repeat the *Jin Ping Mei* but is rather motivated by Pan Jinlian's resolve to seek retribution from Wu Song. The ending reminds the spectators of the film's first scene, in which Pan Jinlian refuses to drink from the glass that would make her forget her past life, spills the potion, and screams: "I want revenge!"

Li Bihua deliberately bases her plot on *Jin Ping Mei*, the erotic fiction that extends the *Water Margin* episode into a full 120-chapter novel. *Jin Ping Mei*, more than *The Water Margin*, portrays Pan Jinlian as the victim of patriarchal society. Through perceptive descriptions of Pan Jinlian's psyche, the novel presents a complex portrait of a cruel, sex-crazed woman who is at the same time abused and maligned. *Jin Ping Mei* also develops the retribution narrative and includes abundant stock phrases about the inescapable power of retribution.[65] Ximen Qing's death in *Jin Ping Mei*, through his own excess rather than at Wu Song's hands, is clearly portrayed as atonement for the death of Wu Song's brother.[66] The plot of Law's film further explores the connection between karmic retribution and narrative dynamics.

Reincarnations of Golden Lotus also follows the modern example of Ouyang's and Wei's plays, notably in reevaluating the protagonist's misogynistic image. The film focuses on Yulian's viewpoint as a woman abused by beliefs—from traditional views to Maoism—that repress female desire.[67] Yet far more poignant is the film's message that even though Pan Jinlian would probably have been exculpated in a modern context, the ideological rehabilitation of her desire would bring her little comfort, as demonstrated by Yulian's fate. Wu Long pays Wu Song's karmic debt to Pan Jinlian, but Shan Yulian does not benefit from it. As her beloved Wu Long dies in her arms, she loses control over the car and crashes to her death. Yulian becomes yet another victim of Pan Jinlian's revenge, as the earlier avatar drags down the later one against her will. Li Bihua's script, like earlier plays, shows understanding for the protagonist but does not give her modern incarnation any respite.

What makes the twentieth-century textual dynamics just as lethal for the film's heroine is that in contrast to the classical retribution narrative, karma carries no ethical value in the modern plot. In fact, adherence to karmic principles proves fatal, and Yulian's tragedy lies in her misinterpretation of karma. Li introduces karma with a Hegelian twist, so to speak—it could not have determined Yulian's destiny had she not acquired historical consciousness and a drive for self-realization, which makes her interpret her life in terms of the earlier novel. Yulian's death cannot be attributed to fate but results rather from her own misreading of the relationship between *Jin Ping Mei* and reality. She reads the premodern novel as a factual description of historical events; furthermore, she believes that the story might repeat itself through her own life. Ironically, in so doing, she gives the literary text power over her destiny. As in Li Bihua's later *Farewell My Concubine*, the protagonist clings to the premodern literary text in order to avoid confronting the implications of contemporary history.

Notwithstanding its soap-opera gloss, *Reincarnations of Golden Lotus* addresses the same issues that have preoccupied Ouyang's and Wei's more highbrow plays, in particular the role of historical consciousness in shaping modern identity. Like her predecessors, Li Bihua portrays historical consciousness as the cause of misreading the relation between past and present. Yulian's tragic mistake consists of interpreting history in terms of karma and regarding the *Jin Ping Mei* plot as an immutable pattern bound to repeat itself. She fetishizes the novel as a historical record that provides the key to her life. First, she does not identify herself as a reincarnation of Pan Jinlian and cannot read the literary text in a way relevant to her experience. Her second mistake, however, is graver: she overreads the text, interpreting it too literally and excluding the possibility that the plot may be modified.

The final tragic moment comes when Yulian realizes her misreading, only too late. She gradually acquires consciousness of her origin and becomes aware of her mistakes as various verbal and visual stimuli trigger her recollection of the *Jin Ping Mei* plot. She achieves a form of awakening, following the tradition of stories of Buddhist enlightenment in which the protagonist is illuminated after being reminded of former incarnations.[68] Wu Long's last words, "I am—I truly—am fond of you! If—we could start all over again—," make Yulian experience a final flashback, reminding her of Pan Jinlian's oath of revenge that brought about her present incarnation. Only when she has already met her tragic end can Yulian recognize her tragic flaw, namely, that she has consistently misread the current historical events as decided by fate. Wu Long's last wish, to "start all over again," points precisely to the lack of such a possibility. History cannot repeat itself, and Yulian has been fatally mistaken in believing that she is reliving what has already taken place once.

The question of whether the present should be interpreted in light of narratives determined in the past had been particularly relevant to Hong Kong since the early 1980s. The memorandums of 1984 stipulated that the British colony would be handed over to PRC control in 1997. Shan Yulian's trajectory symbolizes the ambiguous relation between the mainland, which lays claim to authentic and hegemonic Chinese culture, and Hong Kong, characterized by its fast-paced stress on the here and now but also by preserving traditions repressed in Communist China. As the handover was approaching, writers and filmmakers were anxious to determine a Hong Kong indigenous culture in terms of both affinity to and difference from mainland China. It is therefore significant that Shan Yulian awakens to her past, defined through a Chinese classic, only after arriving in Hong Kong—only the colony seems to provide a truthful reinterpretation of Chinese tradition. In this sense, the film reflects "the politics of disappearance" that Akbar Abbas identifies in 1980s Hong Kong culture.[69]

Reincarnations of Golden Lotus reacts against presenting historical events as evidence of the fulfillment of a prescribed narrative. The handover was touted as redressing history, paying Britain's debt and bringing a colonial retribution narrative to closure. Yet Shan Yulian's experience refutes such rhetoric. Neither tradition nor modernity provides an explanation for her entrapment. Li Bihua's script reflects a reevaluation of the May Fourth legacy specific to Hong Kong's circumstances, and Law's film bears witness to the futility of seeking to use the colony's example to reverse or correct Chinese national history.

HISTORY'S VERDICT

From their respective places and times, Ouyang Yuqian, Wei Minglun, and Li Bihua reworked the May Fourth definitions of modernity, not to find reaffirmation for historical progress, but rather to point to a cultural crisis. Pan Jinlian acquires an awareness of her place in history, reclaims her voice as a woman, and asserts her modernity, but time and again, she cannot be saved. Suspended between a hermetic karmic cycle and the Enlightenment narrative of progress, she cannot resolve her predicament. Even the modern text does not provide an appropriate space for proclaiming social progress and bearing witness *for* history.

Significantly, the three pieces provide multilayered spectacles—legal hearings and executions are placed within stage and screen performances. The dramatic medium stresses that nothing can be done to change the plot—as Stanley Cavell notes, a tension arises from sitting in a theater and witnessing a crime, fully aware that only a yokel would jump on stage to prevent Othello from killing Desdemona.[70] One may argue that the spectators may develop resentment at their helplessness and look for ways to act out justice outside the theater. Yet though the plays at hand seem to entertain more hope than Lu Xun's airtight parables (see Chapter 1), the choice to fashion bearing witness against history as legal testimony and place it on stage has important implications. The theater also stands for the abstract space where opinions may be aired and discussed. Thus the plays function as courts of appeal for the case of modernity, and the literary sphere of debate is shown to be an ineffective place to plead that cause. Pan Jinlian's judgment puts on trial, not only literary tradition, but also China's modern public discourse.

The recourse to drama and film reflected May Fourth's Enlightenment-inspired interest in providing a space where audiences would be imbued with a collective consciousness that would propel change (hence also the burgeoning of literary societies and magazines in the 1920s and 1930s). The trend arguably culminated in the "left-wing cinema" of the 1930s, but doubts about bearing literary witness to history and, in particular, about the dynamics of the spectacle did not abate.

3 Revolution and Revulsion

Ideology, Monstrosity, and Phantasmagoria in 1930s Chinese Cinema

In the 1930s, a growing number of novels and films displayed a more militant stance in the political strife and reformulated May Fourth ideals through images taken from the battlefield. The theme song in Xu Xingzhi's 1935 film *Fengyun ernü* (Children of troubled times), "Yiyong jun jinxingqu" (March of the volunteers)—later adopted as the anthem of the People's Republic of China—starts with the following lines: "Arise, those who refuse to be slaves! / With our very flesh and blood / We shall build a new Great Wall!" Although there is an invigorating pathos in the lyrics, the macabre image of a wall made of flesh and blood is hard to ignore. It draws its heroic appeal from the reference, metaphorical as it may be, to mutilated human bodies. This and similar descriptions of cruel spectacles and physical violence, as well as images of bodily deformity and monstrosity, show a lingering disbelief in the promise of social utopia and the viability of public debate in the revolutionary rhetoric of the 1930s.

The themes of mutilation and sacrifice are foregrounded in *Yeban gesheng* (Song at midnight), directed by Ma-Xu Weibang (1905–61). The film's production began in 1935, and it was released in February 1937. It is no coincidence that the film resonates with the PRC's anthem: Tian Han, who also wrote the lyrics to the "March of the Volunteers," was the co-writer of the script, under the pseudonym Chen Yu.[1] Like *Children of Troubled Times, Song at Midnight* has often been classified as part of "left-wing cinema," yet it presents revolutionary ideology in a roundabout manner. The hero is fashioned after the title role of *The Phantom of the Opera*, resulting in a curious grafting of Chinese revolutionary discourse onto the Hollywood horror movie.

The fashioning of revolution through the hero's facial deformity literally fleshes out the inner contradictions of revolutionary utopia and underscores contemporary doubts about appealing to the masses. On the one hand, the

1930s were characterized by a growing engagement by the arts in the political sphere. Internal political strife since the massacre of communist sympathizers in Shanghai by Chiang Kai-shek's forces in 1927, and growing Japanese aggression in Manchuria since 1931, contributed to a strong nationalist agenda, largely identified with the left wing of the KMT and the CCP. The literary scene came to be dominated by the Chinese League of Left-Wing Writers (Zhongguo zuoyi zuojia lianmeng), established in 1930. On the other hand, doubts that were not made explicit in ideological debates surfaced in film. The fate of Ma-Xu's scarred hero is of special interest, since it provides a self-reflexive assessment of cinema's role and in particular questions its efficacy as a propaganda tool. While the League of Left-Wing Writers called in 1931 for "making literature available to the masses" (*wenxue de dazhonghua*),[2] *Song at Midnight* challenges the assumption that the masses would collaborate with revolutionary writers and filmmakers. The protagonist, significantly portrayed as a stage artist and author, is doomed to alienation from and conflict with his audience. Suspended between the genre conventions of the horror film and revolutionary cinema, *Song at Midnight* is a parable about the tension between film's ideological function and the popular allure of cinema.

Although I deal here primarily with a single movie, the genealogy and reception of *Song at Midnight* point out its relevance to understanding other works from the 1930s. The film's spectacular success demonstrates the efficacy of the plot in appealing to both social sensibilities and the demand for entertainment, but critics have tended to privilege one plotline over the other ever since the film's first release. When the newspaper *Dawanbao* reviewed the film soon after its premiere, the critic distinguished between the two plotlines and warned that simply producing a horror film would be a "mistake." Yet the columnist did not find fault with *Song at Midnight*, since horror films were permissible in his view as long as they also "encouraged humanity to struggle for the well-being of the masses."[3] The distinction between the plot elements along a clear-cut ideological divide was taken a step further in 1963 by Cheng Jihua, whose Party-endorsed *Zhongguo dianying fazhan shi* (History of the development of Chinese cinema) condemns the homage to *Phantom of the Opera* in a would-be revolutionary piece and criticizes the main character's "individual heroism, struggle with oneself, petit bourgeois fervor, and sentimental love."[4] On the other hand, the revolutionary plot has been played down by recent studies, including, notably, Leo Oufan Lee's landmark reevaluation in his book *Shanghai Modern* (1999) of the "decadent" streak in Chinese films and literature of the 1930s, which laments the "implausible and forced" patriotic message in an otherwise well-crafted horror film.[5] Critical views have largely dismissed the combination of revolution and entertainment and attributed it either to Ma-Xu's relenting to Tian Han's ideological intervention or to the Left's insincere currying of favor with audiences. Such approaches tend to lose sight of the profound implications of coupling the revolutionary and the revolting. The protagonist's scar becomes a privileged sign, connoting the preeminence of the revolutionary hero's speech and the triumph of ideology. At the same time, while a contemporary short story describes the revolutionary mission as "tearing off the evil faces" of the "demonic" reactionary forces,[6] in Ma-Xu's film, it is the revolutionary protagonist who regards himself as a monster and masks his face. Rather than take for granted the incompatibility of revolutionary rhetoric and popular "bourgeois" media, one should acknowledge their symbiotic coexistence.

Contrary to contemporary rhetoric and later official reasoning, socially engaged filmmakers did not draw a clear line between their ideological agenda and popular techniques of representation. As Yingjin Zhang notes, it is to a large extent later critics who have made political classifications prevail.[7] The ideological bias, I argue, also reveals the paradoxical position of public discourse in the 1930s and in mass media in particular. Despite a deep-rooted suspicion of entertainment, left-wing circles promoted cinema because of its appeal to a broad audience. The protagonist's double role as revolutionary hero and fantastic apparition concedes that even revolutionary ideology must rely on the allure of the spectacle. At least in the major coastal cities, where *Song at Midnight* was screened, revolutionary strategies of representation gained a following precisely because of the plots' internal tension and narrative heterogeneity. Other contemporary popular films affirm this view. For example, *Shizi jietou* (Crossroads) and *Yasui qian* (New year's coin), both released in 1937, also combine a social message with an entertaining plot. Another example is Sun Yu's *Daybreak*, which blurs revolutionary heroism and concern for the viewers' visual pleasure, as discussed in the Introduction to this book. If, as Paul Pickowicz argues, many left-wing cinematographers "became captives of melodrama,"[8] they were willing captives of this and other popular cinematic devices. The publicity brochure for the showing of *Song at Midnight* in the Luguang [Capitol] Movie Theater in Chengdu during the Hundred Flower Movement of 1956 recaptures the possibility that the two plots are complementary: "At the time, people called

[*Song at Midnight*] 'a great horror film,' but in fact the movie's author in-tended to use the 'horror film' genre to . . . encourage a new generation to [embark on] a new struggle. It is the most outstanding, representative film of its period since May Fourth."[9] To this assessment one may add that in seaming together the two plotlines with coarse stitches, the film continues May Fourth's undercurrent of bearing witness against unmitigated faith in historical progress.

REALISM AND "ICE CREAM FOR THE EYES"

Song at Midnight is set in the China of 1937.[10] It recounts the exploits of Song Danping, a member of the revolutionary underground (played by Jin Shan). Danping's portrayal as a "comrade" (*tongzhi*) fighting against warlords and landlords establishes his left-wing allegiance.[11] The movie focuses on the process by which Danping hands over his mission to a younger man, Sun Xiao'ou (Shi Chao). Through the relationship between Danping and Xiao'ou, the film explores the issues of communicating the revolutionary message and transmitting ideological authority.

In this respect, *Song at Midnight* follows the general narrative pattern of the Soviet novel. As Katerina Clark shows, many Soviet novels share a similar "master plot." They start when the hero arrives in a new place that needs to be set right and mobilizes the "people" to the task but encounters resistance from counterrevolutionary forces. Having overcome these obstacles and his own doubts, the hero completes his mission, and the novels typically end in mourning the dead victims and celebrating the bright future. Ma-Xu Weibang could avail himself of model novels such as Fedor V. Gladkov's *Cement* (1925), which had been well-known in China since its translation in 1930. Sun Xiao'ou's persona is modeled on the Soviet plot: Xiao'ou's opera troupe moves into a rundown theater but fails to draw spectators; mentored by Song Danping, Xiao'ou successfully stages the revolutionary piece *Warm Blood*. An evil landlord, Tang Jun (played by Gu Menghe), interferes and tries to rape Xiao'ou's beloved Lüdie (Xu Manli), but Danping comes to the rescue. Although Danping and Lüdie die in the ensuing fracas, at the end of the film, Xiao'ou surveys the rising sun, looking toward bright horizons.

The plot, thus far fully indebted to the Soviet model, is complicated by the theme of the scar. Danping is a talented opera singer whose face has been turned into a horrifying cicatrix by Tang Jun's men. Danping's scar becomes the mark of the historic battle between feudal and revolutionary forces. Insofar as the facial deformity signals its bearer's sacrifice and the reality of his struggle, the scar is an icon of ideological virtue. It is easy to recognize in this echoes of the contemporary rhetoric of realism, which, as Marston Anderson notes, uses the injured body to invoke pity for the hero and revulsion for the events depicted.[12] In accordance with what I have referred to in the Introduction to this book as the affectation of writing in blood, the scar may function as an irrefutable sign of reality, as if it articulated the revolutionary's message better than words. Yet the scar also stands in counterpoint to the revolutionary message, inasmuch as Danping is prevented from carrying out his mission because he does not want to show his face in public. Throughout the film, the scar threatens to become a sign of condemnation and ruin, an external feature that contradicts the redemptive message.

Here *Song at Midnight* draws on an alternative genealogy, namely, the aesthetics of the Hollywood horror film. Ma-Xu's plot takes after the film version of *The Phantom of the Opera* (known in China as *Gesheng moying*, 1925) directed by Rupert Julian. Like Julian's protagonist, who lives hidden in the cellars of the Opéra de Paris, Danping leads a phantomlike existence in the theater attic. Ma-Xu's career bears an uncanny resemblance to that of Lon Chaney, the actor and makeup artist who co-directed and played the title role in Julian's *The Phantom of the Opera*. It is no coincidence that the magazine *Yingxi shenghuo* (Cinema life; also known by its English title *Movie Weekly*) frequently called Ma-Xu the "Lon Chaney of the East."[13] Both Ma-Xu and Chaney rose to directorial status from careers as makeup artists— Ma-Xu played the title role in his own film *Hunshi mowang* (Human devil, 1929), wearing demonic makeup.[14] As a pioneer of the Chinese horror film, Ma-Xu should also be compared to James Whale, who helped define the horror genre as director of *Frankenstein* (known in China as *Kexue guairen*, 1931), *The Old Dark House* (*Guwu qi'an*, 1932), *The Invisible Man* (1933), and *The Bride of Frankenstein* (1935), all of which seem to have influenced the plot and camera work of *Song at Midnight*. Like Julian's *Phantom* and Whale's *Frankenstein*, which have often been remade and alluded to, Ma-Xu's film has left a lasting imprint on cinematic tradition. *Song at Midnight* inspired at least a dozen remakes and spin-offs in China, Taiwan, and Hong Kong, from Ma-Xu's own 1941 *Yeban gesheng xuji* (Song at midnight, part II) to Ronny Yu's 1995 *Xin yeban gesheng* (The new *Song at Midnight*; English title *The Phantom Lover*).[15]

Ma-Xu's experience as filmmaker demonstrates a commitment to both social criticism and the Hollywood horror genre. He is remembered mostly for his horror films, starting with his first silent film, *Qingchang guairen* (Monster in love), in 1926, but revolutionary zeal and visual monstrosity are inextricably interwoven in his plots, notably in *Qiu Haitang* (1943) and *Qiong-lou hen* (Rancor at a luxuriant mansion), also known as *The Haunted House* or *A Maid's Bitter Story* (1949). Later, Ma-Xu distanced himself from the CCP line, and he left Shanghai in 1949 for Hong Kong, where he directed *Xin yu guangqu* (The new *Song of the Fishermen*), a film with anti-communist undertones (1955). Yet even his late films, such as the 1958 *Liulang er* (Young vagabonds), introduced social messages.[16]

Song at Midnight, deemed by its director in 1945 to be his best film,[17] encapsulates these complementary interests. Ma-Xu deftly combines the revolutionary plot with a melodramatic love story. After Danping is scarred, he hides in the attic of the opera house to conceal his scar from his beloved Li Xiaoxia (played by Hu Ping). Since he can appear to her only as a disembodied voice, singing under her balcony, Danping recruits Xiao'ou to impersonate him and sing for the bereaved woman. The two plots run in parallel: Xiao'ou is urged to take Danping's place both as a revolutionary hero and as Xiaoxia's lover.

The scar's double function, as a bridge between the ideological and sentimental plotlines as well as a marker of the tension between engaged and commodified art, should be understood in the context of critical debates in the 1930s. Left-wing artists were wary that texts and films originally intended to shock readers and spectators into class consciousness might instead turn into fascinating diversion and further detach the audience from social issues. Critics made increasingly strong demands for art with a clear ideological message and introduced the Soviet term "socialist realism." Genres that did not comport with their definition of realism were labeled "self-indulgent" or "romantic" and were considered detrimental to the nation's interests.[18] The debate over "realism" and "romanticism" carried over from literary to film circles. In 1933, a group of critics called for "soft film" (*ruanxing pian*), cinema as a form of entertainment employing light-hearted love stories. The scriptwriter Huang Jiamo made the catchy claim that "movies are ice cream for the eyes, a sofa for the soul." Left-wing critics, who were interested in film as a vehicle of political ideology, rejected the "ice-cream theory," as it came to be known. Instead, they adopted a line akin to socialist realism and promoted "hard film" (*yingxing pian*), emphasizing cinema's mission to awaken the masses.[19] In 1934, for example, the "hard film" advocate Wang Chenwu, who saw the two approaches to film as mutually exclusive, proclaimed that "form is determined by content [alone]," asserting a Soviet-style hierarchy.[20]

The love story and the revolutionary plot of *Song at Midnight* represent the "soft film" and "hard film" approaches respectively. Giving Danping's scar center stage risks allowing form to dictate content and cinematic device to compromise the ideological message. Yet perhaps even more problematic from the social critics' point of view, the scar challenges the very distinction between "soft film" and "realism." The wound is both a symbol of Danping's struggle and a fantastic image that fascinates spectators. The film's cinematic and ideological concerns cannot be neatly separated; they are even complementary.

MELODRAMA AND THE VISIBILITY OF TRUTH

Danping's scar introduces a dialectic of exposure and concealment, signaling the protagonist's need both to face reality and to conceal his identity. As a wound that has healed but yet remains visible, the scar is an apt metaphor for the underground revolutionary's liminal presence. The climactic scenes appropriately focus on stripping off Danping's disguises one by one. The plot reaches a decisive turn when Danping unveils himself and displays his scar to proclaim his mission. Xiao'ou pursues the phantom to the attic, where the latter discloses his identity and exposes his face to his would-be heir. He had been thought dead for the past ten years and now reappears to take up an unfinished project.

The hero first establishes his hidden virtue by naming himself and divulging his identity. Here the plot enlists the melodramatic device of identifying the protagonist by explicit statements. Following conventions established in early nineteenth-century French theater, melodrama assumes that unadulterated truth is manifest in every staged word and image. Heroes and villains alike announce their names, qualifications, and moral identities in clear form, as if it were a revelation.[21] In this vein, Danping tells Xiao'ou: "The renowned Song Danping of ten years ago is me. But the revolutionary pioneer Jin Zhijian, who ran for his life thirteen years ago in the Yangtze River region, sacrificing himself in the struggle for liberty, is also Song Danping. This devoted revolutionary fighter did not die."[22] Danping stages his identity and declares it melodramatically in the third person. He reinforces his claim by showing Xiao'ou photographs of his previous personae as a singer and a revolutionary. Danping's rectitude is evidenced both verbally and visually.

These signs prepare the setting for the ultimate proof of the hero's probity, when he takes off his hood. When Xiao'ou hesitates to take Danping's place, the latter shows his scar, the sight of which compels the younger singer to do his ideological duty. Danping demonstrates that Xiao'ou is his legitimate heir by various signs, including mentoring his singing and handing over the libretto of *Warm Blood* to the younger man. It is, however, by baring his scarred face that Danping initiates Xiao'ou and confers his revolutionary mission upon the younger singer. Showing the scar complements Danping's authorial acts and helps communicate his ideology to Xiao'ou.

Flaunting the facial disfiguration has a clear melodramatic effect. The scar establishes an aesthetics of excess, a theatricality, reminiscent of Diderot, that justifies itself by histrionic exaggeration. Danping's revolutionary credentials are bolstered by overdramatizing the performative nature of revolution and showing off his monstrosity. Comporting with the conventions of melodrama, the plot builds toward the moment of final revelation, when all secrets will be disclosed, intrigues unraveled, and masks torn off. The climactic conclusion, to which I shall return later, starts when Danping exposes himself to the evil Tang Jun as a sign that the final moment of retribution has come. The scar is a secret mark, revealed only when the time is ripe to demonstrate the identity and virtue of its bearer, and it obliges the reactionary landlord to recognize the force of the coming revolution. The melodramatic dynamics call for overt testimony, and bearing witness is rewarded with an immediate, unquestioning response.

As the film draws to a close and Danping's face is unmasked once and for all, the naked revolutionary truth is also revealed to the audience in explicit words. "We must strive harder to struggle against these dark forces, smash them, and fight for the freedom of the masses," Xiao'ou declares. The final exposition of ideology is also enhanced by the cinematic composition. After two hours of dimly lit scenes, a dazzlingly bright shot shows Xiao'ou and Xiaoxia (whose name means "daybreak glow") standing heroically on a cliff, facing the rising sun. Truth inevitably surfaces from the dark and shines upon an enlightened world.

THE DISEMBODIED VOICE OF IDEOLOGY

In contrast to the plot's progression toward exposure, the scar is first depicted as forcing the protagonist into hiding. Tang Jun, who covets the singer's beloved Xiaoxia, sends his men to splash acid over Danping's face, after which the latter cannot bear to show his deformity in public.[23] Danping asks a messenger to inform Xiaoxia that he is dead and retreats to the attic. The need to conceal his inner virtue lends a heroic aura to Danping's actions—he is a visionary ahead of his time, tragically misunderstood and persecuted. The scar fashions Danping as a revolutionary forced underground, working literally behind the scenes as the disembodied voice of ideology.

Danping's dramatic agon is appropriately announced in the theater. His ubiquitous sonorous singing reaches from his hiding place, foretokening the triumph of his ideology. The lyrics of the title song both promote the romantic plot at face value and emphasize that the hero's revolutionary voice cannot be quelled. Every night, Danping hides himself in the attic opposite Xiaoxia's balcony and sings to her:

> You are the moon in the sky,
> I am the lonely star next to the moon;
> You are the tree on the mountain,
> I am the withered vine on that tree;
> You are the water in the pond,
> I am the weed floating on the water![24]

Danping is only a shadow, but his voice transcends his blemished body and continues to resound through the images shown on the screen—a moonlit sky, a vine entwined around a tree, floating duckweed. The lyrics not only proclaim Danping's everlasting commitment to Xiaoxia but also insinuate that he will communicate the revolutionary message even after his physical annihilation. The song's last line is especially significant—the revolutionary message will stay afloat like duckweed, unperturbed by the flux of events, in synchrony with the flow of history. Danping's name, literally "Cinnabar Weed," alludes to the same theme and compounds it with the red color of mercuric sulfide. The red of love and left-wing ideology is destined to last forever, possessing the immortality that Daoist alchemy associates with cinnabar elixir.

Danping continues to stage his message vicariously from his hiding place by mentoring others' operatic art. He helps Xiao'ou to rehearse and later teaches his protégé the melody to be sung to Xiaoxia. Lastly, he hands over his own revolutionary libretto, *Warm Blood*, to be performed by Xiao'ou's troupe. The three episodes indicate Danping's growing success in overcoming the silence imposed on him and in spreading his message to an increasingly large audience.

Danping's uncontained voice compensates for concealing his face and announces the coming eruption of revolution in visible form. In a symbol-laden scene, Xiao'ou fails to reach the high notes, at which point Danping appears as a shadowy figure behind the sets and helps Xiao'ou through the difficult phrase. A duet develops between the younger singer on stage and the voice in the dark.[25] The voices respond to each other by repeating the lyrics again and again, creating a dialogue of echoes. Significantly, the phrase they sing is:

> The pursuing soldiers are coming!
> What shall I do?
> Mother, I am like a fledgling that cannot
>   return to the nest,
> Cannot return to the nest.

The exchange anticipates how Xiao'ou (whose name literally means "Little Seagull") will grow wings and join the Revolutionary Party. At the same time, the aria stresses that the ideological truth cannot remain nested in hiding but must rather come out into the open.

REVOLUTIONARY TRANSFERENCE

The transmission of revolutionary authority from Danping to Xiao'ou foregrounds the fact that the ideological revelation will materialize through the young singer, whereas the bearer of the scar will remain hidden forever. Here the scar violates the parameters that have so far, through Danping's injury, preserved his right to speak. The concealed face signals not only the hero's revolutionary mission but also his deficiency. Danping sees himself as a monster: "I am a demon, I am a beast, I can no longer stay together with you!" His forced retirement introduces the suspicion that the revolution cannot be truthfully represented and, moreover, that it is marred by shortcomings. The scar's revolutionary significance slips quickly to it being regarded as a repugnant monstrosity and a fascinating object of consumption. The scar's aesthetics take precedence over its ideological value and haunt the revolutionary plot.

The scar's compromised position is underscored by the title song, which Danping sings to his beloved every night. The relevant lines go:

> In form I am a demonic monster,
> But my heart is as steadfast as iron . . .
> O maiden,
> Only your eyes can see through my life,
> Only your heart can understand my sorrow!

The song connects the themes of love and revolution, as the description of Danping's love for Xiaoxia—"my heart is as steadfast as iron"—puns on his revolutionary name, Jin Zhijian, literally, "metal-strong will." Even the lyrics, written by the left-wing writer Tian Han, portray the revolutionary author in a compromised position. The romantic relationship shows the author to be caught between the urge to awaken society to historical consciousness and the danger of scaring away his audience. Even when singing the words "only your eyes can see through my life," Danping shows himself as no more than a hooded silhouette. In Danping, the revolution remains an unmaterialized shadow; his testimony is never delivered in person.

The revolutionary sign's failure to transcend aesthetic considerations is indicated by Danping's quest for a more presentable face to substitute for his own. Danping communicates with Xiaoxia through Xiao'ou as proxy. The older singer delegates his mission to another mouthpiece at the cost of erasing his identity and ultimately negating his physical existence. Were it not for the emphasis on the scar's monstrosity, Danping's selfless renunciation of authority could have stood for the transmission of doctrine, based on a revolutionary repudiation of the self and carrying the ideological mission through the collective. Seeing his own scar, Danping gains a critical self-alienation that culminates in transferring the torch to another man. The scar, by contrast, helps identify the flawless double as the heir who will put ideology into practice. Just as the scar serves as a token of Danping's virtue, Xiao'ou's unmarred face signifies that he is Danping's proper and legitimate successor.

Yet the narrative focus on the transmission of revolutionary authority is compromised by an emphasis on visual aesthetics. The deformed face becomes the sign of doom, for which a handsome complexion must be substituted. Xiao'ou is given the privilege of viewing the scar precisely because his own unblemished face is destined to represent the revolution in public. Symbolically, Danping declares Xiao'ou to be his heir soon after a flashback sequence that shows the scarred singer smashing the mirror reflecting his deformed face. Unwilling to see his image duplicated in the mirror, Danping seeks to regenerate himself through a younger, more attractive person.

It is interesting to compare the plot with Ma-Xu's *The Haunted House*, where the facial mark is literally erased after the truth is revealed. Lin Yuqin impersonates Mr. Gao's dead daughter, Lingjuan, and tries to find out how the young woman died (Yuqin's and Lingjuan's roles are played by the same actress, Wang Danfeng). To look like Lingjuan, Yuqin paints a mole over her upper lip. After she has exposed Lingjuan's murderers, she demonstrates to Mr. Gao that she is not his daughter by wiping off the false mole.[26] The easy erasure of the mark in *The Haunted House* stands in stark contrast to the violence and death involved in eradicating the scar in *Song at Midnight*. Rather than let his pursuers see his face, Danping chooses to perish. It is as if the scar must be erased at all costs, even through the death of its bearer. Unlike *The Haunted House*, *Song at Midnight* cannot accommodate the facially marked person. The plot betrays an aesthetic bias that pushes for the scar's annihilation and prevails over its ideological significance.

BENEVOLENT MONSTERS:

A CINEMATIC GENEALOGY

Insofar as *Song at Midnight* draws its force from attributing a double meaning to the scar—as a sign of virtue and as a repulsive flaw—the film relies on important precedents. The works that inspired Ma-Xu's piece also use deformity as a sign of both heroism and evil.

Hollywood's *The Phantom of the Opera* and *Frankenstein* are known as horror films and are associated with vampire stories.[27] Nevertheless, these productions also show compassion to the "monsters," a trait emphasized in the original novels, Gaston Leroux's *Le Fantôme de l'Opéra* (1910) and Mary Godwin Shelley's *Frankenstein, or the Modern Prometheus* (1818). Erik, the "phantom" who inhabits the Opéra de Paris, is a man cast out by society because he was born with repulsive deformities. Leroux's novel depicts the mentoring of the singer Christine Daaé as a tragic attempt on Erik's part to find the love that no woman would be able to give him. The protagonist of Shelley's work is equally pitiable. Victor Frankenstein's scientific experiments inadvertently create a humanoid monster. The Creature, although terrifyingly ugly, is at first kind-hearted and longs for friends, and he becomes murderous only after being abused by humans.[28] The monsters' ugliness always belies a benign innate character.

Fantôme and *Frankenstein* both depict their protagonists' deaths as acts of self-sacrifice. In Leroux's novel (unlike in Julian's film), Erik perishes for Christine's sake; in Whale's *The Bride of Frankenstein*, the Creature altruistically takes his own life. Ironically, "the modern Prometheus" of the novel's subtitle, the one punished for saving humanity, may not be the scientist but the Creature, who commits suicide to spare humanity from his own wrath. *Song at Midnight* follows the outline of these plots in depicting Danping's scar as a sign of the injustice done to him by society, as well as by concluding with the protagonist's heroic death, Danping's Promethean martyrdom.

Not only is Danping's self-sacrifice fashioned after Hollywood horror films, but the last scenes of *Song at Midnight* clearly imitate the concluding sequences of *Phantom* and *Frankenstein* almost shot by shot. Like the Creature in *Frankenstein*, Danping is chased by a torch-carrying crowd and trapped in a burning hilltop tower. Like Erik in Julian's *Phantom of the Opera*, he jumps into a river. Finally, the awkward ending of *Song at Midnight* becomes less mystifying when one recognizes it as a reenactment of the last shot in *The Bride of Frankenstein*. Xiao'ou and Danping's beloved Xiaoxia stand shoulder to shoulder, seemingly looking toward a bright future (together?!).[29] Whale's film concludes with a similar image, where Frankenstein and Elizabeth stand on a hill, finally delivered from the monster's menace.[30] It is as if the conclusion to Ma-xu's film were determined by its antecedents.[31]

Song at Midnight also draws on the films *Phantom of the Opera* and *Frankenstein* in portraying the scar as a mark of Promethean virtue and sacrifice and in eliciting a dynamics of visual fascination. Ma-Xu embraces the strong filmic effect of the apocalyptic conclusion, although it might compromise the revolutionary message. His use of artistic license to bend the plot in the service of the filmic spectacle resonates with James Whale's *auteur*-like attitude toward *Frankenstein*'s conclusion. After the producers forced him to add a happy ending in which Frankenstein survives, Whale proceeded to defend the new plot, saying: "This semi-happy ending was added to remind the audience that after all—it is only a tale that is told, and could easily be twisted any way by the director."[32] If Ma-Xu reworked the ending to satisfy his viewers, he could claim, like Whale, that foregrounding the cinematic drive ultimately benefits the ideological message. Yet the ambiguous ending

of *Song at Midnight* raises the same issues that haunted the Hollywood productions. Is the hero's death a moral necessity, or is it rather the climax of
the horror film's spectacle? And if so, does the viewers' thrilled reaction
make them complicit in persecuting the hero?

SHANGHAI SILVER-SCREEN GOTHIC

As a cinematic production, *Song at Midnight* relies on its horror imagery and
emphasizes it to captivate the audience, following the tradition of the gothic
novel and its silver-screen descendant, the horror movie. From film's early
days, make-believe monstrosities were welcomed as the ultimate use of
cinematic resources. Horror film quickly became a major genre, with artists
such as Lon Chaney elevating camp to the status of high art.[33] Shanghai studios were adept at manipulating the gaze, and Ma-Xu's makeup art took
them further toward cinematic voyeurism. Ma-Xu pays tribute to Julian's
Phantom of the Opera by imitating classical horror shots, such as a black cat
slipping down the stairs and a door slowly opened by long, menacing fingers.
Ma-Xu's camera lingers on Danping's deformity in lengthy close-ups and invites the spectator to watch the scarred face over and over again.

The use of hallmark horror film camera work was also backed by a public
relations campaign that played up the lurid aspects of the piece. Warnings
from left-wing critics notwithstanding, the reaction of moviegoers proved
that the audience liked *Song at Midnight* precisely for the sentimental plot
and visual effects.[34] Xinhua Studio seems to have played both sides in promoting *Song at Midnight*, presenting the movie as a patriotic piece, on the
one hand, and at the same time exploiting ideological resistance to cinema as
entertainment and popular fears of horror films to stir public interest, on the
other. Reception of Hollywood productions inside and outside the United
States had demonstrated that while audiences would often denounce horror
films for being "unwholesome and ghastly, morbid, inhuman and pointless,"
distribution also benefited from the free advertising generated by the films'
bad name.[35] Shanghai producers followed suit; unfazed by a government ban
on ghost films, Ma-Xu promoted a public image that would tease out scandal and draw large crowds.[36] Ma-Xu's effigy as a monster often appeared in
magazines. The first issue of *Movie Weekly* displayed a photomontage of Ma-
Xu in demonic attire, holding Chaplin's head in his hand and with the actress
Wang Xieyan's head depicted on his belly (fig. 1). Three issues later, the
magazine featured a "before and after" montage of Ma-Xu's well-groomed

Fig. 1. Photomontage of Ma-Xu Weibang holding Chaplin's head in his hand, with the actress Wang Xieyan's head depicted on his belly. *Yingxi shenghuo* (Cinema life) 1, no. 1.

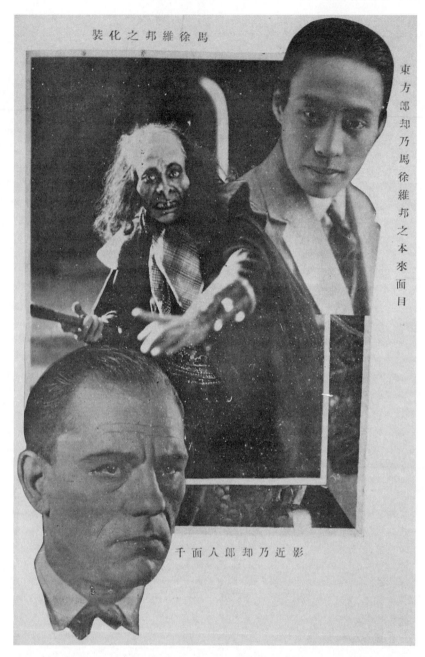

裝化之邦維徐馬

東方郎却乃馬徐維邦之本來面目

千面人郎却乃近影

Fig. 2. Ma-Xu Weibang, with and without makeup, and Lon Chaney. *Yingxi shenghuo* (Cinema life) 1, no. 4. The legend identifies Ma-Xu as the "Lon Chaney of the East."

Fig. 3. A Shanghai street advertisement for *Song at Midnight* at the time of its premiere in February 1937. The billboard's scale is indicated by the man walking up a ladder in the middle right. Notice also the hands protruding in front of the board. The figure was reported to have scared a child to death. "*Yeban gesheng guanggao niangcheng renming*," *Diansheng zhoukan* 6, no. 11 (Mar. 19, 1937): 521.

looks and horrifying makeup (probably for the film *Human Devil*) (fig. 2). Soon after the release of *Song at Midnight*, the cover of *Xinhua huabao* (Xinhua illustrated magazine) showed Ma-Xu as Song Danping, with his hands stretched out menacingly.[37] Ma-Xu probably relished an article that described him as a pervert who drew pleasure from people's terror, an ascetic who released his repressed desires through his films.[38]

It seems that the distributors of *Song at Midnight* took to heart the advice given by *Movie Weekly*: no matter how bad a movie may be, all one needs is a good copywriter. To get a full house, advertise the film's sexual appeal and weird effects. Do not fail to advise against bringing children under sixteen years of age to see it.[39] All of these elements appear in a news article published approximately a month after the film's release, which reports that an eleven-year-old girl had literally died of fright after seeing a large billboard ad for *Song at Midnight*. Although the details cited—the date and time of day, the girl's name, and her parents' occupation—appear to add credibility to the report, the story was most likely a concocted publicity stunt. The girl's repeated pleas—"Father! The man over there frightens me!" "The black man is back!" "Oh, I am afraid!"—and her father's incredulity are taken straight out of folktales such as the one that inspired Goethe's ballad "Der Erlkönig" (The elf king). The story emphasizes the sensational aspects of the movie and its unsuitability for young children (newspaper ads stated clearly: "Children under six not admitted").[40] At the same time, the article implicitly reassures Shanghai readers that they will not be affected like the poor girl, who had just arrived from the countryside and spoke Ningbo dialect. Neither does the article fail to credit the Xinhua Studio and mention that the film is currently playing at the Jincheng Movie Theater.[41]

The cunning use of what may be called reverse advertisement, warning people only to draw them in, was accompanied by sophisticated street advertising. The billboard that purportedly scared the girl to death was placed across from the Horse Race Club in downtown Shanghai. A photograph illustrating the *Movie Weekly* article (fig. 3) provides some visual clues—the billboard featured an effigy of the Phantom stretching out long arms that protruded in front of the board and swayed in the breeze (the darker stripes in the photo are the arms and their shadows). The Phantom billboard towered higher than a four-story building and was a spectacle in its own right. The billboard did not mention the revolutionary plot but bore the word "horror" in large characters. It is probably precisely these advertising tactics that allowed newspaper ads to stay close to the truth in claiming with feigned alarm, "The audience is so large that it spills into the street; movie fans fill the theater's every nook and cranny."[42] The promise of scandal and horror was surer to attract audiences than any prospect of edification.

HORROR AND FASCINATION

The appeal of the much-advertised horror imagery was manipulated consciously not only by the advertisers but also by Ma-Xu's camera work, which shows clear awareness of the implications of voyeurism. This is well demonstrated in the mirror scene, which deserves detailed examination. It is in this scene that the deformed face appears on screen for the very first time. The bandages are taken off Danping's face in an act resembling the shedding of a cocoon, stressing his metamorphosis. The people in front of him recede in terror, and the singer goes to the mirror, where he discovers that the acid has left his face covered with swollen cicatrices, disfiguring his eye sockets and mouth especially. Upon seeing his face, he shouts, "No!" five times, with increasing agony. Unable to bear the sight of his deformed face, he breaks the mirror. This episode could have been exploited as a turning point in the revolutionary plot, the moment when Danping loses all individual aspirations and awakens to the self-alterity of revolution. By breaking the mirror, Danping literally loses the opportunity for self-reflection. The scar serves as a figure of excess, however, not as a mark of ideological allegiance. Danping—like Frankenstein before him—abhors his own image.[43]

The mirror scene invites the spectators to empathize with Danping yet at the same time stresses the scar's graphic horror. Ma-Xu's lens builds up the suspense and shows the doctor removing the gauze strips one by one, while Danping's head remains outside the frame. In the next shot, the camera moves behind Danping to show four terrified grimaces as those present set eyes on the scar (the reaction shot of a young girl's face is especially manipulative). Danping is taunted by the horrified response to his face, which he himself cannot see—"What is it? Why do you all look scared?" he asks.[44] The film's spectators share Danping's point of view and, like him, want to gaze at the face that has emerged from under the bandages.

Ma-Xu employs Hollywood cinematic devices, borrowing specifically from Whale's *The Invisible Man*. This film, made immediately following *Frankenstein*, portrays a scientist who has become invisible. When the man takes off the gauze that covers his head, the camera shows the bandage apparently wrapped around thin air where the man's head should be. In this episode, the scarred face known from other horror films vanishes altogether. In a symbolism too rich to explore in this study, *The Invisible Man* illustrates the nature of filmic fascination, a desire that can never be satisfied because it aims at figures of the void.[45]

Ma-Xu is mindful of the spectators' fascination with the scar. To cater to this voyeuristic desire, the camera follows behind Danping and captures the singer's deformed face as he looks in the mirror.[46] Ma-Xu uses the same "zooming" technique employed by Whale, closing in on the terrifying sight in consecutively narrowing frames. First, Danping is seen in a medium shot that shows his expression of disbelief; when the singer grabs a candle to get a better look at the scar, Ma-Xu jump-cuts to a close-up that records the man's despair. Significantly, even then the camera stays behind Danping's head rather than offering a point-of-view shot, careful not to conflate Danping's and the spectators' gaze. Danping is shown in the act of looking at himself. The scar is portrayed as the object of spectacle, subjected to others' observation, including Danping's own gaze of disbelief. At this point, *Song at Midnight* employs facial deformity to create what Tom Gunning calls the "cinema of attractions," using visual stimuli to the point of overriding narrative concerns.[47]

The appeal to the audience's fascination is even clearer in Ma-Xu's sequel, released four years after *Song at Midnight*. The first film was structured as a complete and autonomous work and was viewed as such by contemporary audiences. Yet to satisfy the spectators' urge to see more glimpses of the uncanny facial makeup, the sequel gives Danping a new lease on life. Like Whale's *Bride of Frankenstein*, which revives the monster, Ma-Xu's sequel reveals that Danping survived his jump from the burning tower. It turns out, however, that Danping was rescued from the waters only to fall into the hands of a mad doctor, whose experiments have made the singer's face even more monstrous.

At first glance, the sequel seems to reinforce the heroic message of *Song at Midnight*. The film starts by showing Lüdie's epitaph, which extols her death as a glorious sacrifice. Danping's death at the end of the film, this time suicide, stresses the theme of self-sacrifice. Still echoing Soviet novels, the sequel ends with Xiao'ou saluting the double tomb of Danping and Xiaoxia in tribute to the fallen heroes.[48] Yet although the plot portrays Danping and Xiao'ou fighting in the service of the Revolutionary Party, the sequel foregrounds even more the cinematic allure of horror. Like *Bride of Frankenstein*, Ma-Xu's sequel is racier than the first installment and uses even campier sets and makeup. Danping's monstrosity is blown up into a veritable skull, echoing the "death mask" in *Phantom of the Opera* and *Frankenstein*.[49] *Song at Midnight, Part II* accentuates the camp that made *Song at Midnight* a success, particularly in the mad doctor episode. The doctor who takes charge of Danping also wears grotesque makeup, and his laboratory adds a voyeuristic streak by displaying nude sculptures. Nude art had been a sure way to stir up scandal in twentieth-century China ever since the Shanghai Painting Academy exhibited nude drawings in 1917,[50] but Ma-Xu adds an especially daring touch in using naked live models for the sculptures.[51] Sex and horror are combined in the eventual disfiguring of the statues: they are broken, and the camera lingers on their mutilated limbs.

The voyeurism of *Song at Midnight, Part II* is complemented by a thematic concern with the protagonists' eyesight. Danping is once again thought to be dead, and Xiaoxia falls ill and goes blind. Danping visits Xiaoxia on her deathbed and commits suicide after she dies. In the original *Song at Midnight*, it is Danping who is unable to come to terms with the scar and conceals it from his beloved; in the sequel, she conveniently goes blind before the two are reunited, and Danping's image remains unblemished in Xiaoxia's eyes.[52] Romance and horror take precedence over the revolutionary plot, and the scar is rendered invisible.

REVOLUTION AS PHANTASMAGORIA

Considering the elusive dialectic between images of revolutionary revelation and the concealment of the scar, and in view of the unresolved tension between the ideological and entertainment functions of cinema, the seeming contradiction between revolutionary plot and horror imagery cannot be explained away as the result of the co-writers' ideological differences or as a marketing compromise. Several implied messages must be taken into account. The director uses the filmic voyeurism with irony, suggesting that no mass medium, not even cinema, can be fully enlisted in the service of ideology. The revolutionary message can at best be reflected in film's broken mirror and distorting lens.

The scar's ambivalent reference to both revolution and horror also points to pent-up historical forces that erupt with uncontrollable violence. Danping's veiled face becomes a symbol of repression, not only of unconscious desires as Chen Huiyang would have it,[53] but also of unresolved contradictions within the revolutionary drive. Marshall Berman draws attention to the contradiction in Marx's thought—although it calls for a new subject divested of bourgeois illusions, "the newly naked modern man may turn out to be . . . even more elusive, because there will no longer be any illusion of a real self underneath the mask."[54] Danping's uncovered scar demonstrates the doubtful nature of the revolutionary forces about to be unleashed.

In its critique of the revolution, *Song at Midnight* is yet again indebted to the Hollywood horror film. Slavoj Žižek locates *The Phantom of the Opera*, *Frankenstein*, and *Dracula* within the nineteenth-century discourse on terror and the sublime and argues that the face's resistance to verbal description is a sign of repressed social anxieties.[55] *Frankenstein*'s Creature may represent the French Revolution as perceived in Mary Shelley's England—a monstrous excess, a dangerous experiment that generated growing disorder.[56] *Phantom* tells that Erik's abode in the cellars of the Opéra served as torture dungeons during the 1870 insurrection of the Paris Commune. Erik's voice, surging up from the cellars, symbolizes the resurgence of the historically repressed. In Žižek's words, the phantom "is a kind of 'fossil' created by the Enlightenment itself as a distorted index of its inherent antagonism."[57]

Danping's monstrosity (whose form is never verbalized aside from triggering a guttural "no, no") serves as an equally powerful sign of the residual terror of revolution. As a mark left by Danping's confrontation with the landlord, the scar connotes the unfinished class struggle. The film's conclusion demonstrates how the contained violence is bound to resurface with brutal force. In the final apocalypse, the scar's revolutionary significance is reasserted and enunciates itself in a crescendo of mad pursuit, fire, and killing. In imitation of chase scenes in Whale's films,[58] Danping flees out of the theater and is pursued by a torch-wielding crowd. The burst of violence into the hitherto carefully regulated ideological structures is emphasized by the destruction of physical barriers. A mob, joined by soldiers, breaks through each of the theater's three entrances, causing a stampede; the crowd proceeds to shatter the doors to Lüdie's dressing room and to Danping's loft. Danping hurls Tang Jun through a window and escapes through the skylight; his escape route leads him straight through the stage curtain, which he tears down. The audience storms across the stage and out of the theater to chase Danping through a tunnel. Danping climbs the tower and breaks the ladder, but the crowd sets a fire that burns through the floor partitions and forces the singer to jump out of the tower into the torrential river. The chase carries a revolutionary message of shattering the existing social order. It brings down the theatrical boundaries that distinguish between actors and audience, as well as between spectators of different classes. As Elias Canetti remarks, since the fall of the Bastille, mobs forcing their way out of contained spectacles have been associated with the triumph of revolution.[59] Demolishing the theatrical divisions vividly symbolizes revolutionary resistance to the regulating, dominant ideology.

The concluding scene, ending in Danping's death at the hands of the crowd, points, however, at a violence hidden even within the revolutionary force. The final scene shows that the mob might turn against the harbinger of revolution. The revolutionary artist is unable to communicate his agenda to the unruly spectators. The masses to whom the singer addresses his message turn against him; after finding Danping's Revolutionary Party membership card, they become a lynch mob that chases the hero to his death. The response to Danping's message literally spreads like fire, inasmuch as the chasers are armed with torches, which they use to burn down Danping's place of refuge. Danping has dedicated his life to bringing the fire of revolution to the people, but at the end of his Promethean mission, he himself perishes in the fire. When "the masses" expel darkness in a carnival of fiery violence, Xiao'ou's final words, "We must strive harder to struggle against these dark forces . . . and attain liberty for the masses," take on an ironic undertone.

The unfavorable portrayal of the crowd in *Song at Midnight* betrays a suspicion of the mob and questions the left-wing emphasis on "making literature available to the masses." In one of the last shots, Danping is shown seized by agony, looking down from the burning tower at the angry mob. The physical structure that might have served as a podium or a witness stand—and by extension, the social structure through which he could address the crowd—becomes a mortal trap. Danping's singing is supposed to communicate with his audience, heal its spiritual illness, and mobilize the nation in the revolutionary cause. Instead, he is driven to quasi-insanity, confined to the dark attic, and eventually hunted to death. One should note the similarity of the tropes of insanity, confinement, and persecution to those in Lu Xun's "Diary of a Madman." The burning tower also brings to mind the parable of the iron chamber (see Chapter 1). Like Lu Xun's well-known depiction of the author as unable to communicate with his audience and save them, Ma-Xu's film shows the revolutionary trapped, helpless, and in tragic dissonance with the crowd.

The hero's martyrdom during the struggle for social justice is a common concluding trope in 1930s films. One recalls, for example, the hope-shattering death of the heroine in *Xin nüxing* (New woman, 1934) after she has regretted her suicide attempt and wishes to continue fighting. Yet Danping's death is exceptionally disheartening, for he never wins the sympathy of the crowd, which continues to persecute him even when his revolutionary identity is made known. Such doubts about the revolutionary agent's ability to communicate with the masses and bear witness to the social reality of the time may reflect the dispirited atmosphere of the 1930s, when civil strife demonstrated the extent to which China's 1911 revolution and the May Fourth reforms remained unfinished projects. These circumstances questioned the ability of writers, filmmakers, and other intellectuals to contribute to public debate, let alone stir the masses into action.

Song at Midnight questions the communist vision of revolution in particular. The first sentence of Marx and Engels's *Manifesto of the Communist Party* likens communism to a phantom: "A specter is haunting Europe."[60] Marx ridicules those who fear the growing shadow of communist ideology, but by tongue-in-cheek presenting his own philosophy as a monstrosity, he opens up a space for a dialectic relationship between ideological consciousness and fear. Marxism is the dominant ideology's other, and any attempt at harnessing it to a singular vision must fail. Marx also uses the metaphor of the phantom to warn against the escapist denial of historical experience. In *Capital*, Marx explains that commodification covers up for an abusive mode of production: "the particular social relation between people . . . takes on the phantasmagoric form of a relation between things."[61] "Phantasmagoria" was the name of a specific form of optical illusion, a projection mechanism used to produce half-transparent phantoms on stage.[62] By referring to this theatrical device to illustrate the need to awaken the masses from the collective dream of commodification, Marx shows a mistrust of mass culture and especially of make-believe spectacles.

Song at Midnight portrays the revolutionary hero as a specter and at the same time entrusts the revolutionary message to the cinematic medium, the descendant of theatrical phantasmagoria. There is profound irony in that a spooky apparition materialized on screen is charged with the mission of awakening the masses from the capitalist mirage. It is difficult to decide whether in Ma-Xu's mind, film is a specter in Marx's sense or simple phantasmagoric shadow play. This is perhaps the film's most poignant critique— that cinema and other mass media cannot be enlisted fully in the service of the revolution. The film implies that cinema is like "Song at Midnight," the tune that Danping sings to his beloved—there is no telling whether it will cure the audience or lull it deeper into insane fantasy. The melody can be either a shrill shout that should awaken the masses to action or a soothing lullaby. *Song at Midnight* leaves unresolved the troubled relation between revolution and monstrosity, between historical consciousness and phantas-magoria, between bearing witness and public discourse.

It does not seem coincidental that Song Danping reveals himself after ten years of absence, which—if the narrated time corresponds to the date of the film's release—dates his disappearance to 1927, the year of the rift between the KMT and CCP that conventionally marks the end of May Fourth's initial drive. *Song at Midnight* calls for ignoring the programmatic fervor of the 1930s and revisiting the ideals and contradictions of May Fourth. Within five months of the film's release, the attempt to reintroduce a nuanced debate was doomed by the Japanese invasion of China. The subsequent patriotic fervor and growing influence of the CCP, culminating in the establishment of the PRC in 1949, made it difficult to criticize either public discourse—now identified with war propaganda—or the idea of historical progress, a central Marxist tenet. As the next chapter shows, with the ascent of Maoist ideology, witness against history not only lost impetus but was also directly censored and suppressed.

4 The Purloined Lantern
Maoist Semiotics and Public Discourse in Early PRC Film and Drama

Until recently, histories of literature and film in twentieth-century China have largely ignored the Maoist period—both the seventeen years from the establishment of the PRC in 1949 to the beginning of the Cultural Revolution in 1966 and the "ten years of chaos" that followed until Mao's death in 1976. Few good works, it was implied, were created during that period. The intellectual and literary discourse initiated by May Fourth was only taken up, it seemed, by the avant-garde of the late 1980s, giving rise to comparisons between "May Fourth" and "June Fourth." This view does justice neither to the diversity of the early PRC years nor to the intricate artistic production during the Cultural Revolution. Moreover, many cultural issues and literary themes retained their relevance in the Maoist period. Notably, Ban Wang shows how the sublime remained a central criterion from Wang Guowei's aesthetics to Mao Zedong thought and avant-garde fiction.[1] Yet the question remains, in what ways did Maoism disrupt the May Fourth project? How were Enlightenment ideals transformed under the system of thought adopted by the CCP? What were the implications of the PRC's political culture for the critical practice I call "witness against history"?

I argue that in literary terms, the Maoist break with May Fourth was most palpable in the control over artistic production and censoring of public debate. The particular genres and themes condoned by Mao and his wife Jiang Qing were buttressed by a theoretical framework for delegitimizing dissent. While free literary expression was both celebrated and challenged until the 1940s, Mao's "Talks at the Yan'an Literary Conference" ("Zai Yan'an wenyi zuotanhui shang de yanjiang," 1942) barred writing altogether from becoming a semi-autonomous space for social and political criticism. Maoist ideology effectively silenced the voices that had previously dominated the Chinese literary scene. Arguably, the "modern revolutionary operas," or "model plays," of the Cultural Revolution were the culmination of Maoist art. The revolutionary operas demonstrate the effect of the totalitarian system, which

promoted only literature deemed accessible to the proletariat and denounced all other texts as "poisonous weeds" (*ducao*). Moreover, as recent
studies of drama during the Cultural Revolution have shown, the machinations that accompanied Maoist productions clarify the behind-the-scenes
dynamics of the larger political arena.[2]

This study, however, examines not the extraliterary attitudes to writing
but rather how literary works point to the Party as the sole hermeneutic
reader and supreme arbiter of ideological correctness. Literary and cinematic
productions played an active part in suppressing public debate. The plays
and films advanced by Mao's propaganda apparatus employed complex
textual strategies to denounce the sphere of debate and point to the Party as
the sole arbiter of ideological content. As a medium dependent on production facilities and financial backing monopolized by the state until the mid
1980s, and as an art form easily controlled even at the stages of postproduc-
tion and distribution, cinema and filmed drama were sure to reflect the current Party line and became a favorite propaganda tool.

The case of the revolutionary opera *Hongdeng ji* (The red lantern, 1963,
rev. 1970) shows how Jiang Qing's coterie monopolized control, not only
over repertoire and stage production, but even over critical reception and
aesthetic criteria. The opera's prominent themes of transmitting undeci-
phered codes and handing down secret signs, I argue, reflected a totalitarian
semiotics that abrogated the public sphere of debate and handed overall interpretive authority to the Party.

STAGING THE CULTURAL REVOLUTION

The emergence of a clear Maoist doctrine in the 1940s and the establishment
of the PRC in 1949 literally transformed the Chinese political stage. Party
leaders frequently held parades and other public spectacles to mark political
turning points and targeted drama and film specifically to serve as paradigms
of art compliant with their demands. Many theater and cinema pieces were
either blacklisted for their incorrect ideology or conversely made into exem-
plars of revolutionary tenets. The attempt to achieve absolute control of
stage production culminated in the Cultural Revolution. It is of symbolic
value that the first event in the Cultural Revolution may be identified in a
November 10, 1965, article in the Shanghai *Wenhui bao*, commissioned by Jiang Qing and approved by Mao, that criticized the new Beijing opera *Hai Rui*

baguan (Hai Rui dismissed from office, 1961).[3] The play, perceived as an oblique criticism of Peng Dehuai's dismissal from office in 1959 after he had opposed Mao's Great Leap Forward policy, came under fire as early as July 1962. The 1965 article was employed to circumspectly attack the opera's author Wu Han and his political patrons. The pattern of using literary criticism to discredit political rivals would grow fiercer as the Cultural Revolution progressed.

Political intervention in drama production reached a new level with the creation of the model plays. Jiang Qing had long taken an interest in restructuring traditional opera into a form that would suit popular taste and bolster revolutionary content. The process of "modernizing" opera culminated in the National Conference on Performing Modern Beijing Opera (Quanguo jingju xiandaixi guanmo yanchu dahui) held in Beijing in June and July 1964.[4] From the pieces presented, Jiang Qing and Lin Biao (at the time minister of defense) picked out four exemplary works in the genre dubbed "revolutionary modern Beijing operas" (*geming xiandai jingju*) and canonized them in a memorandum in February 1966.[5] Eventually, eight exemplary pieces were endorsed as "model plays" (*yangbanxi*) in an article in *Renmin ribao* (People's Daily) on December 9, 1966, and performed in Beijing on the twenty-fifth anniversary of the Yan'an Talks, starting May 16, 1967. The eight works were proclaimed to be Jiang Qing's "model plot" (*yangban tian*), a term borrowed from agriculture that implied that the plays would be continuously reworked by Jiang, with the results disseminated as a model for other productions.[6] The plays provided not only a model for other works of art—to the point where virtually all other productions were taken off the stage and screen—but also the ideal of how one should act and live. The model plays shaped people's aesthetic and political judgment. They were performed all over the country time and again, often by work units, so that as many people as possible would actively participate in the spectacle. As Ban Wang notes, the repeated staging of the model plays introduced their rhetoric and even bodily gestures into daily life, which began to some extent to replicate the plays.[7]

The first play chosen by Jiang Qing as a model of her aesthetics was *The Red Lantern*. The plot was based on the film *Zi you hou lairen* (Where one falls, another rises, 1962, released 1963). Within a year, the script was modified into the Beijing opera *Geming ziyou hou lairen* (In revolution, where one falls, another rises; staged by the Harbin Beijing Opera Troupe), the *Kunqu* drama *Hongdeng zhuan* (Story of the red lantern), and the Western-style play (*huaju*) *Sandairen* (Three generations). These productions served as the inspiration for the opera *Hongdeng ji* (The red lantern) staged by the Patriotic Shanghai Opera Troupe (Aihua hujutuan).[8] Jiang Qing saw the latter on February 22, 1963, and as part of her attempt to integrate Shanghai's heritage with the culture of the political center in Beijing, immediately set out to modify its Shanghai idiom and stage conventions to turn it into a standard Beijing opera.[9] The Beijing version was first staged in November 1963. After a performance on June 11, 1964, it was given Mao Zedong's seal of approval as an exponent of the aesthetics appealing to "workers, peasants, and soldiers."[10] Comporting with its function as a model play, it was sent on tours through the country beginning in February 1965. *The Red Lantern* was in fact the first play in conjunction with which the word "model" (*yangban*) appeared—the March 16, 1965, issue of *Jiefang ribao* (*Liberation Daily*) claimed that *The Red Lantern* was "a prominent model of revolutionizing Beijing opera." Articles in *Guangming ribao* (*Guangming Daily*) and *Xiju bao* (Drama journal) followed suit in using the term.[11]

Conflicting accounts exist of the successive modifications of the plot, controversial due to the involvement of Jiang Qing, condemned after 1976 as the leader of the Gang of Four.[12] As a sympathetic contemporary account tells it, "Comrade Jiang Qing directed that [*The Red Lantern*] be endlessly revised and performed."[13] Madame Mao insisted on changing the original production and intervened in decisions about tunes, dresses, makeup, and other details. Those who objected, among them the scriptwriter Wen Ouhong and the director A Jia, would be thrown into "cowsheds," the Cultural Revolution's combination of jail and torture camp. The lead actor, Qian Haoliang, who cooperated with Jiang Qing, was handsomely rewarded, put in charge of later revisions of the opera, and made deputy minister of culture in 1975.[14] While other versions appeared—accompanied by piano and by a Western-style orchestra—the Beijing opera version served as the basis for the 1970 revision. As part of the movement to "vigorously popularize the revolutionary model plays" (*dali puji geming yangbanxi*), *The Red Lantern* was adapted into a movie by the same title (production began in May 1970, and the first screening took place in January 1971).[15] It was one of the first three model plays to be filmed, and as such the first feature to be produced since virtually all film studios had been closed down four years before. Paralleling political developments, *The Red Lantern* pushed all competing forms of drama offstage.

THE AESTHETICS OF DIFFERENTIATION

The plot of *The Red Lantern* also reflects the monopoly of the new political agenda. As suggested by the title of the originary film, *Where One Falls, Another Rises* (the full proverb is given in the concluding lines of the Shanghai opera: "Those ahead fall, but those behind continue; there is always someone to follow"),[16] the plot revolves around the question of succession and legitimacy. *The Red Lantern* takes place in occupied Manchuria during World War II, or the Anti-Japanese War, as it is known in China (the Shanghai version specifies the year as 1938). A messenger arrives in a village and gives the local communist contact man, the railroad switchman Li Yuhe (played by Qian Haoliang), a telegraph code that has to be delivered to the communist guerrillas in the mountains. One of the underground Party members betrays Li, and he is executed by the Japanese, but his daughter Tiemei (Liu Changyu) slips away and delivers the code.[17]

The plot had immediate implications for the political situation in the 1960s, and bore in particular on the need to identify enemies of the state—both external and internal—according to current agenda. Since the establishment of the PRC, a barrage of novels and films had tackled the "imperialist" danger and especially the threat posed by infiltrators collaborating with the Taiwan-based KMT.[18] The result was a large corpus of films on counterespionage. *Wuxing de zhanxian* (The invisible battlefront, 1949), probably the first movie in this genre, depicts the capture of a KMT-supported network. The film starts and ends with a quotation from Mao: "After the armed enemies have been eliminated, the unarmed enemies still survive. We must struggle with them to death; we should not take these enemies lightly." *The Red Lantern*, originally given the subtitle "A Revolutionary Detective Story,"[19] continues in the same vein and emphasizes the role of the turncoat Wang Lianju, who turns Li over to the Japanese. Just as the play presents Li Yuhe as a model hero, it depicts Wang as an exemplary enemy of the people.[20]

Differentiating between CCP sympathizers and enemies in *The Red Lantern* was part of a larger project of rewriting China's revolutionary history. The original eight model plays cover among them the entire period of the communist revolution in China, from 1927 to the 1960s. *The Red Lantern* addresses an especially sensitive and controversial period, namely, the Anti-Japanese War. The years 1937–45 were key to building popular support for communism (owing mainly to the CCP's reorganization in the loosely controlled Japanese-occupied territories in the northeastern provinces, where *The Red Lantern* takes place). Moreover, after the war, the Party refashioned itself as the only patriotic force to have fought the Japanese. Chiang Kai-shek's decision to avoid armed confrontation with Japan after losing the core of his trained forces was portrayed as the KMT's active collaboration with General Hideki Tōjō's government—for example, in the film *Tiedao youjidui* (Railroad guerrilla, 1956). Such depictions were an important element in CCP propaganda, both for vilifying the KMT government, which continued to rule Taiwan and laid claim to China's entire territory, and for aggrandizing the Party. *The Red Lantern* follows other films on the revolutionary resistance in Manchuria, beginning with *Songhuajiang shang* (Along the Sungari river, 1947).

The mole theme had, however, more urgent targets than the Japanese and the KMT. The representation of the 1940s also alludes to contemporary "turncoats" within the Party. It should be borne in mind that one of the main motivations behind the Cultural Revolution was to purge elements vying with Mao from the Party. The alternative center of power was identified with Liu Shaoqi, who would lose the position of Mao's intended successor to Lin Biao and be tagged as a "revisionist," in analogy to Khrushchev (ironically, by 1971, Lin Biao, the patron of the model plays, would himself be designated as an evil second only to Confucius). The two main themes of *The Red Lantern*—"love" and "struggle,"[21] that is, mutual help among the revolutionary underground and struggle against the traitor—could be conveniently used to foreground the issues of allegiance and succession central to the rivalry between Liu Shaoqi and Lin Biao. In *The Red Lantern*, Wang Lianju's treachery raises the question of whom one should trust. Meanwhile, the collaboration between the people in Li Yuhe's household, who regard one another as family, although they are not related by blood, demonstrates not only the camaraderie among the proletariat but also Tiemei's right to succession due to her correct ideological stance. Tiemei proves her right when she deals with Japanese collaborators while Li is detained by the Japanese. Granny and Tiemei recognize the collaborator for what he is and foil his ruse. Tiemei eventually takes Li's place and completes the mission, whereas Wang is killed by the guerrillas. The happy ending also reconfirms the importance of ferreting out the enemy within.

Although some of the implications could not have occurred to the playwright in 1963, later analyses of the play read the struggle between Li Yuhe and his family against the Japanese and their collaborators retrospectively to refer to intraparty conflict. In 1970, the claim was made that "Li Yuhe's . . . indignant condemnation of the traitor Wang Lianju continues to criticize Liu Shaoqi's sinister revisionism today."[22] Discussion of the play also served as an occasion for criticizing the prominent figures in the cultural bureaucracy labeled "the four villains" (*sitiao hanzi*)—the literary critic Zhou Yang, the film director Xia Yan, the playwright Tian Han and the author Yang Hansheng.[23]

Identifying Mao's true heir also had direct implications for literary hermeneutics. The contrast between Li's heroism and Wang's transparent villainy parallels the distinction between exemplary literary works and "poisonous weeds." Jiang Qing and her cultural bureaucrats claimed to know an ideologically correct work from an erroneous, "revisionist" one. Party scheming and paranoia among the leadership reappropriated Marxist class theory to distinguish friend from foe. All artistic devices were categorized as either beneficial or detrimental to the dominant ideology and justified or condemned accordingly. Plots were written and works criticized based on an aesthetics of differentiation.

THE REVOLUTIONARY SUBLIME

The apparatus in charge of production further tightened its control over the model plays by providing an aesthetic theory to support the political agenda. A clear example is to be found in the lead role, who is given a privileged space onstage; moreover, Li is described as comporting with the sublime, which endows him with absolute authority. Li Yuhe is often cited by contemporary critics as the exemplary "sublime heroic image of workers, peasants, and soldiers."[24] Portrayed in accordance with Jiang Qing's directives on "understanding the sublime realm of thought of the heroic persona,"[25] Li provides a model for adoration akin to Mao. Li Yuhe's prominence is promoted through long arias in the execution scene (which takes up 21 of the filmed version's 112 minutes). The plot focuses on Li Yuhe and uses the other personae to foreground his distinctive features. Li Yuhe's heroism is accentuated by his family's self-sacrifice, which is in turn brought to the fore by the other underground members. This structure, which not only draws a clear line between heroes and villains but also stresses the gradations of revolutionary rectitude, comports with the dramatic theory of the Three Prominences (*san tuchu*). As expounded by Yao Wenyuan in 1969, the theory stipulated: "Among all characters, give prominence to the positive characters; among the positive characters, give prominence to the heroic characters; among the heroic characters, give prominence to the main heroic characters."[26] Li Yuhe, who in earlier versions was portrayed as a fallible man, literally towers above all the other characters and performs the best and most numerous arias. He is given especially many occasions to strike heroic poses during scene 8, "Struggle at the Execution Grounds." As members of the troupe that staged the model play *Zhiqu Weihushan* (Taking Tiger Mountain by strategy) note, the execution scene was rewritten to "present more clearly the brilliance of Li Yuhe's thought, in text, music, dance, and sets."[27] Critics from the August First Film Studio, the PLA studio that produced the cinematic version of *The Red Lantern*, describe the execution scene in Maoist hyperbole as "the utmost climax."[28]

The firing squad also demonstrates *The Red Lantern*'s debt to the themes and aesthetics of earlier revolutionary literature and film. His clothes tattered after torture by the Japanese, Li offers his body as well as his voice to bear witness to the coming triumph of the communist revolution: "My bones are broken, my flesh is torn, / But my will is as firm as steel." Revolutionary rhetoric had long employed the injured body to stress the reality and ideological rectitude behind the hero's enunciations. I have pointed to a similar dialectic between bodily mutilation and mental resolve in the theme song of Ma-Xu Weibang's *Song at Midnight*: "In form I am a demonic monster, / But my heart is as steadfast as iron" (see Chapter 3). Yet if the execution scenes in Lu Xun's, Ouyang Yuqian's, and Ma-Xu's texts doubt whether the executed achieve anything in their deaths, the aesthetics of the model plays avoids any irony. In this sense, the model plays reflect the contemporary demand made upon society at large to "take suffering as honor, hardship as pleasure" (*yi ku wei rong, yi ku wei le*). *The Red Lantern* follows the martyrdom scenes in preceding theatrical productions, notably the opening scene in the musical *Changzheng zuge—Zhongguo geming lishi gequ biaoyan chang* (The Long March chorus: The history of the Chinese revolution in song and dance, 1963; dir. Hua Chun), which portrays chained communist heroes striding defiantly to their execution at the hands of KMT soldiers. In both pieces, the heroic act is accompanied by the tune of "The Internationale," a common theatrical trope in the PRC (see Chapter 9). Li Yuhe's defiant glance, which strikes terror into the executioner's heart, is also modeled after the 1963 musical.[29] The major difference is that *The Long March Chorus* takes after Soviet stage conventions, while *The Red Lantern* introduces Beijing opera style. Yet the ideological emphasis of the model play diverges sharply from its precedents. What sets *The Red Lantern* apart is that the unmitigated adulation of Li Yuhe, required by the Three Prominences theory and stressed by his suffering and death, is put in terms of the hero's sublimity. Qian Haoliang describes how Jiang Qing directed him to portray Li Yuhe so as "to make this heroic image more prominent, more ideal, and more sublime."[30] Li Yuhe's sublimity allows him to command the stage and demand submission from enemy and fellow revolutionaries alike.

The protagonist's attributed sublimity demonstrates Li's monopoly on ideological rectitude. Kant's concept of "the dynamically sublime" associates the sublime with terrifying experience that arrests the mind and excludes reasoning.[31] The revolutionary sublime takes from the Kantian category the idea of an experience that terrorizes and overwhelms the witness and leaves no room for contemplation or discussion. Lin Biao accordingly instructed model play actors: "Do not describe the cruelty of war but rather play up and exult in the terror of war. Do not describe the difficulty of the revolutionary struggle but rather play up and exult in the difficulty."[32] Whereas Kant expects the subject to react to the sublime by developing a "moral law" on which to base personal judgment, Lin Biao's exultation of terror excludes individual critique. In his book-length study of the sublime in twentieth-century Chinese aesthetics, Ban Wang shows how the category of the sublime was used in the PRC to privilege the authority of "the masses" over individual will.[33] Using "the sublime" as a term of praise and adoration rather than a tool for eliciting critical thought implements a totalitarian strategy of silencing the audience and privileging the role model on stage.

IN THE NAME OF THE MASSES

Li Yuhe's dominant position extends beyond the stage, inasmuch as it signals the abrogation of the spectators' judgment and legitimates the leadership's actions in the name of the masses. The mise-en-scène emphasizes the hero's ability to reach to the audience and at the same time to dictate the desired emotions. At the execution grounds, Li Yuhe enunciates in clear and unequivocal terms the coming triumph of the communist revolution: "New China will shine like the morning sun, / Red flags will fly all over the country." "His eyes gaze into the distance, his hands stretched forward," explains a critic, "as if he sees the red flag of revolution waving everywhere."[34] Li looks over the heads of his executioners and beyond the spectators. His privileged gaze unites his will, the audience's aspirations, and the country's future. The spectacle makes Li into the primary witness to revolutionary ideology and at the same time bars any dialogue with the audience.

The transparent spectacle, which places the leader at an advantage precisely by pretending that no barrier stands between the revolutionary and the masses, has its underpinning in Mao's Yan'an Talks, which served as the ideological foundation for literature in the PRC, and whose twenty-fifth anniversary in 1967 served as the occasion for inaugurating the model plays. The Yan'an Talks, delivered as introductory and concluding remarks to a writers' conference summoned in May 1942 in the Yan'an base area, constituted Mao's response to dissenting voices and a reaffirmation of the Party's hegemony over literary production.[35] With the rest of Mao's writings, the Yan'an Talks became part of official PRC policy. The political importance of the Yan'an Talks lies in their proscription of any space for ambiguity. Even though Mao makes a qualified concession to some unspecified forms of satire, the Talks are intolerant of oblique speech and demand "the unification of politics and art."[36] As the writer becomes one of the proletariat, class identity erases linguistic, ideological, and other differences that might give rise to ambivalent meaning. Mao's call for writers to learn from the masses is tantamount to conflating author and audience, requiring that writers should always express the will of the masses. Since the opinion of the masses would be ventriloquized by the state ideologues, the Party would thus be able to maintain absolute control.

The Cultural Revolution allowed the leaders to further appropriate the voice of "the masses." Mao's initiation of the Cultural Revolution to ensure a state of perpetual political flux was paralleled by Jiang Qing's use of the model plays as her "model plot," an experiment in need of constant alterations. Just as the political turmoil gave Mao total power, the radical experimentation in opera put Madame Mao in a position of total authority over the arts. Constantly stating that she based her alterations of The Red Lantern on hundreds of letters from worker, peasant, and soldier audiences,[37] Jiang Qing assumed control over operatic production in the name of the people. The abrogation of agency even away from those involved in the production is evident in the words of Zhao Yanxia, who played the role of A Qing's wife in the model play Shajiabang: "Under the brilliant radiance of Chairman Mao's thought, I shall never be content with the present situation."[38] The task of interpreting Maoist ideology and continuously modifying the current version fell to Jiang Qing.

Jiang Qing's absolute power not only over production but also over the apparatus in charge of literary interpretation was achieved with Machiavellian manipulations. In the case of *The Red Lantern*, the edited proceedings of meetings organized in academies, film studios, and military units were published, along with commissioned articles, to give a specific spin to the drama. The meetings and discussions were no doubt carefully orchestrated, and the regulated reception ensured that the piece would reaffirm Mao Zedong Thought and the Yan'an Talks in particular. The "discussion group" of the opera troupe that staged *The Red Lantern* mentions how "the revolutionary modern Beijing opera *The Red Lantern* was created under the bright light of Chairman Mao's Yan'an Talks,"[39] while the August First Studio referred to the opera as "one of the bounteous achievements of the great art proceeding in the direction shown by the Talks at the Yan'an Literary Conference."[40] Analysis in the resulting documents is restricted to demonstrating how the opera comports with the Chairman's words. The troupe's acclaim—the term used is "praise" (*zan*) rather than "criticism" (*pinglun*)—quotes extensively from Mao's writings, in bold type. The full chain of theatrical production—choice of repertoire, staging, discussion in art circles, and public criticism—was mobilized. The published outcome of this process was not left to chance, and the doctrinaire statements should come as no surprise.

The inversion of public discourse, where the audience were informed of their own opinion as "the masses," was finally accomplished when the model plays were reenacted in daily life. Ban Wang argues that presenting Mao and the socialist motherland as sublime figures enabled the masses, and the Red Guards in particular, to identify with these entities. Leader and country were seen as sublime enlargements of the Red Guards. In Wang's words, "By loving these objects, [the Red Guards] loved themselves even more."[41] The Maoist principle of "the unity of politics and art" entailed in practice that the state could claim to embody the collective sublime. In the name of the aesthetic category of the sublime, Mao's apparatus could privilege the masses (read: the People's Republic and its leaders), exclude individual agency, and advance the slogan "Destroy the individual and establish the public" (*posi ligong*).

Both *The Red Lantern* and the critics' praise for the play identify the Party and Mao as the supreme arbiters of meaning. Viewers were required to suspend all judgment of their own. The beginning of the film version presents a quotation from Mao to the effect that communist progress is achieved at the cost of martyrs' blood. Implicitly, the audience is directed to attribute its own achievements to others, conveniently deceased, whose portrayal as "selfless" (*wuwo*) entrusts their legacy to the collective agency represented by the People's Republic. The slogan "Unity with the masses" did not make any demand on the leaders but rather required the spectators to fully identify with the enunciator of revolutionary ideology. By virtue of its supposed sublimity, the state could present itself as the ideal subject, to which each individual should aspire and yield all will and authority.

THE CODED MESSAGE

The Red Lantern's totalitarian aesthetics goes far beyond simply asserting the hero's (read: the Party's) monopoly on ideological rectitude. In focusing on secret signs and codes, the plot deals directly with the theme of interpretive authority. *The Red Lantern* centers on the revolutionary underground's task of delivering a secret telegraph code from the Eighth Route Army Pine Peak Base Area to the guerrillas on Cypress Mountain. Li receives the code from a messenger but is compromised before he can hand it over to his contact. The traitor Wang Lianju informs the Japanese of the code's existence, and they try to obtain it by coaxing, torture, and underhand ploys. All of these fail, and Tiemei completes the mission. The successful transmission of the code supports the claim that the revolutionary truth is bound to travel safely to its destiny, namely, the masses, who will understand and accept it. No doubt is expressed as to either the qualifications of the author of the message or the capacity of his audience to receive it.

Aptly, a telegraph code—that is to say, a substitution table—is central to a plot in which objects are exchanged and interchanged. Rather than arms or a specific missive, the underground fights for something that has no significance of its own, but is a tool that will enable the guerrillas to send and receive other messages. As a text void of specific content, the code suggests an eternal truth that transcends the specific circumstances of the moment. Moreover, the code's importance lies in that both sides must possess it in order to encipher and decipher messages. The code makes transmissions impermeable to the enemy, yet easily legible by the revolutionary forces. As the code signals who is allowed to yield interpretive authority, it resonates with the leaders' concern with controlling public discourse and delegitimizing other centers of power.

The Revolutionary Committee of Sun Yat-sen University noted that the revolutionary mission in *The Red Lantern* was "to guard the secrets of the Party."[42] What is at stake for Li and the underground is not possession of the secrets but rather their safe delivery. "It is through Li Yuhe's reception and transmission of the secret telegraph code, and through his unswerving and unyielding struggle with the enemy to protect the code, that the entire profile of this hero is displayed," a tribute to the play from the August First Film Studio declared. When the code reaches its destination, Li Yuhe's death is vindicated and the narrative achieves closure.[43] The message lies in the very act of communicating the Party's commands. "The script deftly uses the singularity of the 'secret telegraph code' as a link between the Party's underground work and the armed revolutionary struggle," a study group at Fudan University observed.[44] The code's lack of content allows the plot to focus on distinguishing friend from foe, to emphasize the ease with which the revolutionary message is conveyed, and to play up the Party's crucial role in these processes.

The Red Lantern's crafty use of the code theme can be traced to a number of earlier films that focus on secret messages that must be smuggled across enemy lines. Shi Hui's prize-winning Jimao xin (The urgent letter, 1954), set in the "liberated base areas" in Japanese-occupied northern China, tells the story of a twelve-year-old shepherd, Haiwa (played by Cai Yuanyuan).[45] Haiwa's father, commander of the villager guerrilla band, must deliver a message to a neighboring Eighth Route Army company. As the Japanese presence hinders him from making the journey in person, he entrusts the mission to his son. The child is intercepted by Japanese soldiers and cannot slip away, but he leads them into a minefield, where they are annihilated by the guerrillas. He hands over the hidden letter to the guerrilla company commander, who then uses an intelligence tip contained in the missive to overrun a Japanese fortified post.

Although The Urgent Letter is a propaganda piece aimed at a younger audience, "a feature film shot for the children of New China,"[46] the film makes the most of the theme of a son who follows his father's revolutionary mission, learns in the process how to overcome the enemy, and is eventually accepted into the ranks of the fighting guerrillas. Audiences of all ages learn of the formation of a younger corps of revolutionaries, the transmission of revolutionary experience to the new generation, and the latter's readiness for self-sacrifice. It is not surprising that in the period when the Red Guards were fashioned as the next revolutionary wave, the theme of a young hero appealed to the propaganda apparatus and was taken up in the character of Tiemei.

Another film depicting the delivery of intelligence information is Yong bu *xiaoshi de dianbo* (The undying transmission, 1958; dir. Wang Ping). The movie focuses on Shanghai's wartime underground and tells the story of Li Xia, a communist sent from Yan'an to the coastal city in 1939 to operate a clandestine communication post. The traitor Yao Wei turns him in to the Japanese, but after the latter surrender, he is released from jail and continues his work, this time against the KMT.[47] Li Xia makes two important contributions. First, he receives from Yan'an a verbatim transcription of an accord between the KMT and the Japanese government and helps make the secret document public. Later, in 1949, Li transmits to Yan'an the battle formation of the KMT defense line around Shanghai and thereby facilitates the communist takeover of the city. Operating the Morse code telegraph is portrayed as an important wartime task, at the forefront of combating both the invading army and the internal enemy.

Li continues to broadcast, although he knows that the enemy is drawing near. He finishes his last communication with KMT soldiers pointing their guns at his head and ends with the words, "Farewell for ever, Comrades! I miss you." One recognizes in this scene the model martyr who proclaims the revolutionary message while facing his executioners. The next and last shot shows Li's translucent image rising over the sky, implying that although he died in the line of duty, his revolutionary spirit survives in a more ethereal form, akin to his airwave messages. As the film's title suggests, the revolutionary message cannot be silenced. The telegraphic transmission is an apt metaphor for ideology's existence in a sphere that defies all barriers. The message is conveyed through the literally transparent medium of the airwaves, conveniently portrayed as controlled by the Party.

In the mid-1960s, Jiang Qing declared *The Undying Transmission* to be an unworthy model. Party members who had worked in the Shanghai underground under Liu Shaoqi were being targeted as traitors simply for having survived Japanese and KMT jails, and Li Xia could hardly serve as a model revolutionary.[48] Yet the theme of the coded broadcast proves useful when set in the countryside, in *Where One Falls, Another Rises,* which inspired *The Red Lantern.* This film is less jubilant than later versions. For example, *Where One Falls, Another Rises* ends simply with the successful transmission of the code, whereas the opera version adds a victorious battle. Yet although *The Red Lantern* was made more cheerful under Jiang Qing's supervision, the model play retained the basic premise of passing on a vital coded message.

Where One Falls, Another Rises and early counterespionage films demonstrate the centrality of the code theme. By portraying the code as precisely the message that must be delivered and by focusing on how the code changes hands, the plot circumvents the possibility that the missive might be misunderstood. The only threat to transmission is that the enemy may intercept the code and thereby interrupt the flow of communication between the headquarters and the fighters in the field. Once the code is secured, the enemy cannot divert the broadcast, corrupt it, or abrogate its meaning. By extension, the code ensures an open space for exchanging information and an ideal sphere of communication—that is, ideal in that it is governed by the code alone.

Celebrating the dissemination of information is, however, belied by the code's implications for the distribution of interpretive power. It is worth noting that the mechanism that ensures the telegraph code's safe use is its mathematical randomness. As part of the code's lack of an organizing principle, it must not in any way replicate the order of the enciphered content, least of all the linguistic attributes of the message. Unlike the coded message, the code itself is meaningless and undecipherable even to its users, and only its originator knows how it is generated. When *The Red Lantern* describes how the code remains in the possession of the underground, it not only leaves the task of decoding in the hands of the communist forces but also implies the ultimate unintelligibility of the message even to the field activists. Moreover, the model play depicts the delivery of an unopened codebook (the heroes never even glance at it), demonstrating that the guerrilla commander keeps control of decoding the messages. In the concrete political context of the 1960s, concealing the code even from revolutionary fighters signifies that the leadership will determine the ideological correctness of all content. Moreover, like the code, which depends on logical and linguistic arbitrariness to remain invulnerable to cracking, the leaders' power does not submit itself to logical scrutiny and does not need to comport with their verbal statements. Even within the Party, a power structure exists to curb the wide distribution of information and critical authority.

Presumably no more than a random substitution table, the code does not stand for specific content but rather signals a space to be filled with directives from above. *The Red Lantern* establishes a particular system of reference, a semiotic economy that defers signification indefinitely. The code marks the absence, not only of meaning, but also of the interpreting subject. It is a sublime sign that displaces all interpreters in anticipation of a hermeneutic intervention from a different plane, namely, the realm of power. Whereas linguists have referred to words as "floating signifiers" that allow social inter-

action to decide their meaning, the code is, rather, an empty sign that prohibits the target audience from exercising interpretive authority, a symbol
awaiting forceful employment by the Party. *The Red Lantern* invokes a totalitarian relationship between the work of art and its audience, one that anticipates freedom of interpretation and nullifies it ahead of time.

In suggesting a hermeneutic framework for its own reading, the model
play is no different from many literary works that propose how they may be
read. A text about strategies of secrecy, *The Red Lantern* insinuates both
strategies of reading and the strategic reading fitting the contemporary political situation. If only in this sense, *The Red Lantern* comports with the legacy
of the May Fourth movement. Like the modernist fiction written in the 1920s
and 1930s, the revolutionary opera is preoccupied with the hermeneutic
process to which it will be subjected and with preempting its readers. *The
Red Lantern* adds a Maoist twist, however, in providing an allegory of the in-
validity of allegories unless approved by the keepers of the code. This last
modification nullifies the May Fourth argument for a free public sphere and
upholds the Party's monopoly on interpretation in general and literary criticism in particular.

THE LANTERN AND THE SUN

The code's importance is further borne out by the fact that the telegraph
code is only one of several codes that advance the plot. The most dramatic
instance involves the eponymous red lantern. The revolutionaries identify
each other with the newcomer saying: "I sell wooden combs." The host responds: "Any made of peach wood?" to which the other answers: "Yes, for
cash down." The host then raises a red railroad lantern, saying, "Comrade!"

Before continuing to explore the lantern's function within the semiotics
of the code, it is important to note the more concrete allusions of the prop
that gives the opera its name. The attributes of the lantern make it a direct
reference to Mao. The libretto mentions the leader explicitly only once—in
the final version, Li's last words are, "Long live Chairman Mao!" Yet the ico-
nography of the lantern clearly invokes the Great Helmsman. Possessing the
essential elements of Jiang Qing's aesthetic—red, shining, and bright (*hong,
guang, liang*)—the lantern becomes the *lux et veritas*, the touchstone of
genuine revolutionary loyalty. These qualities also suggest an affinity between the lantern and Mao, often described as the bright red sun. Popular
lyrics from the period portray the Chairman as "the reddest, reddest red

heart in our hearts." One song in particular reached the status of the unofficial anthem of the Cultural Revolution: "The East is red; the sun has arisen; a Mao Zedong has appeared in China." Some paintings, apparently modeled on images of Lenin, show Mao with solar rays radiating from his head. Book illustrations and stage sets for *The Red Lantern* presented similar radiant images, with the lantern at the center.

Critical references to the opera further used the metaphor of brightness to contribute to Mao's cult. Li Yuhe is depicted as "feeding on the light and dew of Mao Zedong Thought."[49] The hero in *Taking Tiger Mountain by Strategy* is also described as blessed by "rays of powerful sunlight . . . [that] symbolize Yang Zirong's advance under the brilliance of Mao Zedong Thought."[50] Praise for *The Red Lantern* often asserts that Li—a thinly disguised stand-in for Mao—"is a most brilliant [*guanghui*] model of the Chinese proletarian class"[51] and "sparkles with the dazzling brilliance of communism."[52] The opera is claimed to be "a brilliant paradigm of the union between the political nature of proletarian art and artistic elevation,"[53] "resplendent with the light of revolutionary romanticism."[54] The stage lighting takes these attributes to the literal level. After the bleak lighting of the first nine scenes, symbolizing the darkness of Japanese occupation, the last two scenes lighten up "with resplendent colors and splendid brightness [*huihuang canlan*]," depicting the invigorated new spirit in the revolutionary bases, according to one critic.[55]

The bright lighting is particularly pregnant with meaning in two scenes. As a critic styled Ding Xuelei (literally "A Nail Learning from [model soldier] Lei Feng") observes, "Li Yuhe's sublime political ideal of the proletarian class radiates with especially shining brilliance [*canlan de guanghui*] in the scene 'Struggle at the Execution Grounds.'"[56] In this scene, red spotlights follow Li Yuhe as he strides to the tune of "The Internationale." The lighting, one critic proclaimed, expressed "Li Yuhe's crimson gall and red heart, boundlessly loyal to Mao Zedong, boundlessly loyal to the Party, and boundlessly loyal to the work of the proletarian revolution." Li Yuhe's "dazzling glow" (*guangcai zhaoren*) signals that his spirit will survive his physical death.[57] The bright red light, like the radio signals in *The Undying Transmission*, points to the persistence of revolutionary ideology even beyond the grave.

Stage lighting also contributes to the striking effect of the scene at the beginning of the model play when Li Yuhe raises the red lantern to welcome the messenger. A bright red spotlight rests on Li as he strikes an operatic pose of brave resolution. The lighting helps "express Li Yuhe's brave fighting spirit—fearless, breaking through the darkness, 'like fleeting clouds unconstrained.'"[58] The critic's quotation from a poem by Mao foregrounds the analogy, drawn by the red light, between Li and Mao.

The importance of the red lighting becomes evident when the scene is compared with earlier versions of the play. In *Where One Falls, Another Rises*, the exchange of codes takes place in a radically different setting. Li Yuhe sends Tiemei out of the room to watch some boiling water and whispers to the messenger. The scene is dark, the characters are wary, and the dialogue is spoken unconfidently. Much is left unsaid, and the passwords are heard from off-screen while the camera follows Tiemei into the kitchen. It remains for the viewer to figure out, together with the young woman, who peeps at the scene from behind the curtain, the meaning of the secret procedure. The canonized version of *The Red Lantern* rewrites the scene and fully dramatizes the exchange in which the code smoothly changes hands. While the original script features a liaison officer from the occupied areas, the later version modifies the messenger's provenance to the more glorified Eighth Route Army Pine Peak Base Area. The change may, as the Shanghai opera troupe argued, "foreground our Party's underground tactics of struggle and particular ways of keeping secrecy" and "express more profoundly the anti-Japanese struggle of the Chinese people under the leadership of Chairman Mao and the Communist Party."[59] At the more evident level, the modification endows the scene with a heroic atmosphere. Significantly, in the earlier film (as well as in the Shanghai opera version), the messenger dies at the end of the episode, while in the model play, he recovers from his temporary weakness and strides off the stage to his next mission. The red light stands for unmitigated triumph.

The lantern scene emphasizes Li's (read: Mao's) authority and sublimity. The libretto, rewritten in accordance with the Three Prominences theory, centers on Li Yuhe. The early versions balance Li's heroism with Tiemei's initiative. *The Red Lantern*, on the other hand, floods Li Yuhe with red light. *Where One Falls, Another Rises* already portrays the lantern's light as miraculously bright, bringing a glimmer of hope to the ailing messenger's eyes. Yet the cinematic version of the model play, which unlike the earlier film is shot in color, inundates the corresponding scene with red. The effect stresses Li's almost supernatural powers. The messenger glares transfixed at the lantern, with an ecstatic gaze. His field of vision is completely filled by the lantern, as if he is blinded by its light.

The red lantern, which according to contemporary critics stands for "the bright light of communist thought" and "the 'red lantern' of the literary revolution of the proletarian class,"[60] displaces the messenger's vision. The stage lighting illustrates how the revolutionary sublime takes over individual will. The messenger will believe and entrust himself to whoever holds up the lantern. The cinematic rendition of the scene emphasizes the totality of Mao Zedong's thought as a red light that divests the messenger—and, by extension, the movie spectators—of any interpretive authority of their own. The red lantern folds together Mao's cult, the aesthetics of the sublime, and the totalitarian semiotics of the code, so that they complement one another.

THE SEMIOTICS OF THE LANTERN

Like the undecipherable code, the lantern reaffirms Maoist control over public discourse. "The signal lamp" (*haozhi deng*), as Granny calls the red lantern, is used at the end of a series of passwords that lead to transferring the secret signals. As a symbol of revolutionary allegiance, the lantern adds further complexity to the system of codes. The lantern procedure is first used in scene 2, when a messenger is hurt while jumping off a train and is brought to Li Yuhe's house. The Li household has developed a variation for an extra measure of safety—after the "wooden comb" repartee, and before Li raises the red lantern, his mother shows an ordinary kerosene lamp and says, "My neighbor!" It is only when the guest believes that he has made a mistake and hurries to leave that Li approaches from the other side and holds up the red lantern. The routine for recognizing a fellow revolutionary is elaborated to include a method for detecting pretenders. The latter use is made clear in scene 5. While Li Yuhe is being detained by the Japanese, a collaborator visits the two women and is about to win their confidence. When the grandmother holds up the other lantern, however, the fake messenger fails to react with disappointment and is thrown out unceremoniously. The lantern signal is duplicated in two forms, to elicit a possible correct response as well as an incorrect one. The double-edged routine stresses the need to distinguish friend from foe and upholds the politics of differentiation.

The lantern is a sign as well as an actual railroad traffic signal. It is painted red, the symbol of revolutionary rectitude (one is reminded that the Red Guards tried to change traffic lights so that the revolutionary color red would signal "go"). Yet the lantern stands also for another, more important concern, namely, the succession of authority. As Granny explains to Tiemei, the lantern was salvaged from a massacre, in which the young woman's parents were killed, during the brutal suppression of the 1923 Beijing-Hankow Railroad worker's strike. In the Shanghai opera version, Tiemei adds after Li Yuhe's and Granny's execution: "The blood has painted the red lantern with even redder light."[61] The red lantern, their "heirloom" (*jiabao*) as Granny describes it, stands for the red of the slain proletarians' blood, a class martyrdom that binds together the revolutionary family more than their blood relationship and unites them in their struggle. As praise for the model play fleshes out, "The red lantern is also the heirloom of the Chinese proletarian class."[62] As the lantern theme points out, what is at stake in Li's family based on ideology rather than blood is primarily revolutionary succession. The play's depiction of an imagined familial community, the "Maoist model family" as Xiaomei Chen calls it,[63] stresses the ideological affinity. Yet the lantern's provenance underscores that Tiemei is heir to both Li's revolutionary family and her dead proletarian parents, an important pedigree in a period when the official "bloodline theory" (*xuetonglun*) justified persecuting the descendants of tagged "counterrevolutionaries." The heirloom lantern validates the successor and thereby enables handing over authority to the next generation.

Like the Soviet novel and its early Chinese derivatives, the opera centers on the education of a new revolutionary generation (a similar pattern may be noted in Xiao'ou's tutelage in Ma-Xu Weibang's *Song at Midnight*—see Chapter 3). Tiemei's name, literally "Iron plum," designates her as Li Yuhe's heir. "Once the storm has passed, flowers will bloom," Li sings at the execution ground, and the Shanghai opera notes "small Tiemei, resilient as a red plum branch in snow."[64] Tiemei's act of taking over the lantern and the code, left by her parents and adoptive family respectively, may allude to the struggles within the Party over Mao's succession. After almost being fooled by the fake messenger, Tiemei observes Granny expose him and learns the lesson. The lantern provides the young woman with the necessary revolutionary experience for ferreting out the enemy from within and prepares her for shouldering the task ahead. By extension, revolutionary education prepares the younger generation to recognize and denounce purported traitors such as Liu Shaoqi.

Knowledge of the correct codes, which ensures control over the dissemination of information and distribution of power, also plays a vital role in determining the proper succession of authority. Tiemei's newly acquired qualifications, which allow her to take over Li Yuhe's mission, depend spe-

cifically on her skilled manipulation of codes and passwords. Granny's pres-
entation of the kerosene lamp instead of the red lantern is the first in a series
of exchanges and displacements taught to Tiemei. When the Japanese soldiers ask for the codebook, Tiemei gives them an old almanac. (The Shanghai version extends the episode into a humorous dialogue in which Tiemei
first pretends that the Japanese are after a delicacy—"Too bad, I've already
eaten it!")[65] In so doing, she takes after her father—when the chief gendarme
asks Li Yuhe for the code, the latter pretends to misunderstand, taking the
word for "telegraph code" (*dianma*) for the homonymous "electric horse"
("Ha, electric horse, electric donkey . . . never got to play with any of those").
The displaced pronunciation stresses how mastery of the code betokens Li's
superiority over the enemy. A contemporary critic singles out Li's transposi-
tion of the code as a clear sign of valor: "In the original opera, Li Yuhe brings
the telegraph code home, but this was modified so that Li Yuhe relocates the
code and puts it under a stone next to an old locust tree on the western river
bank. This expresses Li Yuhe's high level of revolutionary alertness and rich
experience in struggle."[66] As Li Yuhe's profession as a switchman demonstrates, he is adept at diverting and relocating passing missives. Likewise, Tiemei's knowledge of signs, such as the red lantern, a knife-grinder's signal call,
and a butterfly pasted on the window as a prearranged indication of safety,
demonstrates her role as heir to Li Yuhe (in *Where One Falls, Another Rises*,
Tiemei also recognizes the signs of the enemy and detects Wang Lianju's
concealed wound). In fact, she proceeds to invent her own dislocated signs—
first, she gives the almanac (an apt substitute, since it also contains numeric
tables) to the Japanese gendarme, and later she steals out through the neighbor's door after exchanging coats. The Shanghai version stresses Tiemei's
learning process—in scene 1, she suggests to Li Yuhe that he exchange his red
lantern for her simple lamp, unwittingly trying to effect an erroneous displacement of signs. It is only with revolutionary experience that she learns
the correct exchange, and by the end of the Shanghai opera, she uses yet another decoy for the code, fooling even the underground fighters.[67]

The signs in the model play are "purloined" in the same sense that the
object of search is displaced in Edgar Allan Poe's "The Purloined Letter." In
Poe's story, a letter is hidden by being put in plain view, only folded inside
out. As Jacques Lacan and other critics have pointed out, the purloined letter
functions as the center of a complex semiotic system in which each player
derives power from his or her assumptions about the letter's whereabouts.
The letter's contents become unimportant in and of themselves; it is the

ability to recognize the letter, and if necessary replace it, that preoccupies the plotters.[68] Similarly, the way in which the underground in *The Red Lantern* makes use of visible props as secret signs becomes their very meaning. The codes establish an abstract web of relationships that demonstrates the revolutionary possession of power but does not specify the way in which it will be employed. Like the telegraph code, the lantern implies, not a system that facilitates the free exchange of messages and opinions, but rather a structure that upholds the Party's arbitrary interpretation of all signs. Since the lantern's provenance emphasizes that shared class consciousness is stronger than blood relationship, the revolutionary leaders can invoke collective consciousness to reserve all rights to assigning meaning.

Compared with the ideals promoted by May Fourth, the circulation of signs in *The Red Lantern* parodies the free exchange of ideas. The more transparent the mechanism for ascribing meaning seems, the less conducive it is to the formation of a space in which opinions can be openly circulated, commented upon, and reshaped by all participants. It is worth noticing that the plot eventually abandons the use of the password. When Tiemei meets the guerrillas, among them a liaison man she recognizes, she foregoes the elaborate verification routine and hands over the code without hesitation. Tiemei cannot question the revolutionary fighters' authority even by means of the secret identification process, and she cedes the treasured object. In line with the Yan'an Talks, public debate is abandoned in the name of total identification of individual aspirations with the will of the masses.

The Red Lantern, praised for "portraying the sublime rectitude of the revolutionaries,"[69] exemplifies the Maoist hermeneutics that stopped the May Fourth project of instating critical public discourse in its tracks. On the one hand, May Fourth ideals were preserved in vulgar form, since the utopian communication between author and audience was proclaimed to have been accomplished. On the other hand, Mao practiced an aesthetics of differentiation that functioned as an ideological and practical means of denying free debate. Literature and art were curbed from inquiring into past or current events. Bearing witness against the dominant view of history was effectively silenced.

PART TWO

Wounded Memories

5

A Blinding Red Light
The Displacement of Rhetoric in the Cinema of the Early 1980s

The film *Ku'nao ren de xiao* (Bitter laughter, 1979) signaled a response to the Maoist obstruction of critical discourse. The plot describes a journalist's distress at having to write a false piece of reportage during the Cultural Revolution. In a key scene, Fu Bin (Li Zhiyu) asks for his journalism professor's advice and the latter refers him to a short piece by Lu Xun, "Li lun" (Establishing an opinion, 1925). Lu Xun tells of a man who is asked to comment on a newborn child's future. The man neither wants to lie and promise the child riches and good fortune, the way other people do, nor to limit himself to unpalatable certainties such as saying that the child will die sooner or later. To avoid these options, the man is advised to say, "Oh! This child! Just look at him! So . . . Ha-ha! Ho ho! Ho, ho ho ho ho!"[1] The professor's complaint in *Bitter Laughter* that "they don't even let you answer with a ha-ha," criticizes the Maoist monopoly on hermeneutic codes. There is also rich symbolism in that *Bitter Laughter* reappropriates Lu Xun's parable to describe the plight of print culture during the Cultural Revolution. Lu Xun shows how one's words might be self-incriminating and how a turn of phrase, based on performance rather than content, can produce half-truths. In paying tribute to Lu Xun's piece, the scene comments on the doublespeak of the authorities, demonstrates the limitations imposed on public debate under Mao, and revives the ambivalence found in Lu Xun's writings and other texts of the May Fourth period.

Bitter Laughter is emblematic of how, following Mao's death and the demise of the "Gang of Four" in 1976, texts and films started challenging totalitarian aesthetics and the delegitimation of debate that had taken place under the Great Helmsman. While celebrating the newfound opportunity to convey silenced experience, writers and filmmakers were aware of the lingering effects of the prolonged mutilation of critical debate. Moreover, literary expression continued to be monitored and constrained. Trauma, split voices, impaired memory, and temporal disorientation haunted literary production in the PRC and Taiwan, from the scar literature of the 1980s to the

avant-garde fiction and even the "hooligan literature" of the 1990s, and reshaped conceptions of public discourse.

The success of avant-garde fiction and the "fifth-generation" films associated with it (see Chapter 8) has somewhat overshadowed scar literature and
especially its cinematic equivalents. Yet in a recent monograph, the first
dedicated to film between 1976 and 1981, Chris Berry persuasively argues that
"these films constitute the first site in which a significant and sustained
cinematic construction of postsocialist Chinese culture occurs."[2] Although
they toed the Party line, the films of the early 1980s directly challenged the
symbolism and hermeneutic structure of Maoist art and of the so-called
"model plays" in particular. By addressing the consequences of the Cultural
Revolution in symbolic terms rather than by simply testifying to the "ten
years of turmoil," the films in question also struggle with the aftermath of
the literary tropes and stage aesthetics of the Cultural Revolution. They take
the first steps toward inventing a cinematic vocabulary for dealing with the
trauma and establishing the narrator's position as a witness. At stake in these
films is the resuscitation of critical debate. The films do not, however, simply
celebrate the new dialogue with the audience. The Maoist monopolization of
all art production and interpretation in the name of the unity between the
artist and "the masses" had already given the lie to the naive belief in free exchange of ideas. Instead of endorsing a discourse that might turn out to be
illusory, the films take a more cautious position. They find the response to
Maoist rhetoric in characters' inner thoughts, where mutually incompatible
and even absurd viewpoints may coexist beyond the reach of ideological censorship.

Here I examine four films in particular, starting with *Bitter Laughter* (literally "The laughter of the man in distress," the 1979 directing debut of Yang
Yanjin and Deng Yimin), and ending with Yang's *Xiao jie* (The alley, 1981),
including also *Bashan yeyu* (Night rain in Bashan, 1980; directed by the veteran filmmaker Wu Yonggang together with the young Wu Yigong) and
Tianyunshan chuanqi (The legend of Tianyunshan, 1980) by the established
director Xie Jin. Although five filmmakers of various backgrounds were involved, their works reveal similar concerns. All four films were produced at
Shanghai Film Studio and describe political persecution during the Cultural
Revolution, including to varying extents depictions of the aftermath in the
"new era." The films also converge in presenting the political events from a
more personal point of view, emphasizing subjective experience. Fantastic
hallucinations, flashbacks, and alternative endings are conveyed with the

help of experimental music, novel camera angles, and jittery editing. These formal innovations not only stand in direct opposition to Maoist aesthetics but also directly challenge the authorities' interpretive codes. The shift of emphasis to formal device and new themes also entailed a refashioning of public discourse.

A NEW LANGUAGE FOR A NEW CINEMA

Cinema production entered a new stage after 1979, when filmmakers, critics, and the government all called for cinema that would mark the demise of the Cultural Revolution. After Deng Xiaoping's rise to power in 1978, the Eleventh Party Plenum recognized the "mistakes" made during the Cultural Revolution and before. A period of looser control followed, under the slogan "Let a hundred flowers blossom, a hundred schools contend"—the same slogan as that used in the mid-1950s, before the clampdown of the Anti-Rightist Campaign of 1957–58. The second "Hundred Flowers Movement" allowed films to reverse the trends set during the Cultural Revolution. The aesthetics of the revolutionary operas was abandoned, and production of Western-style drama and feature film resumed quickly. The year 1979 saw the revival of the first play to be attacked as part of Jiang Qing's ascent to power, *Hai Rui Dismissed from Office*, and the re-release of previously banned films, including *Where One Falls, Another Rises*, which had been replaced by the more upbeat *The Red Lantern* (see Chapter 4). Film production and viewing boomed.[3] The reopening of the Beijing Film Academy in 1978 allowed filmmakers active before the Cultural Revolution to train a younger, "fifth" generation of directors. Before their students started dominating the screen, however, veteran directors reintroduced filmic and narrative techniques neglected during the Cultural Revolution and addressed their experience of the period of brutal repression.

The more immediately felt departure from Maoist paradigms was thematic. Literature and film of the late 1970s explore love from a formerly taboo viewpoint, describing affection that has little to do with patriotic duty and often involves conflicting allegiances.[4] As such, the plots return to the May Fourth movement's unfinished project of rewriting Nora's fate (see Chapter 2). Some films dealing with love became overtly political. The acclaimed *Lushan lian* (Love in Lushan, 1980) shows the son of a venerated cadre fall in love with the daughter of a renegade general who has defected to the KMT and fled to the United States. The happy reunion at the end coincided not only with Deng's agenda of reviving the ties with the economically powerful overseas Chinese communities but also with the contemporary reversal of the Maoist "bloodline theory" mentioned in Chapter 4. The protagonists demonstrate how love can cross class lines and overcome their parents' enmity.[5] Another "love" film, *Taiyang he ren* (The sun and the man, also known as *Kulian*—Unrequited love, 1980; dir. Peng Ning), presents a bleaker view and draws an analogy between the Cultural Revolution and pre-1949 China. The script came under attack, and the film was never released.[6]

The change in cinema since 1979, however, constituted not only a thematic shift but also recognition that there is a discrete cinematic idiom that determines the film's message no less than the director's allegiance or the script's political innuendoes and includes the introduction of new stylistic devices. The theoretical breakthrough was marked by Zhang Nuanxin and Li Tuo's milestone essay "The Modernization of Film Language," which appeared in *Dianying yishu* (Film art) in 1979. Stating that Chinese film should follow Deng's Four Modernizations policy, the essay gives examples of innovative techniques from Italian neorealism and the French New Wave.[7] In declaring that "we do not concern ourselves with the issues of film content in each era, nor with political or economic aspects that may stimulate (or delay) its development,"[8] the authors make a claim for a sphere of debate that is not controlled by the state but rather by artistic device. Filmmakers responded by binding together political messages and new technique. Zhang Zheng's war film *Xiaohua* (Little flower, 1979) notably diverges from earlier films on the anti-Japanese resistance by interweaving color and black-and-white sequences to represent the viewpoints and memories of multiple protagonists.[9] Yet only with *Bitter Laughter* did post-Maoist Chinese film venture beyond realism.

FROM PHOTOGRAPHIC MEMORY TO
FILMIC IMAGINATION

Bitter Laughter explores the paradoxical situation of the witness in Mao's China at length. As the scene alluded to at the beginning of this chapter evidences, the film is emblematic of the revival of the May Fourth critique. Despite the professor's recommendation that he follow Lu Xun's advice, the journalist makes some incautious remarks, and he is subsequently arrested. The film ends with the man's release after the Cultural Revolution, and the very last frames show opening flowers, alluding to the renewal of the slogan

"Let a hundred flowers blossom, a hundred schools contend." *Bitter Laughter* may therefore be said to celebrate the newfound freedom of those oppressed by the Gang of Four. Yet the film also strikes a bittersweet note in showing the released reporter as a white-haired man who has lost the better part of his life. Moreover, *Bitter Laughter* shows how even the protagonist becomes an accomplice to lies when he commends his young daughter for telling the truth precisely when, unbeknownst to her father, she learns how to use a false confession to her advantage. The film serves as a reminder of the abuse of testimony and the caution that must be exercised when expressing one's opinion in public.

In this context, the homage to Lu Xun in Yang's film, as in other contemporary works, is especially interesting.[10] Lu Xun's legacy was appropriated by Mao, who concluded his Yan'an Talks on Literature and Art by proclaiming, "All Party members, all revolutionaries, all revolutionary literature and art workers, must follow the model of Lu Xun and be 'oxen' for the proletariat and the popular masses."[11] Recalling the other, critical Lu Xun, who places the witness in a position where he is compelled to utter nonsense, resuscitates a more complex view of public discourse. Furthermore, *Bitter Laughter* picks up Lu Xun's borderline consciousness, between dream and awakening (see Chapter 1). "Establishing an Opinion," like many of Lu Xun's short stories, is related as a dream and as such is relegated to the writer's inner mind. Expressing one's opinion, it is implied, can only take place in a dream. The reporter in *Bitter Laughter* is barred from his vocation of disseminating information through the print media and would do best to share his thoughts with no one.

Bitter Laughter proceeds to depict the reporter's anxieties and inner thoughts through his fantastic hallucinations. After talking about keeping a balanced reportage, he imagines himself falling from a tightrope. Later, he imagines himself climbing a pyramidlike structure above the clouds to reach an important cadre. Finally, the same cadre is integrated into a dramatization of Lu Xun's short story, which turns into a Kafkaesque chase, full of mazes and grotesque faces. *Bitter Laughter* comports with Zhang Nuanxin and Li Tuo's above-mentioned essay, which calls for representing the protagonists' psyches rather than their actions: "Thoughts, fantasies, memories, ideals, wishes, and even the subtle and complicated subconscious can all be reflected through visual images. These representations are more direct, vivid, ardent, real, and more emotional than speech or the performances of dramatic actors."[12] The director Yang Yanjin explains: "During the 'Gang of

Four' period, [due to] the high pressure and the introversion of spiritual life, many people got used to having nightmares. . . . People dared to be angry but not to speak out, so that resistance often took place inside their minds. In order to represent people's state of mind during that period, we use dreams, remembrances, fantasies, and associations in our film."[13] Ma Ning notes that Yang Yanjin was among the first to use new cinematic language to visualize subjective perception.[14] The film theorist Bai Jingsheng also praised *Bitter Laughter* for integrating different techniques for expressing reality, fantasy, and memories.[15] The hallucination scenes explore film's ability to visualize images that are not part of material reality. Against Maoist revolutionary realism, Yang places subjective perceptions on a level with everyday situations.

The hallucination scenes insinuate that visual images—and by extension films as well—at best serve as evidence to events, but cannot bear witness to the complex reality of the inner mind. Although the reporter's wife refers to his eyes as "sincere," his journalistic photos are left unpublished, together with his essay on "lies, facts, and news reportage," which he is forced to burn. Instead, the corrupt cadre manipulates the medium by posing for the camera, posturing as a manual laborer. In other films of the same period, photos introduce unresolved issues. In *Legend of Tianyunshan*, shots of a man wrongly persecuted as a counterrevolutionary prompt a fight for his rehabilitation. In *Love in Lushan*, a family photo triggers a tense situation that ends with forgiving the former KMT officer and accepting his daughter. Yet *Bitter Laughter* is more explicit than these pieces in probing the relationship between facts, personal perception, and testimony, to the point of questioning the veracity of visual media. As I shall show later, *The Alley* explores at length the implications of vision (and blindness) on cinema's role in bearing witness. Yet even the earlier films challenge the possibility of presenting a clear narrative or reliable evidence to the past and instead emphasize the importance of the rich imagery of the inner mind.

"THINK IT OVER!"

The turn to inner reflection as an alternative way to remember and give testimony also arises in *Night Rain in Bashan*, winner of the first Golden Rooster Award for Best Feature. The plot takes place in the early 1970s and depicts the journey of the poet Qiu Shi (played by Li Zhiyu), who is transported incognito down the Yangtze River from Chongqing to be punished—

most likely executed—by the henchmen of the Gang of Four. As it turns out, all the other passengers on board have suffered during the Cultural Revolution and sympathize with the persecuted poet. The only one to resist their logic is the "small revolutionary general," Liu Wenying (Zhang Yu), assigned to guard the poet. Yet even Liu Wenying abandons her Red Guard stock phrases and convictions when faced with the honest poetic language of Qiu Shi. Qiu Shi tells her: "Think it over . . . it is as if the world does not need sunshine, forests, flowers, colors. That would be a dead world!" After the poet tells the young woman to think for herself, she changes her mind and even helps him escape to the shore.

Night Rain reflects the contemporary Party line of criticizing the Gang of Four, but like other films of the same period, it retains many of the themes of the revolutionary operas. For instance, Liu Wenying relinquishes her mistaken beliefs after observing an elderly woman mourning her son's death, presumably during a clash between Red Guard factions. As in Cultural Revolution productions, notably *The Red Lantern,* discussed in Chapter 4, the memory of the martyrs sets ideological priorities straight. The film also replicates the language of revolutionary productions to mock and counteract the effect of official rhetoric. The bereaved mother deplores her son's death: "He didn't die while resisting the Japanese and fighting Jiang [Chiang Kai-shek], but at that moment [of internecine Red Guard fighting] . . . he died." The words resonate eerily with the accusations leveled at "revisionists" during earlier campaigns. The commander in *Tiedao youjidui* (Railroad guerrilla, 1956), for example, utters a politically charged insinuation when he hisses: "I got away unwounded by the Japs but was wounded by the capitalist revisionist KMT!" *Night Rain* reappropriates tropes from the model plays to portray the people united in their hatred and active subversion of the enemy—in this case, the Gang of Four. If the Li household in *The Red Lantern* stands for the people's struggle against the Japanese invaders, the people on board the steamer in *Night Rain* are paragons of the resistance to Jiang Qing and her collaborators. The film depicts how young and old, simple folk and officials—including the boat crew and a high-ranking plainclothes policeman—all lend a hand to protecting Qiu Shi. Whereas Jiang Qing's productions engaged in rewriting the history of the CCP, *Night Rain* sets out to rewrite history yet again, this time to show the Cultural Revolution as the doing of a numbered few.

Despite its stylistic affinity with Maoist productions, *Night Rain* resembles *Bitter Laughter* in its concern with the influence of writing on a wide readership and a new vision of public discourse. The original script included a scene in which Qiu Shi posts poems criticizing the Gang of Four in public—in reality, a feat impossible during the Cultural Revolution, as the critic Chen Huangmei points out in a letter to the scriptwriter, Ye Nan.[16] The film's title itself is borrowed from ninth-century poet Li Shangyin, and as Ye Nan explains, alludes to the protagonist's will to weather any storm.[17] Qiu Shi's poetry becomes a vehicle for "seeking truth from the facts" (*shi shi qiu shi*—the slogan for Dengist pragmatism; the poet's name, taken from Li Shangyin's poem, may also be a homonymous allusion to the slogan). Poetry is also portrayed as a vehicle of anti-Maoist dissent through the character of Song Minsheng. As a Red Guard, Song raided the poet's house, but he has since grown up to regret doing so. As it turns out, Song saved Qiu Shi's work when looting his house, and he now tells the poet: "The poetry manuscript is still with me . . . it should not be lost." Poetry is portrayed as a political force that cannot be suppressed, resonating with Mikhail Bulgakov's famous anti-Stalinist retort, "Manuscripts don't burn."[18]

Too sentimental and individualistic by Mao's standards of revolutionary realism and revolutionary romanticism, Qiu Shi's poetry possesses a liberating quality that allows his spirit to remain free even when he is in shackles. He can turn the tables on his guard, telling her that she is the true captive: "You are a prisoner of your mind." As the transforming nature of Qiu Shi's poetry suggests, the true drama takes place in the protagonists' minds (paralleling the plot, the film's director told the actors to act not with their "faces" but with their "hearts").[19] Contrary to Mao's demand for unity of thought and action, where every inner thought finds its external manifestation, the film presents a psychological drama. The enclosed space of the steamer and the constricted time frame—a mere twenty-four hours—further enhance the reliance on the characters' inner mental dynamics, presented through flashback sequences. The interior working of the mind is privileged over public performance.

The importance of individual judgment is emphasized in Qiu Shi's words to Liu Wenying to "think it over." The poet places the burden of reflection on the young woman and tells her to think for herself. It is useful to compare how the phrase "think it over" (*ni xiang yi xiang*) is employed here, in contrast with its use in the execution scene in *The Red Lantern*. The heroic Li Yuhe, a surrogate Mao figure, admonishes the Japanese commander: "Hatoyama! The Chinese people and the Chinese Communist Party cannot be killed. I want you to think carefully over the outcome!" Li's tone is similar to that of a Red Guard asking for a detailed self-criticism from a "counter-revolutionary." Li demands that Hatoyama "carefully think over" (*zixi xiang yi xiang*) his position. While in the model play, the injunction implies submission to the communist line, in *Night Rain* "think it over" gives individual judgment free reign.

The new way of using the phrase after the Cultural Revolution can also be glimpsed in the Urumqi Political Bureau Drama Troupe's *Tianshan shenchu* (Deep in Tianshan Mountains, 1981). The piece follows the relationship of two young people—she lives in Beijing, while he is posted to a remote Xinjiang labor camp. Even when the opportunity to unite comes up, both find it hard to part from their respective places. At the end of the play, the man decides to stay in Xinjiang and invites his beloved to come and live with him. Just before the curtain drops, she answers: "Let me think it over!" The critic Lu Mei draws attention to the implications of the statement. The undecided ending and the woman's retort, Lu writes, "leave it to the audience to 'think it over' and put the pressure of answering this difficult problem on each and every member of the audience."[20] Lu remarks that since the PRC was established, theater has avoided ambiguous endings. In other words, only in the post-Mao period can literature present an ambivalent situation and bestow interpretive authority on individual readers and viewers. Lu Mei's call to "let the entire society 'think it over'" ("quan shehui dou lai 'xiang yi xiang'") is tantamount to a plea for revising the experience of the Cultural Revolution through texts that stimulate the audience to think for themselves and through works that support an artistic realm of free thought.

The ending of *Deep in Tianshan Mountains* anticipates the *Rashōmon*-style narratives that would become popular in the mid-1980s, discussed in the next two chapters.[21] Unlike Mao's totalitarian aesthetics, which reduced all meaning to a single blinding, authoritative sign, literary and cinematic works after the Cultural Revolution ask the audience to form their own opinions. Qiu Shi's gesture in *Night Rain in Bashan*, asking the young woman to relinquish formulaic revolutionary phrases, turn to her inner thoughts, and use her own judgment blatantly diverges from the rhetoric of Maoist stage productions.

Through the early 1980s, critical interest developed in characters' inner thoughts and especially film's expression of the psychological dimension. In 1981, Yu Qian drew attention to the distortion of the mind's workings in filmic representation of reminiscences, fantasies, nightmares, and other visualized images.[22] Disregarding Yu's simplification of how cinematic language might reify subjective experience, the article signals the emergence of psychological trauma, and memories of the Cultural Revolution in particular, as a major filmic trope. Yu refers specifically to *Legend of Tianyunshan*, which shared the major Golden Rooster Awards of 1981 with *Night Rain in Bashan* and was hailed at its release for presenting the most uncompromising depiction on screen to date of the Great Leap Forward and the Cultural Revolution.[23] Directed by the film veteran Xie Jin (b. 1923), whose works were attacked and shelved during both movements, the film portrays some of the most painful features of the Cultural Revolution with blunt directness—the physical brutality of labor camps, the ruthless mental manipulations by the cadres, and the complicity of the many who betrayed even their friends and lovers.

The Legend of Tianyushan tells how Song Wei (played by Wang Fuli) is sent to the countryside and falls in love with the cadre Luo Qun (Shi Weijian). After Luo is targeted as a "rightist element," however, Song "draws a clear line" between Luo and herself, marries his persecutor, Wu Yao (Zhong Xinghuo), and enjoys the comfortable life of a high official's wife. Yet reports and photos from the "special area" to which Luo has been confined remind Song of the wrongs done to Luo. When she finds out that her husband has continued to suppress Luo's case, she appeals to a higher authority and confronts Wu with the reversed verdict. Although Song's actions come too late to allow her to reconcile with Luo, the film's message is clear—some officials are still covering up for past wrongs, but they will be ferreted out. As Song Wei's friend says defiantly to Wu Yao, "Look, a new history has already begun—and what about you?" The film comports with Deng's policy of eradicating the practices associated with the Gang of Four and rehabilitating older Party activists. As Chris Berry notes, the film avoids direct criticism by placing the original conflict in the late 1950s.[24] Yet the plot implicitly challenges the very way in which the CCP has written its history.

Most saliently, *The Legend of Tianyunshan* employs the subjective perspective of multiple narrators, complemented by especially dynamic camera work. A contemporary critic points out how seeing the story through the eyes of various narrators helps reveal their "inner world of the mind."[25] Instead of having a single authority, typically identified with the Party, recount the entire story, Xie Jin's film presents the events through the eyes of three different persons. Moreover, the film begins in 1978, and the three points of view are offered after the fact, in flashbacks. Luo Qun's case is first recounted by Song's friend Zhou Yuzhen; the story is then picked up by Song's own reminiscences, and it is completed with a letter from Feng Qinglan (played by Shi Jianlan), Song's former friend, now married to Luo. Although Song puts the pieces together, coming to terms with her past involves no reconciliation, for she arrives after Qinglan has already died. Even as the protagonist revisits Tianyunshan, it becomes clear that the past cannot be recaptured and will continue to haunt the memories and inner thoughts of the people who went through the Cultural Revolution.

BEYOND THE TOTALITARIAN SYSTEM OF SIGNIFICATION

The use of novel themes, plot structure, and cinematography to counter Maoist narratives is taken even further in *The Alley*, a film praised by the writer and Cultural Revolution victim Ba Jin as uniquely successful in recapturing the emotions of the period of turmoil.[26] The story takes place during the Cultural Revolution and follows the friendship between two people. What starts as an idyll of two young men spending a day in the countryside ends abruptly when one of them confesses to being a woman. The woman, Yu (played by Zhang Yu, who also plays the female lead in *Love at Lushan* and *Night Rain in Bashan*), has pretended to be a man so as not to draw attention to her short hair, which was brutally clipped by Red Guards. Yu's male friend, Xia (Guo Kaimin), searches for a wig for her, but when he tries to steal a braid used as stage prop, he is caught and beaten blind. The last part of the film presents several possible endings and different outcomes to Xia's search for Yu.

Although *The Legend of Tianyunshan* had already employed multiple viewpoints through which to present the plot, Yang uses the device in a more radical manner. Whereas in Xie Jin's film, the three narrators complement one another, the endings of *The Alley* are mutually exclusive. In one, Yu has become a loose woman, a product of the emerging consumer society, leaving no place for Xia in her life. In another ending, Xia finds Yu at her old place and is at first led to believe that she has already married. In the third conclusion, Yu comes back to take care of Xia. Even more jarring than the three coexisting endings is the narrator's final statement, which rejects all the resolutions and leaves the story open-ended: "This is not the ending but a new beginning. Let the audience imagine and complete the story according to their own lives." *The Alley* fleshes out the implications of the undecided plotline for public discourse—the incompatible endings stress the audience's agency of interpretation. The contemporary critic Zhang Zhongnian remarks explicitly on this aspect: "The three projected conclusions provoke the audience to fresh imaginations and thoughts more than any stimulant and allow the audience to soar freely in the boundless realm of thought." Drawing a parallel with Italian neorealism, Zhang quotes Fellini: "I believe that . . . by not providing [the audience] with a happy ending, you make them think, . . . after which they *have no choice* but to look for their own answers."[27]

Responses to *The Alley* suggest that old critical practices kept some spectators from discerning the significance of Yang's new cinematic language. Zhang Junxiang, for example, dismisses the ending and "show-off" camera work, stating that the film's innovation resides in its message that "the human quest for the good will not be quenched by any fascist regime such as Jiang Qing's anti-revolutionary bunch."[28] Yet *The Alley* distances itself from such simplistic messages. Unlike *The Red Lantern*, which points at a single authoritative meaning of the text, *The Alley* internalizes the polysemic scheme that allows plural readings and returns interpretive agency to the individual members of the audience. To emphasize that the account depends on the spectators' reading, the film frames the plot within a metafictional framework. Yu and Xia's relationship is told to a film director surnamed Zhong, as material for a possible script. Although Xia is played by the same actor as the narrator, arousing the suspicion that Xia's story is the narrator's autobiographical account, the narrator repeatedly insists on the story's fictionality. Later, the narrator and the fictional director imagine the three endings. Frequent interruptions in the narrative ensure that the viewers are aware that it is only a story being told and that the film represents no more than the young man's subjective point of view.

In another self-referential twist, *The Alley* presents a frame narrative that tells how the story came to be filmed. The movie starts as Director Zhong (played by the director, Yang Yanjin) signals "Action!" and the camera starts dollying to follow the narrator, who heads to Zhong's house. Although Director Zhong explains, "my appearance in my film is merely for the sake of the story's veracity," the viewers may question the "veracity" of a sequence that disregards continuity, starting with presenting Director Zhong on the set and ending with showing the same man at his home, talking to the narrator. The audience may further wonder to whom it is that the director refers in the first person. If the film's purported veracity does not benefit from Director's Zhong's presence, does the fictional director refer to the film's director, Yang Yanjin? Can either the narrator or Director Zhong speak with authority, considering that they are fictional characters? The film further blurs the lines between the various fictional layers as the narrator looks for Director Zhong in the same house used, in the story-within-a-story, as Yu's residence. Is it that the narrator uses Director Zhong's home as a prop in his story? This option is refuted by the second ending, which shows that the narrator is indeed Xia, who has come to Director Zhong's place in search of Yu. The less clear it is just how factual the story may be, the more it is left for the spectators to find their own solutions.

To the extent that *The Alley* suggests how the film should be interpreted, it aims at excluding Maoist reading practices. Even before suggesting the three conclusions, the narrator and Director Zhong contemplate a perfect happy ending and a tragedy, both of which they reject out of hand. In other words, an unambivalent plot of the kind characteristic of revolutionary aesthetics does not even merit serious consideration. The themes and structures of Cultural Revolution productions are consistently challenged. The protagonists are no longer characterized by ideological stereotypes but are rather portrayed through what Yang Yanjin and his assistant Wu Tianren repeatedly refer to as the "inner world of the mind" (*neixin shijie*). The directors note that *The Alley* "does not have a fascinating plot, describe amazing events, include heroes of a colossal scale or use earth-shattering brave words." In fact, they claim, it is Xia's humanity that makes him more real and emotionally complex than any heroic figure.[29] The heroes of the model plays give way to fallible human beings. Presenting a non-hero is perhaps the most radical divergence from the aesthetics of the Cultural Revolution.

Instead of bravery, the characters in *The Alley* resort to the post-Maoist trope of professing individual emotions and even erotically charged love. Xia vows: "I want to tell everyone that you are a woman." There is rich symbolism in that the only artificial hair he can find for Yu is a braid used as a stage prop for staging *The Red Lantern*. When he tries to buy one, he is turned away, because they are for use in the model play alone. The dominant aesthetics did not acknowledge the use of the human body for stressing one's femininity except as a revolutionary metaphor. The model plays monopolized the use of the body and reappropriated signs of gender to demand love for the motherland and the Party. In stealing the braid, Xia retaliates with his own reappropriation of signs. The braid that designates Tiemei's revolutionary resolution becomes the object of desire. The ideological model is substituted for by an attractive woman of "black" class background, and revolutionary romanticism is replaced by romantic love.

The braid scene is emblematic of the ways in which *The Alley* consistently redirects and subverts the symbolism of *The Red Lantern*. Most conspicuously, the film mocks the model plays and exposes the affinity of Maoist drama with the violent street spectacles of the Cultural Revolution. After being caught, Xia is brought back to the stage where the opera was performed. The unflinching representation of the Red Guards' violence on the same platform used for the model play brings home the parallelism between the meticulously regulated Maoist drama and the highly theatricalized "struggle sessions." The state-sponsored violence took the form of staged spectacles that followed a clear script, with main characters, foils and sidekicks, and fervent rhetoric to match the aesthetics of the revolutionary operas. In venturing behind the platform, Xia exposes the backstage of the model plays, literally and metaphorically. Although in the preceding scene Tiemei sings on stage the concluding lines of scene 5—"Generation after generation we shall fight on / Never leaving the field until all the wolves are killed"—the model play is portrayed as encouraging the bestial brutality. Significantly, the model play in *The Alley* is staged across from the zoo's vultures, which watch the scene greedily.

The mise-en-scène of the beating scene presents a jarring discord. The senseless violence parodies heroic scenes in the model plays. Moreover, whereas the operas employ grand scores, the sequence in *The Alley* is set against a song in a minor key: "When I was a child, mom left me a poem, where there is no grief, no sorrow. Whenever I sing, my heart fills with joy." Xu Jingxin's sentimental melody is incongruous with the brutal images and makes even more jarring the piercing cry of pain that follows when Xia is beaten blind and unconscious. The cognitive dissonance between sound and image is left for the spectators to resolve.

The scene plays directly off the themes of *The Red Lantern*. Xia is beaten with a heavy belt and kicked in the face. As blood runs into his eyes, a point-of-view shot shows his vision immersed in red before going blank altogether. Whereas *The Red Lantern* uses a red filter to flood the room with color when Li Yuhe raises the lantern, symbolizing the hope and sense of direction given by communist ideology, in *The Alley* the tinted lens signals the contrary. Xia's red vision targets the Red Guards and their bloody violence. The color red forces itself on Xia as a victim of the Cultural Revolution, dominates his field of vision, and leaves him with no alternative view or vision.

Significantly, it is at the moment of being blinded that Xia regains agency. The narrator, who has previously refused to identify himself as the protagonist and refers to Xia as "he," starts after the injury to speak in the first person. It is also when Xia is blinded that the film first provides a visualization of his thoughts. In a series of quick cuts, the film juxtaposes cheering crowds during the Cultural Revolution, war scenes (presumably from the sanctified battles leading to the establishment of the PRC), and the injured Xia and Yu. Paradoxically, Xia is still blindfolded with bandages when he searches his inner mind and gains insight into the futility of Maoist history. The sequence is shot in black and white, in stark contrast with the rest of the film and especially with the beating scene, inundated in red. Xia's field of vision is symbolically de-Maoified. The black-and-white images also foreground the cinematic medium and imply that film can provide a more objective narrative, one that resists the pathos of bloody visions (and that claims access to History, as I mention in the Preface to this book).

The Alley continues the bleak portrayal of the Cultural Revolution's aftermath presented in Yang Yanjin's previous work, *Bitter Laughter*. Xia's incurable semi-blindness points to the irreparable scars of the Cultural Revolution. No matter which conclusion Chinese society chooses, the Cultural Revolution's outcome will be tinted and marred by a lingering pain and blind spots. Although Mao's death meant increased freedom of interpretation, the effects of the Cultural Revolution introduced new obstacles to reading the past. Despite the relaxation of the totalitarian system of signification, the externally imposed censorship of the public debate was replaced by an internalized resistance. "Couldn't they see that my eyes were shedding not tears but blood?" Xia wonders. Yet the question points out not only the torturers' insensitivity but also how the physical and mental scars continue to impair the victim's vision. *The Alley*'s incompatible alternative endings demonstrate the witness's failure to narrate his own past. Although the film's three endings all emphasize that one should "let bygones be bygones," the wounds of the Cultural Revolution have not healed. The traumatic experience resurfaces through a complex reappropriation of symptoms and mental codes. While the films of the early 1980s resist Maoist rhetoric by parodying it and displacing public debate to the inner world, they also pave the way to later works that acknowledge the post-traumatic involuntary displacement of speech.

6

Disjointed Time, Split Voices
Retrieving Historical Experience in Scar Literature

Whereas in the late 1970s and early 1980s, writers and filmmakers made tentative inquiries, checking the limits of expression under Deng, exploring the potential of public discourse and assessing the inner resources needed for speaking up and bearing witness, from the mid 1980s on, memoirs of the Cultural Revolution were published in growing numbers. Entire monographs have been devoted to sorting out major tropes and genres within the industry of Cultural Revolution testimony.[1] As Xiaomei Chen notes, one may even discern a discrete variety of accounts written in English for popular consumption outside China, which often celebrate the author's newfound freedom of expression.[2] Yet other writers have perceived a tension between personal memories and public expression. In this chapter, I focus on a single text, namely, Zhang Xianliang's (b. 1936) *Wo de putishu* (My bodhi tree, 1994),[3] which addresses the conflict between the inner mind and the public sphere. I argue that Zhang finds a space for testimony neither in attesting to factual events nor in reclaiming his private thoughts, but rather in the interstices where narrative, time, and history cease to exist.

Another writer who explores the relationship between time and testimony is Ji Xianlin (b. 1911), former head of the Department of Oriental Languages and Literatures at Beijing University. Ji prefaces his autobiographical account of the Cultural Revolution, *Niupeng zayi* (Memoirs from the cowshed, 1998), with a description of how he came to write the book:

Memoirs from the Cowshed was written in 1992. Why, then, is it only now in 1998, six years later, that I have fetched it out to be published? This is not what writers usually do, and the reader may well suspect that there must be some explanation. . . . In fact, initially I had no intention of writing such a book. Otherwise, considering that the ten catastrophic years officially ended in 1976, why was the book written only in 1992, sixteen years later, with so many years in between? For sixteen years, I reflected, inquired, hesitated, and waited. . . .

I expected that some one would write about the calamity that has befallen them personally. . . . I waited days, months, years, and eventually lost hope. No one was willing to take up a pen and write, or narrate the story for someone else to write it down. . . . Waiting for myself was better than waiting for others, so I had rather to make an attempt on my own. This is how *Memoirs from the Cowshed* came to be. . . . I hope that what I waited for may come about.[4]

There is as much to learn from Ji's silences—before and after writing his manuscript—as from his highly articulate testimony. Addressing the Cultural Revolution entails not only depicting the "ten years of turmoil" in detail but also explaining the effects of what Ji calls their "residual poison," which extends into the present. As Ji writes, for many "the Cultural Revolution has never passed."[5] Ji confronts the unresolved issues of the Cultural Revolution, and his first task is to face his own silence. His preface fails, however, to provide satisfactory answers to the questions that he himself poses. Considering the perceived urgency of testifying, Ji does not clarify why it took him sixteen years to write the book.[6] Moreover, he never explains why he waited for another six years after he had written it to publish it.

Ji's evasion of these questions is especially interesting, because his attitude is an exemplary case of what I have called "witness *for* history." Ji claims that "this small book is begotten in exchange for blood" and distances himself from the trend of Cultural Revolution memoirs known as "scar literature" (*shanghen wenxue*) because of its purported neglect of the harshest experience, that of the older intellectuals.[7] Yet even though Ji is in search of a straightforward record and expresses faith in bearing witness, *Memoirs from the Cowshed* demonstrates how all testimony is belated. It is that time gap between his experience and the eventual testimony that allows Ji to reflect not only on the events but also on the process of writing. Just as in the preface to *Outcry*, Lu Xun introduces himself as an author sixteen years after the event that has allegedly made him write (see Chapter 1), so Ji Xianlin lends authority to his voice precisely by demonstrating that even so many years have not diminished the urgency of his words.

Ji's preface to his memoirs introduces the questions that I address in this chapter. In what ways does literature bear witness to historical events that cannot be conveyed in real time? How does past experience change with the writer's deliberate and subconscious delaying, repressing, and forgetting? What was the effect of the Cultural Revolution's "residual poison" on the relationship between writers and their readership? How does one participate in public discourse when one's voice and identity still suffer from past trauma?

Moreover, Ji's reflections accentuate the problems that arise when speech is tainted by traumatic experience. Under Mao, language was not only censored but also co-opted as a tool of control and oppression. Repeated confessions were forced out of those tagged as the people's enemies. As illustrated by K's story, quoted in the Introduction to this book, the recurrent linguistic coercion often resulted in blurring the sense of reality. Ji, too, recounts how the Red Guards would punish the "cowshed" inmates for any error in memorizing Mao's "supreme directives."[8] The abuse of language to the point where it became meaningless except as a means of inflicting pain and producing false witness would reflect on the language of later testimony. I argue that taking into account the damage to linguistic expression is crucial to understanding the gap between the time of narration and the narrated time. When writing can no longer be assumed to be either truthful or therapeutic, silence—or, as in Ji Xianlin's case, writing for the drawer—becomes a logical choice.

This chapter examines also how linguistic repression is addressed in autobiographical writing. Fiction and film have addressed the return and retrieval of voices silenced in many ways during the Cultural Revolution. Yet autobiographical accounts seem in hindsight to have constituted a more sustained trend of looking back at Mao's era. Some authors dedicated their writing to semi-autobiographical accounts of the Cultural Revolution. Prominent examples of such works include reportage by Liu Binyan and Zheng Yi, nonfiction by Wuming shi (Pu Ning's pen name), as well as fiction and essays by Ah Cheng (Zhong Acheng's pen name).[9] Arguably the writer most renowned for using the testimonial genre to describe Maoist repression is Zhang Xianliang, who wrote half a dozen semi-autobiographical novels about his experiences in the camps between 1957 and 1979 and has been compared to Primo Levi and Aleksandr Solzhenitsyn.[10] I turn to Zhang's *My Bodhi Tree*, subtitled "a nonfictional novel in diary form,"[11] because its form stresses the problems of retrospective writing and negotiating past trauma with one's present voice. *My Bodhi Tree* combines Zhang's labor camp diary—from July to December 1960—with commentaries written in the 1990s. While the diary tersely records the daily routine, the lengthy commentaries both elaborate on the diary and offer Zhang's deliberations on his past experience, as well as reflections on the diary itself. The novel is written at two different points in time, in two different idioms, by two different authorial personae, and shuttles back and forth between the two texts, playing them one against the other. As such, *My Bodhi Tree* expresses anxiety about the author's task when facing the past as an abyss, a gap that defies verbal representation. Since it attempts to reconstitute events that have not been committed to writing, the novel foregrounds the need to overcome a mental trauma that has ruptured one's perception of time.

WRITING BEYOND LANGUAGE

Unlike Zhang's earlier writings, the publication of *My Bodhi Tree* in 1994 did not cause a stir in literary circles. Zhang's short story "Ling yu rou" (Soul and flesh, 1980) had been widely welcomed by readers and critics,[12] and his novella *Lühuashu* (Mimosa, 1984) and its sequel, the novel *Nanren de yiban shi nüren* (Half of man is woman, 1985) caused a controversy because of their explicit depiction of sexual desire among camp inmates. By 1994, however, the writing of former sent-down youth (*zhiqing*) had evolved in other directions. The scar literature of the early 1980s, which straightforwardly described experiences in the countryside, gave way to the more experimental forms dubbed "root-seeking literature" (*xungen wenxue*) and "avant-garde fiction" (*xianfeng xiaoshuo*). Zhang Xianliang himself tried using a less linear narrative in *Xiguan siwang* (Getting used to dying, 1989). By the late 1990s, the author would find himself increasingly marginalized in literary circles and turn to a successful business career, running a film-set theme park in Yinchuan, Ningxia Province.[13] *My Bodhi Tree* marks a return to realistic narration, however, giving expression to the many unresolved issues still haunting Zhang and his generation.

Zhang was born into the well-educated family of a KMT official in Nanjing. In 1957, the Anti-Rightist campaign targeted his poem "Dafeng ge" (Ode to the gale), and he was condemned to labor reform. He was rehabilitated only in 1979. In 1993, he was sentenced to three more years in connection with his attempt to commemorate the Tiananmen crackdown. Perhaps even more than the victims of the Cultural Revolution, Zhang personifies the difficulties of coming to terms with the "lost years" of the Maoist period.

Zhang's entire work is consistently written in the first person and clearly uses autobiographical testimony as a way to overcome silence. Yet *My Bodhi Tree* frustrates any expectation that testimony should strive for a coherent point of view or a single meaning. Whereas Zhang's previous accounts reveal how basic human joys and sorrows survived in the camps, *My Bodhi Tree* focuses on the disruption that shatters the testifying subject. Zhang describes the pain and subsequent damage to his perception of reality inflicted by incarceration: "A sharp knife had severed me at the waist—the half of which I was now conscious had been tossed into this barren wasteland. Where the other half was I had no idea; I wasn't even sure if I had ever been whole before" (MBT, p. 3).

Zhang's reference to dismemberment to explain his geographical dislocation is key to understanding his experience. The camps, where deceit, violence, hunger, and death reigned, are perceived as otherworldly. They lay far "outside the range of usual human experience," to quote the American Psychiatric Association's definition of the conditions that induce post-traumatic stress disorder (PTSD).[14] Inmates like Zhang were exposed for long periods to mental and physical violence. They felt the proximity of death, existing on the brink of starvation, while others perished around them. Zhang repeatedly refers to his experiences inside and outside the camps as having taken place in different "worlds" and tells how "Today, only [the diary] has remained as a link between me and that other world" (MBT, p. 6). In describing the camps as another world, Zhang emphasizes how the prolonged assault on his mind violated his perception to the point where he came to rely on altogether different experiential parameters. Zhang's description calls to mind the testimony at the Eichmann trial of Yehiel Dinur ("K. Zetnik"), who described Auschwitz as a "planet of ashes [that] stand[s] in opposition to our planet Earth," where "every shard of an instant moves . . . on the wheels of a different time."[15] Similarly, a central trope in Zhang's witness is the cognitive dissonance that places the camps outside the continuum of his former life—spatially, temporally, and linguistically.

Indeed, Zhang details the role of language in creating the dissonance between his past and the camps, as well as between the material conditions and how they are perceived. He stresses that his traumatic experience included not only the physical suffering of starvation and hard labor but also the mental torture of being forced to deny his hardship: "You had to forget all about the man who had died beside you right away. Next time, when 'another' died, he was still the first. You had to get accustomed to this method of accounting: no matter how many died in the labor reform company, it was just one who died" (MBT, p. 45). The camps used language to reverse experience. Zhang lists various ways in which the authorities employed language as an active tool of surveillance and incrimination. His own travesty started when his poem was declared counterrevolutionary. He comments on Maoist doublespeak with irony: "a new social condition necessarily produces a new semantic structure" (MBT, p. 34). An entire chapter in *My Bodhi Tree* is devoted to the evil of words, and a fellow prisoner draws an etymological affinity between the Chinese characters for "speech" and "harm" (MBT, pp. 95–103). Zhang shows how the camps relied on the enslaving power of language:

[I]n Europe, ... castles [were] built of durable stone, with gates made of iron or bronze. However, when they lock people up in China, they have fallen into the habit of using simple buildings of mud and wood, none too solid, labeling them "prisons" or "labor reform companies" and locking people up inside them. Once having entered [such] barracks labeled "prison" or "labor reform company," an incarcerated Chinese will never deny being a criminal merely because these buildings do not look like a prison. (MBT, p. 267)

It is important to note the author's willingness to ascribe his suffering to language. Although others had clearly inflicted pain on him, Zhang credits his condition to the walls within one's own mind. He attributes the torture of incarceration, not to political power, but to the victims' excessive belief in the power of language. If only as a rhetorical gesture, Zhang fashions the trauma of the camps as submission to a literal prison-house of language.

THE HEALING POWER OF TESTIMONY

Recognizing the linguistic roots of Zhang's trauma, one can better understand his choice of writing as a means to overcome the lingering effects of his camp experience. As Zhang explains in the first pages of *My Bodhi Tree*, he wrote the diary in an effort to survive. Since he had already traded everything he could for food and was left with only a pen, an unwanted commodity, he tried to tap inner forces through that pen: "The pen signaled that I could still use the skills I had acquired in that world to do something in this world. After I had exhausted all the ways for staying alive, it tempted me from another world" (MBT, p. 4). Writing functions in this case as a form of communication, not with another person but with Zhang's other self, his persona as an author. In a turn to the inner mind reminiscent of the strategies of resistance in texts and films immediately following the Cultural Revolution (see Chapter 5), Zhang uses the diary to imagine himself as a free writer, a position that he had briefly enjoyed before the camps and to which he wishes to return. If trauma is experienced as existence in another world, for Zhang, the pen holds the two worlds together.

Zhang keeps his sanity and distances himself from the harsher effects of dislocation by using writing to keep a time of his own and distance himself from the immediate events. "I availed myself of the pen to write this diary in interstices that served as the means for survival. When I wrote in my diary, I would first think . . . of the events and thoughts that I absolutely could not write down in the diary" (MBT, pp. 4–5). As he prepares to write each entry, Zhang uses the opportunity to reflect on the linguistic repression to which he is subjected. The diary may therefore serve later as a mnemonic code that allows the silenced events to resurface in the added commentary.

The diary projects "another world" into the future, which uncannily materializes when Zhang, by now a rehabilitated and widely recognized author, revisits the diary and includes it in *My Bodhi Tree*. In this sense, the novel attests to the power of the written word and expresses faith in the witness for history. Zhang highlights the redemptive value of his suffering by referring in the book's title to the tree under which Buddha Śakyāmuni proved his immunity to the demons of Māra. Moreover, he makes the symbolic gesture of dating the manuscript's completion to his return from Golgotha in Jerusalem. The novel allows Zhang to look back and reevaluate his lifelong project of writing about the camps. Already in *Half of Man is Woman*, Zhang prefaces his narrative with a sense of belatedness akin to that conveyed in the passage from Ji Xianlin's *Memoirs from the Cowshed* quoted earlier. "I wanted to put this experience into writing many times, but I either felt remorse about it or was ashamed of some things and thought it better to cover them up," Zhang writes. "Eventually, I would lay my pen aside. I am often my own adversary."[16] In *My Bodhi Tree*, he finally confronts the adversary in himself, through a second authorial voice. A healing process takes place when Zhang reproduces the diary in an effort to preserve his memories and make the Chinese people "face the past."[17] It is important for the author to reaffirm the genuineness of his testimony, and *My Bodhi Tree* opens with a photograph of the original document. By quoting from this "real diary" (MBT, p. 4), Zhang can testify to the reality of his experience, a proof not only for the readers but for the author himself: "If it weren't for this thin diary, I might doubt that that part of my life was real" (MBT, p. 3).

Zhang's present writing is just as important as the diary, testifying "in original form how low the human world and humans can fall" (MBT, p. 7) and appealing to readers: "Don't ever walk that path again" (MBT, p. 308). Through the compound text of *My Bodhi Tree*, Zhang attests to himself and to his readers that he has overcome the trauma. To paraphrase the definition of the American Psychiatric Association, he also experienced something outside the normal range of *linguistic* experience, and it is his urgent task to demonstrate that he has survived as a writer. Composing *My Bodhi Tree* becomes an exercise in survival, a demonstration that one can write prose after the camps and about them.

WRITING AS A WOUND

Yet in what is possibly the novel's most dramatic departure from Zhang's own expectations, the author finds out that his language has been contaminated by the camps. The diary represents a mutilated text that reinscribes itself into Zhang's present writing. Moreover, language has been abused for so long that writing not only misrepresents his experience but also perpetuates the trauma. Possibly despite himself, Zhang bears witness against history.

It should come as no surprise that the same mechanism that promotes Zhang's mental healing is also the one that triggers post-traumatic symptoms. As Freudian scholars have noted, the victim does not acknowledge the trauma at the time of its occurrence. Instead, the traumatic disruption remains unassimilated and is obsessively repeated, in dreams and hallucinations, as well as in recurrent behavior patterns originating in the traumatizing moment.[18] In Zhang's case, writing becomes a way of returning to the camps and reliving them. *My Bodhi Tree* acknowledges that the act of writing repeats the painful experiences of the past. In order to deliver an authentic account, Zhang aims at reexperiencing the originary event: "to faithfully represent the reality of that time, not only do I need to divorce my mind from present reality and immerse myself totally in the past, but I also have to undergo again the torment of the past" (MBT, p. 6). The author admits that in returning to the diary and rewriting it into *My Bodhi Tree* he subjects himself to reliving the experiences described in it.

The split that makes Zhang Xianliang torn between two worlds, rips his consciousness in two, and forces him to repeat the traumatic moment is also reflected in the novel's form, which stitches together the diary and the commentary. At first glance, it seems that the two texts are complementary and interdependent. The diary consists of terse entries limited to description of daily chores. As Zhang explains later, he kept descriptions to a minimum for fear the diary might be inspected: a suspect phrase could have cost him his life. The commentary passages, on the other hand, are lengthy and detailed, trying to fill in for the self-censored passages. The heading "commentary," preceding each later addition, implies that the recent text is a secondary exegesis, while the diary remains the focus of *My Bodhi Tree*. The commentary is legitimated by the diary entries, and there is no apparent discrepancy between the two texts.

Yet the diary entries are mostly unintelligible in and of themselves, and they leave gaps in anticipation of the later narrative. The commentary keeps referring to omissions and contradictions in the diary and stresses the need to fill in the blanks and reconstitute the experience through a more coherent narrative. Meanwhile, the diary brings up an onslaught of memory that incapacitates Zhang's present voice: "I have written quite a few so-called novels, and yet I am often powerless in the face of this billowing tumult of memories" (MBT, p. 146). The two texts are distinct from and exceed each other, each referring also to events not mentioned in the other. By presenting the diary and the commentary side by side, Zhang acknowledges that his writing cannot be located in either the past or the present alone. There is a gap between the two texts, a silence that cannot be filled in. The authorial voice is forever displaced and divided between the two temporal points of narration, which keep pulling away from each other.

Zhang goes as far as to describe his state of mind during writing in the present as being cut in two: "With irresistible decisiveness, time continues to flow and splits in two the future from the past. As it does, it might not only rip me in two but also tear the entire world to shreds" (MBT, p. 146). By employing the same violent image that he uses earlier to describe his camp experience ("a knife had severed me at the waist"), this time to depict the process of remembering and bearing witness, Zhang draws attention to how writing reinforces the traumatic experience at a nearly corporeal level. In another telling passage, he stresses how memories imprint themselves on the author's body: "In writing this work, I often stop and lose myself in thought as I look at my fingertips on the keyboard. Slowly, I begin to feel as if they emit the slight coolness of death" (MBT, p. 151). In the face of memory, witnessing marks a fault line, a threat to the writer's sense of a wholesome physical existence and a composed mind.

HISTORY AS A SCAR

Zhang's torment seems only to augment when he examines the old diary from his present vantage point:

Today, the more I write, the more I am in deep pain. The pain comes not from the fact that when I write I have to enter the character and immerse myself again in the grief of the past. . . . [the pain comes from realizing that] I really had been a poet before. I had not been short of the ability to compose beautifully structured literature . . . yet in 1960, I was writing such unsightly words. (MBT, p. 236)

Curiously, Zhang chooses to judge his diary by literary standards, and he finds his style lacking: "After copying out the diary text of more than two months, I am very embarrassed. It is hard to believe that these words came from the pen of a poet. I myself doubt whether I ever wrote poetry" (MBT, pp. 235–36). Yet despite his previous claim that the main impediment to writing in his diary was fear of supervision, Zhang does not see the deficiencies of his diary as an indication of political control, but rather as proof of how mental oppression results in the impoverishment of language. He writes:

It wasn't cowardice or the need to avoid inspection. To escape inspection, my skill was good enough to lead the censors in circles and play word games with them. I could have used codelike signs to write down many shocking stories. I could have carved my true impressions in mirror writing, so that there would be absolutely no need for me now to explain the diary of that time. Rather, in one fell swoop, I lost my wisdom, I lost my power of discernment, I lost my intuition, I lost my compassion, I even lost my literary and moral standards. I could recognize characters and write them, but that was merely because I didn't become totally illiterate. (MBT, p. 237)

The split in consciousness and the corresponding doubling of the authorial voice in *My Bodhi Tree* lead Zhang to confront an urgent question: what remains of writing in the wake of a shattering experience such as the labor reform camps? This question is akin to that posed by Theodor Adorno, discussed in the Introduction to this book—can poems can be composed after Auschwitz? At the literal level, the question of whether literature can be written "after" the camps has been answered in the affirmative by numerous survivors' accounts. Yet the heavy toll on language is clear in Zhang's diary— the account is reduced to an emotionless factual report, self-censored to the point where it is intelligible at best to the author alone. Zhang's novel asks what kind of writing can follow after the camp diaries, to what extent he can, as a mature writer, extricate himself from the form of expression he used in the camps. Although he and others have written literature of the camps, *can there be literature after the literature of the camps?*

In the aftermath of the camps, Zhang tries to resuscitate his literary writing but is wary of literary confabulation. Already in 1985, Zhang proclaimed: "I can write fictional stories but I cannot write fiction about myself. Not only while writing, but even in daily life, I am searching for myself."[19] *My Bodhi Tree* responds to Zhang's concerns when the author, after a long career as a fiction writer, accepts a handicap and forbids himself "the skills of writing," explaining that "I discovered that real life cannot be contained in the frame of fiction" (MBT, p. 146). Zhang's ostentatious rejection of fiction underlines the contradictions in his approach to writing. Why does the author counterpose the diary and the commentary, so that each text guards and delimits the other? Can Zhang, who in earlier essays has repeatedly proclaimed a Marxist belief in literature's ability to reflect life experience,[20] resolve his doubt about both diary and commentary as viable testimonies?

My Bodhi Tree demonstrates the paradoxes of testimony after the Cultural Revolution and the dialectics of bearing witness to the untestifiable. The novel's title implies an analogy between Zhang and Buddha Śakyāmuni, who, after withstanding the temptations of Māra and achieving enlightenment, called upon the Earth to witness his survival and new state of awareness. The novel testifies to Zhang's experience—but it does so precisely by acknowledging the unbridgeable gap between the two texts. Although the two authorial voices establish between them a therapeutic relationship, in which the commentary attempts to work through the diary, the diary and the commentary replicate each other's pain and offer no reconciliation. Zhang keeps returning to the same point in time, marked by pain and death, but does not acknowledge the implications for his writing. He tells that the camp inmates had to count each death as the first and only death, yet Zhang is complicit in denying the repeated demise of language, evidenced in the two texts' undermining of each other. *My Bodhi Tree* claims to describe not only the death but also the resurrection of language, yet in the camps, language had died countless deaths, and Zhang's experience can be told only through the silences between his two voices. The split voice in *My Bodhi Tree* demonstrates that the originary experience remains impenetrable to verbal representation. The labor reform camps and the Cultural Revolution join other twentieth-century disasters, such as the Holocaust and the AIDS epidemic, that have been declared to be radically unthinkable and inexpressible. Although the novel is presented as a testimony of redemptive value, trauma bars the author from bearing witness. Furthermore, in the process of recovering his authorial voice, Zhang runs the risk of repeating the traumatic experiences and making his writing a vehicle of trauma.

My Bodhi Tree is literally a case of scar literature, for it addresses not only the wounds but also the elusive distance between the wounded flesh and the scars that cover it. The double-layered structure, in which past and present are each represented by a separate text, provides an allegory of writing after the shattering blow delivered to Zhang's sense of self and perception of history. To recapture his camp years, he needs to reactivate suppressed mnemonic and linguistic skills. The commentary symbolizes the process of this linguistic reconstruction and illustrates how past silences can be overcome only by writing one's testimony over and again. As the novel revisits the traumatic event, it repeats writing itself as a trauma and shows the limits of testimony.

My Bodhi Tree forces the reader to rethink the temporal parameters of historical events. Traumatic experience stretches far beyond the time of the originary injury. As a consequence, the witness must often include the present in which testimony takes place as part of the past trauma. Moreover, as the fragmented text of *My Bodhi Tree* demonstrates, the present and the past are interlinked but do not form a coherent account, so that testimony can only present multiple mirror images. Like the films of the early 1980s discussed in the previous chapter and the novellas introduced in the next one, Zhang's novel retells the same event by several witnesses, a structure that not only challenges each account but also fails to locate experience within a clear historical narrative. The pain of being severed at the waist, as Zhang puts it, conveys, not nostalgia for a lost wholeness, but rather the doubt of any continuum of experience—in Zhang's words, of whether "I had ever been whole before." The passing of time heralds the dissolution of the past and the disintegration of the subject. Under these circumstances, the witness can only testify to the collapse of the authorial voice and against the hope of a meaningful history.

7

Retelling Taiwan
Identity and Dislocation in Post-Chiang Mystery

As the previous two chapters have shown, the literary and filmic response to Maoist censorship included both deliberate and involuntary splitting of the narrating voices. The turn to the protagonists' inner psychological dynamics resisted totalitarian control and at the same time shed doubt on the new-found faith in public debate. In the context of the revival of debates dating back to May Fourth, it is interesting to compare works on the other side of the Taiwan Straight. The lifting in July 1987 of the martial law imposed by Chiang Kai-shek was accompanied by a literary surge that alluded to May Fourth ideals and employed similar narrative strategies involving multiple narrators.

In this chapter, I turn to two well-known novellas, Chen Yingzhen's (b. 1937) "Shanlu" (Mountain path, 1983; henceforth MP)[1] and Liu Daren's (b. 1939) "Dujuan ti xue" (Azaleas cry out blood, 1984; henceforth ACB).[2] Neither of the two can entirely represent the diverse literary scene in post-Chiang Taiwan, and my focus here neglects the important trend of nativist literature, which has striven to reclaim a Taiwanese history. Yet it is precisely Chen's and Liu's respective idiosyncratic political views—the one an old-fashioned Marxist, the other a disillusioned one—that allow them to ignore trendy politics and link the situation in Taiwan to May Fourth's legacy. Paradoxically, Chen's and Liu's fiction, rooted in the outmoded conviction that Taiwan's fate is linked to that of the PRC, reflects Taiwan's crisis of identity in the 1980s. The two texts address concerns central to post-Chiang Taiwan and demonstrate how memories of past repression might be too traumatic to be recorded directly or even acknowledged later. Rather, experience and speech become mutually exclusive, and memory becomes the witness's nemesis.

A TAIWANESE RASHŌMON

Among other vignettes of life in Taiwan in the early 1950s, the 1991 film *Gu-ling jie shaonian sha ren shijian* (English title *A Brighter Summer Day*), directed by Edward Yang (Yang Dechang), features radio announcements searching for missing relatives. News broadcasts were followed by lists of the names of people of whom track had been lost during World War II and the KMT's retreat to Taiwan in 1949. The situation reveals much about the spatial and temporal dislocation of mainlanders in 1950s Taiwan—by dint of their attempt to connect with their past, the past intrudes into the present, through the names of people who may perhaps no longer be alive or who may have stayed behind on the mainland and may never be able to hear the broadcast. The episode also reflects Yang's contemporary concerns and is emblematic of the formation of Taiwanese identity. Just as nations form when people read the same newspapers and novels,[3] a Taiwanese identity has formed around that shared listening, hearing the same names at exactly the same moment. The missing persons announcements linked the here and now of the news update with searching for the past, and the past became urgent news. Radios blared name after name of people unknown to most of the listeners, so that the list became a text that had little to do with individual persons. The broadcast created a collective memory that recalled the past by remembering the absent. Although those who posted the names were anticipating an unlikely reunion, the lists reified the past. The effect on the community of listeners could be compared to that of reading aloud the names of war casualties. The name lists set in motion a dynamics of collective commemoration similar to that of the Vietnam Memorial Wall, Jewish Holocaust ceremonies, and the AIDS quilt.

Yet collective memory often goes hand in hand with collective forgetting. Mainlanders in Taiwan were conjuring up a past through absent people, while at the same time, the KMT made other people disappear and took their names off public records. Reified and repressed memories contended with each other. Chiang Kai-shek's dictatorial rule in Taiwan from 1949 to his demise in 1976 glorified the battles fought by the KMT on the mainland before 1949 and silenced references to Chiang's policy of executions and arrests on the island, especially the White Terror that began with the clashes on February 28, 1947. Neither mainlanders nor native Taiwanese could express their personal sufferings. Taiwan's collective memory formed out of the combination of these multiple versions of the past, making it impossible to create a coherent memory of the present. If Edward Yang's film about the 1950s struck a chord with the audience in 1991, it was because Taiwanese citizens were still struggling in the 1980s and 1990s to present a viable narrative of their past.

Taiwan fiction of the 1980s reflects a similar politics of memory. After the relaxation of the KMT's rule in the mid 1980s, leading to the lifting of martial law, a literary corpus emerged that took it upon itself to forge a Taiwanese identity by reclaiming repressed memories. The unsaid, it seemed, could finally be spoken out loud. Curiously, literature and film turned to mystery at the same time that victims' accounts revealed secrets of past oppression. Texts either dealing directly with the recent past or describing more abstract parables would often end without solving the riddle around which the narrative revolved. The contrast between the political and literary discourses presents important questions. Why do fictional works of that period deny factual revelations the status of uncontested truth? Why have memories continued to be dislocated in unstable narratives? What are the implications of these literary constructions for Taiwanese identities?

The mystery genre, I argue, is a sign of Taiwanese writers' recognition of their inability to redress past wrongs and rewrite history into a narrative of progress and redemption. Memories shape the past in the mold of uncertain and unfinished narratives. It can be presented only as an absence. Like Oedipus, a model mystery detective, the narrators face a riddle to which they themselves are the only answer. No witness can provide the solution in its entirety, and storytellers put the pieces together to form an incomplete reconstruction of past events.

A symbolic manifestation of the breakdown of memory is to be found in the many mysteries that present multiple versions of the same story, in a manner reminiscent of Akira Kurosawa's 1950 *Rashōmon,* which presents four versions of an event, told by different narrators, without reconciling among them. Examples are fiction like Ping Lu's "Yumi tian zhi si" (Death in a cornfield, 1983) and Yang Zhao's *Anxiang miye* (Night of riddles in a dark alley, 1994), as well as films like Edward Yang's 1983 *Haitan de yitian* (English title *That Day on the Beach*) and He Fan's 1990 *Shidai zhi feng* (also known as *L'Air du temps*). The coexistence of alternative stories has been rightly ascribed to the postmodern demise of grand narratives. In post-Chiang Taiwan, one could pick and choose from among many versions of one's own past, and the diverging literary accounts leave the protagonist and readers alike in a position to choose their preferred explanations. Yet the crisis does not arise simply from the proliferation of histories; it lies rather in the present moment of bearing testimony, where memory fails to recuperate the past and generate a coherent version of history. Yang Zhao's *Night of Riddles in a Dark Alley*, for example, illustrates how the multiple viewpoints originate from the witness himself. The text is composed of two narratives presented in interwoven fragments. Yet there is only one narrator, who actively participates in creating two versions of his memory as he talks separately to two women. Memory changes not only according to whom he listens to but also according to whom he talks to. The narrator fails as an interrogator and ends up recounting a mystery because the memories erase the history that they are supposed to reconstruct.

Post-Chiang mystery points out the silences that have continued to dominate narratives of identity and shows that writing memory cannot turn into a historical testimony. These texts do not simply counter the official version but also draw attention to the chronic manipulation of memory that has maimed writers' capacity to bear witness. The resulting testimonies are unresolved detective stories that mystify the reader with accounts that never tally up.

THE PURPLE SMOKE OF TIME

Chen Yingzhen's short stories from the 1980s illustrate the unresolved plots of the post-Chiang period. Chen, a native of Taiwan, has been one of the more conspicuous figures on the island's literary scene since the 1960s. In 1968, he was sentenced to ten years in jail for criticizing KMT rule, but he was released seven years later. His Marxist beliefs also led him to seek inspiration from the PRC, even after June 1989, which cost him the support of many intellectuals. Yet in the 1960s, Chen left his mark by explicitly modeling his social and political activism on that of May Fourth writers and acknowledging the strong influence of Lu Xun, whose writings were banned in Taiwan at the time.[4] After he recovered from his imprisonment and resumed writing in 1978, Chen represented the voice of the KMT's political prisoners. Like those sent to labor camps, reeducation in the countryside, or "cowsheds" in the PRC, Chen had to deal with the temporal and cultural abyss of the years of his incarceration in Chiang's jails. His late fiction draws prominently on his seven years in prison, yet even his implicitly autobiographical writing shows the past to be inaccessible to testimony. Zhang's characters, survivors of the White Terror, cannot bear witness to the years of persecution and imprisonment. Chen's works exemplify the simultaneous turn to recovering the past and acknowledgment of the failure of memory to retrieve the lost voices of the victims.

Of special interest are his three major works of the 1980s, "Lingdanghua" (Bellflowers, 1983), "Mountain Path" and "Zhao Nandong" (1987). An apt metaphor for temporal dislocation is found in the latter story, which tells of the disintegration of a released prisoner's family. Old Zhao and his wife, who participated in the anti-Japanese demonstrations in Shanghai in 1932, are thrown into a Taiwanese jail in 1947. Old Zhao is released thanks to the "special amnesty" following Chiang Kai-Shek's death in 1975, only to find that his younger son Zhao Nandong, born in jail shortly before his mother was executed, has himself been imprisoned—not for political activism but for dealing in narcotics.[5] A friend of Old Zhao's, also a former political prisoner, likens her "anxiety at jumping into a totally different history"—that is, the historical moment of late 1970s Taiwan—to the Japanese tale about Urashima Tarō, who briefly visits the Dragon King's underwater palace. Upon returning to his home town, however, Tarō finds that centuries have passed. Like Urashima Tarō, Chen's protagonists are dislocated Rip van Winkles who cannot reacclimatize to the changes of time. The Taiwanese dissidents have become exiles in their own land.

The belated reaction to historical change, and specifically the inadequacy of writing in coping with change, are addressed in "Mountain Path," set in 1983, which starts with Cai Qianhui, a woman in her early fifties, being hospitalized in critical condition, but for no apparent physical illness. The doctor diagnoses her problem as total loss of the will to live. Li Guomu, Qianhui's brother-in-law, observes that her health started deteriorating after she had read that her friend Huang Zhenbo had been released after spending thirty-two years in jail. Huang had been arrested in 1950 for anti-KMT activities, together with Guomu's elder brother, Guokun, who was executed soon afterwards. After Guokun's death, Qianhui came to stay with his family and help them, explaining that she had married Guokun without his parents' knowledge.

Another version of Qianhui's story changes Guomu's perspective. The woman dies, and when the brother-in-law puts her belongings in order, he finds an unsent letter addressed to Huang Zhenbo. The letter reveals that Qianhui was in fact Huang's fiancée and knew Guokun only as Huang's comrade-in-arms. After the two had been betrayed by Qianhui's brother, the woman decided to atone for her brother's deceit by helping Guokun's destitute family. She concludes her letter explaining that Huang's release from jail had awakened her from the numb, comfortable life she had recently enjoyed thanks to Guomu's support. Taiwan's people, including herself, have forgotten about Huang and his comrades: "I'm afraid that facing this vast, thoroughly 'tamed' world, your fight will be even harder than in the past" (MP, p. 65). As the memories come back, Qianhui loses her sense of purpose and chooses to put an end to her life. Qianhui's awakening exemplifies how trauma is experienced as a rift in time, as a wound that reaches from the past into the present.

One may regard the story of Urashima Tarō as an apt metaphor for Qianhui too. The complete story, already found in the eighth-century *Manyōshū*, tells how Tarō marries the Dragon King's daughter, but after three years is too homesick to stay. Before Tarō leaves, the dragon's daughter gives him a box and warns him never to open it. When he goes back to his village and finds that centuries passed while he was staying in the underwater palace, he opens the box. It releases a purple smoke, which envelops Tarō, who transmogrifies into a crane and flies off to reunite with his wife. The Urashima tale is relevant to Chen Yingzhen's characters, not only because it illustrates the futility of longing for an often-imagined home, but also because it shows the difficulty of coming to terms with the consequences of one's return. Tarō is not transformed (in another version, he ages in Dorian Gray fashion)[6] until he opens the box. In "Mountain Path," the effect of time sets in only when the news about Huang's release opens Qianhui's Pandora's box of memories (incidentally, as a possible echo of the Japanese tale, Guomu finds the unsent letter in a lacquer box). The traumatic effects are unleashed long after the mental wound is inflicted, in response to a seemingly harmless stimulus.

Qianhui breaks down and succumbs to a delayed death-wish, observed in many trauma survivors, because the news awakens her memories as well as her consciousness of the present.[7] Once she puts down her political arms, she also lowers her psychological defenses. Living on no longer counts as a struggle in and of itself and loses its meaning. Moreover, her survival seems immoral when compared to the fate of the long-imprisoned and the dead. Qianhui's very existence in the present and her ability to look back at the past undermine her mental balance more than her past suffering has done. Her newly formed historical awareness only stresses her temporal dislocation, which she can resolve only through death. As David Wang comments, her death "is a necessary means for filling in the blanks of history."[8] Ironically, Qianhui can assert the meaning of the past only through the act of self-annihilation. Her testimony takes the form of silencing and erasure.

Chen Yingzhen's stories show how memory can only exist in the form of split voices. "Zhao Nandong" closely follows the *Rashōmon* structure and presents the plot through the narratives of four persons. In "Mountain Path" Guomu's memories are countered by Cai Qianhui's letter to Huang Zhenbo. Qianhui's testimony from beyond the grave brings to the surface repressed memories and sets the historical record straight, but her testimony comes too late. When Qianhui finally breaks through the long silence, her words remain displaced in the unsent letter.

The letter could have dispelled the unspoken political oppression and psychological repression. Throughout her life, Qianhui has forced herself to keep silent, as becomes evident when Guomu, when still a child, hears his sister-in-law singing a resistance song to herself. When he asks Qianhui what she is singing, she immediately stops humming and answers: "Nothing. . . . You can't sing, you shouldn't sing. For now" (MP, p. 58). Despite the implied anticipation that the time to start singing will come, Qianhui persistently shelters Guomu and steers him away from politics. Later, she commits all her secrets to the letter, but after having written down all that was left untold, she continues to hide her secret. She grows taciturn and stashes the letter away, keeping her thoughts to herself. Neither her voice nor that of her adopted brother is allowed to convey the past.

The fact that the letter remains unsent, that Qianhui may never have intended to send it, is crucial to understanding the paradox of bearing witness to a past known only through silences. In her letter, Qianhui explains that she must speak out, "for both moral and emotional reasons" (MP, p. 61) and attempts to negotiate her and Huang's memories. She concludes by asking that Huang remember her as the young woman he knew. The memories, however, hold her back from delivering any testimony. It is not simply that she is too nostalgic to reach back into the past and shatter its beautiful image. Rather, what drives Qianhui to seal the letter and keep it in her possession is her recognition that memory itself is the source of her suffering. What does her violence is the terror of awakening to memory. Either in the process of writing the letter or soon after, Qianhui realizes that traumatic experience is contained, not in past events, but in present remembering. The letter turns from a testimony to Qianhui's survival into an assertion of the impossibility of surviving in the face of what she has witnessed. As a witness, she cannot go on living, and as a testimony, her letter cannot be sent.

The letter is but one of the symbols employed in "Mountain Path" to convey the written word's failure to provide timely, accurate testimony. Another sign is found in an earlier episode, when Qianhui erects a tombstone for Guokun. Ironically, it is another act of KMT repression—the Kaohsiung Incident of 1979—that breaks the taboo on mentioning political prisoners. Consequently, Qianhui orders a tombstone for the elder brother. The tomb reclaims Guokun's place in memory, but the inscription keeps displacing the events. Truth is partially restored: the engraved list of surviving family members euphemistically includes Guomu's family as the descendants of the deceased, but omits mention of Qianhui as Guokun's purported wife. Yet the tombstone embodies fallacies in its reference to time and place. It dates Guokun's death to 1952, the year in which the authorities declared his demise, rather than to the actual time of his execution almost two years before. Moreover, the tombstone is erected over an empty grave, containing only Guokun's clothes, since his body has never been returned. The words fail to specify the correct time and place; the inscription functions at best as a mnemonic code for the ever-unutterable facts.

The half-truths engraved over Guokun's displaced grave are emblematic of the problems in testifying to a disaster that annihilates its major witnesses and mutes everyone else involved. Furthermore, all testimony must struggle against previous adulterated depositions. A case in point is the concocted story Qianhui tells Guokun's family when she first joins them. Guomu is somewhat impatient with Qianhui's fondness for reiterating her life story, which might be taken for either nostalgia or obsession. Only after reading the unsent letter does it become clear that Qianhui has been retelling her story precisely to cover up its fallacy. Only the unsent letter eventually refutes Qianhui's earlier version.

Qianhui's letter, like her fabricated life story and the inscription on Guokun's tombstone, is a displaced testimony. While its contents may be accurate, the letter fails to reach its addressee; instead, it lands in the hands of the man from whom it was supposed to be kept secret. Qianhui had kept Guomu from meeting Huang Zhenbo and learning the truth, wishing to protect her adopted brother-in-law from the pain of her memories. (Or is it that she deliberately refrains from destroying the letter, knowing that it might resurface, thereby leaving her testimony suspended?) Moreover, the letter fails in a more profound sense when Guomu reads it yet keeps its contents to himself. At the end of the story, he sobs, but when his wife asks him what is wrong, he does not tell: "Nothing. . . . I . . . miss . . . sister-in-law" (MP, p. 66). Qianhui taught Guomu to deny the past, to stifle the songs that she would never teach him. When the time comes to bear witness, the letter can no longer change Guomu's ingrained habit of denial.

Guomu becomes an accomplice to Qianhui's silence, as inept as she is at speaking out. When the doctor asks him the cause of Qianhui's illness, Guomu immediately thinks of Huang's release, yet he repeatedly tells the doctor that he can give no clue. At first his refutation comes "almost instinctively" (MP, p. 38); the next time, he thinks to himself: "But how can I face these doctors and nurses and tell the events of that morning [of the roundup in 1950], speak out my brother's and Huang Zhenbo's affair?" (MP, p. 43). It is not only that Guomu is unwilling to divulge the family secret and reveal his pain; equally important, he cannot face others with his knowledge and put himself in the position of a witness. Insofar as Cai Qianhui's plight reflects Chen Yingzhen's attempt to relocate his writing in the realities of post-Chiang Taiwan, "Mountain Path" points to literary testimony as always-already belated, addressing either the mute dead or the deaf living. The author cannot recover a voice free of the doubts—his own and his readers'—that have been ingrained during years of oppression and suppression.

THE WITNESS AS EXILE

Liu Daren represents a different strain of Taiwanese dissidence. Born on the Chinese mainland, and thus considered a potential KMT sympathizer, Liu nevertheless soon became critical of its policies. As a result of Liu's political activism in the early 1970s, the KMT refused him reentry to Taiwan, and he has since lived in the United States. Liu's activism at times brought him close to Chen Yingzhen, yet Liu's refusal to align himself with any specific group since the early 1980s, compounded by his exile and work for the United Nations, have made him harder to classify. In 1983, Liu was allowed to visit Taiwan for the first time since his exclusion. This visit, as well as two eye-opening tours of the PRC in 1974 and 1977, called for readjusting his political convictions and taking a step back from political activism. "Writing," he said in a 1997 interview, "was my only way out."[9] Liu found out, however, that his writing skills had suffered from his total immersion in politics: "My writing was no longer like literature." Even though Liu was banished to far more comfortable places than Zhang Xianliang, he experienced the same anxiety about the effect on his writing.

In the early 1980s, Liu composed a trilogy consisting of "Fengjing jiu ceng an" (Scenery once familiar), "Guguo shenyou" (A magical journey home), both written in 1983, and "Dujuan ti xue" (Azaleas cry out blood), written the following year. All three novellas portray protagonists who return to the mainland after more than thirty years' absence and encounter the uncanny cognitive dissonance alluded to in the stories' titles. As Wendy Larson notes, the three works show consistent concern not only with exile and return but also with the author's position.[10] In these stories, writing tries—and fails—to assume authority, thereby causing a rupture in the narrator's identity. The protagonist in "Scenery Once Familiar" seals his fate by following his talent for calligraphy. Writing becomes his "karmic obstruction."[11] In "A Magical Journey Home" a man loses his U.S. documents before going through an airport passport check in the PRC. The authorities take him for a Taiwanese spy; consequently, he goes through an identity crisis and a nervous breakdown that paralyze him even as he is asked to sign the papers for his own release.[12] In other words, he is unable to attest in writing to who he is. Once Liu's characters try to reach beyond past traumas, they find that their present identity is distinct from their past one. Trying to anchor their sense of temporal continuity in texts and documents serves only to show that writing cannot set history right. Instead, the protagonists become dependent on earlier written texts to the extent that their present and immediate testimonies are ignored.

"Azaleas Cry Out Blood" was composed shortly after Liu was first allowed to return to Taiwan and expresses the author's endeavors to retrieve his voice in an era of political change and account-taking of memory. Liu addresses the repressed experiences of the Cultural Revolution, but also issues of Taiwanese ideology, specifically the KMT's repression of public debate. The story is set in the PRC during the early 1980s. The narrator, Professor Hu, is an overseas Chinese from Singapore teaching in the United States. Hu follows a clue in a Red Guards bulletin from 1968, *The Luzhou Battle Report,* and finds out that his fourth aunt, Leng Yufeng, of whom there has been no trace for over forty years, is living in the PRC under the name Leng Feng. Hu visits her in a sanatorium for high-ranking cadres but fails to communicate with her. Except for a single unintelligible burst, Leng Feng is incapable of acknowledging her nephew's presence, let alone helping him understand why she suddenly severed ties with her family in the early 1930s or how she lost her sanity during the Cultural Revolution. The little information provided by the sanatorium staff implies that she had been treated brutally in 1968, after which she lost her speech for two years and has said little ever since. Only after Hu leaves the PRC does he find the key to his aunt's past. In Hong Kong, he discovers a hitherto missing part of *The Luzhou Battle Report*, which reveals that Leng Feng had given up everything to follow her teacher and lover Luo Cheng, a communist leader, to the Chinese hinterland. The *Report* further discloses that after Luo Cheng betrayed her and possibly the communist underground in the 1930s, Leng Feng had him executed and ate his heart.

At the center of the story lies madness—Leng Feng's mad revolutionary zeal, subsequent insanity, and the "madness" of the Cultural Revolution.[13] In psychoanalytical terms, the repetitive pattern of Leng Feng's conduct shows how she reenacts the same punitive behavior after each recurring perceived betrayal of a father-figure. Leng Feng shows the need for an infallible father-figure when she abruptly leaves her own family and falls for her teacher, Luo Cheng. When Luo betrays her, she turns cannibal and eats his heart. Later, she projects the emotions previously reserved for Luo Cheng onto the Party and "marries the Chinese revolution" (ACB, p. 179). The Red Guards' physical abuse of her is compounded by what Leng Feng could regard as being betrayed by Mao. The Great Helmsman was portrayed as the nation's father-figure and collective superego, to whom all agency was renounced. Party cadres, the group most protected by Mao and the most inculcated with his ideology, felt deceived when the leader shifted his allegiance from the party apparatus to the Red Guards, who accused the cadres of being covert "careerists and schemers like Khrushchev" (ACB, p. 188). As Wang Shaoguang observes, the Cultural Revolution left most people with a sense of having been "'blinded,' 'hoodwinked,' 'cheated,' or 'used' by Mao."[14] When Leng Feng feels betrayed by Mao, she turns not against him but against herself. She loses her sanity and regresses into aphasia. Turning away from her father, Luo Cheng, and, finally, Mao results in a growing loss of touch with social structures and norms—from severing all family ties to effacing her birth name, to cannibalism, and eventually to giving up all verbal communication. Inasmuch as each crisis is concurrent with a major historical disruption—the civil war, the Anti-Rightist Campaign, and the Cultural Revolution—the woman's mental regression also points to a collective psychosis linked to expectations of and setbacks in China's political discourse.

Leng Feng's mental disorder and the story's location in an insane asylum should, however, be understood not only in psychoanalytical terms but also as an allegory on the post-traumatic displacement of memory. The present repeats past traumas, not only of the Cultural Revolution but also dating to the Anti-Rightist campaign of the 1950s and farther back to the civil war of the 1940s. As in Chen's "Mountain Path," the significance of trauma lies in its return and extension into the present.

THE NARRATOR AS DETECTIVE

The regression to increasingly earlier roots of madness motivates the narrative to establish the originary experience that led to Leng Feng's post-traumatic behavior pattern. Her lack of responsiveness produces a riddle that can be solved only by reading between the lines and through reference to other texts. "Azaleas Cry Out Blood" derives its force from the narrator's need to retrace Leng Feng's history through detectivelike working through his aunt's past.

The narrator, Professor Hu, cannot establish a coherent version of any key event or reconstitute a narrative that would reconnect the various suppressed moments in Leng Feng's life. His only approaches to the past are through his aunt, her physician Dr. Xu, and the text of *The Luzhou Battle Report*. Each of these represents a different manifestation of the crisis of memory. Leng Feng offers inner resistance to recovering the past, as is clearly illustrated when Hu tries to jolt his aunt's memory by placing by her bedside a photograph of her and her sisters taken in the 1930s. Leng Feng ignores the picture throughout his visit and never touches it. She not only disowns her family ties but also ignores the very existence of the historical moment represented by the photograph. She continues to deny the past, to herself, the Red Guards, and her nephew. Unlike survivors such as Zhang Xianliang, who at least tries to reclaim his two "worlds" of experience (see Chapter 6), Leng Feng's psyche disintegrates when she is forced to confront her past, her mental fault lines rupture, and her memory breaks down.

At the sanatorium, Hu is met with another version of denial, namely, the political rewriting of history, represented by the elusive Dr. Xu. Hu realizes from the beginning that he must elicit his information despite Dr. Xu's resistance:

I waited patiently for my counterpart to make the move and get to the main issue. I was convinced that they had a good idea why I was visiting them; the only thing that worried me was that I did not know how much they were willing to reveal. I could only keep cautioning myself that it was better to feign ignorance and pursue any leads my counterpart might reveal unintentionally. (ACB, p. 154)

The scene stresses the plot's similarity to a detective novel, which strives to answer the whodunit through manipulative interrogation. The narrator's account reads as if taken right out of a classical spy thriller, as the two sides exchange pleasantries with each aware that the other knows more than he pretends and is looking for ways to extract information without revealing in the process how much he himself may know. Yet the encounter between Professor Hu and Dr. Xu brings the investigation to an impasse, illustrating the tenacious resistance to resuscitating unwelcome memories.

For his own reasons, Dr. Xu cooperates with Leng Feng's denial of her memory. He not only pretends that her insanity hides no traces of any event worth pursuing but also actively helps repress her secrets. When Leng Feng suddenly utters a few incoherent words—a stunted yet hopeful sign of willingness to communicate—Dr. Xu immediately rushes her back into her room and expresses dismay at her "regression" (ACB, p. 183). Freudian treatment would have encouraged verbal expression, but Dr. Xu refers disparagingly to "this Western idealistic nonsense about psychoanalysis" (ACB, p. 158). Significantly, the only treatment that the sanatorium applies successfully consists of prescribing traditional medication to stop internal bleeding (ACB, p. 181). The authorities keep the symptoms of violence under cover rather than reveal the cracks in the communist utopia.

TEXTUAL VIOLENCE

Of the three sources of information—Leng Feng herself, Dr. Xu, and the *Luzhou Battle Report*—the most complex manifestation of the crisis of memory and public testimony is the *Report*, in which Hu encounters a more insidious form of resistance to memory, namely, textual dynamics that turn testimony against itself. The *Report* replicates Leng Feng's insane silences and the official line of tendentious half-truths, but also in itself becomes the vehicle and victim of brutal oppression. Hu can avail himself only of an incomplete copy of the *Report* kept in a U.S. library—such Red Guard publications, usually mimeographed pamphlets, have rarely been preserved.[15] The *Report* contains the first half of an article that contains testimony about Leng Feng's carryings-on in the mid 1930s. When Hu has no choice but to reveal his cards and ask the official escort for the *Report*, he is given a copy from which the relevant article has been completely excised. The text is repeatedly interrupted and mutilated. First, it is cut short by the editors' frantic interjections, then the censors cut it out completely. Symbolically, the title "Chop off the Evil Manipulator, the Counterrevolutionary Revisionist Two-faced Leng Feng! Destroy Completely the New Counterattack of the Old Provincial Committee!" (such pamphlets typically had long titles) is abbreviated by the narrator to "The 'Chop off' Text." The foreshortened form sounds even more violent than the original title, suggesting a text capable of being dismembered and cannibalized—or of beheading.

The *Report* demonstrates, not only the failure of writing as a carrier of memory, but also how texts can violently interfere in the work of memory. The *Report* plays a major role in driving Leng Feng mad; it is a murderous text that calls explicitly for her death: "the debt of blood has to be paid in blood!" (ACB, p. 172). "The 'Chop off' Text" becomes a tool of violence when the Red Guards use it to incite people against Leng Feng, as well as to open the wounds of her memory and make her more vulnerable. The Red Guards unearth Leng Feng's deposition and reproduce it in the *Report*. Leng Feng had reportedly given her version of the events of 1934 during the Anti-Rightist Campaign of 1957: "[Another Party member] forced me to swallow the warm, blood-dripping heart and liver taken out of [Luo's] disemboweled corpse, in front of the crowd!" (ACB, p. 188). Leng Feng uses the graphic description to arouse revulsion against her political rival and invite pity for her own plight. The Red Guards reappropriate Leng Feng's incendiary testimony and use it as evidence against her. Leng Feng is made, so to speak, to eat her own blood-dripping words. The *Report* article highlights how testimony, especially when committed to the printed media, might end up cannibalizing the writer's voice.

Finally, the narrator locates the crisis of memory even within himself. Professor Hu realizes his own complicity: "Did I so bury myself from the very start in verifying the identity of the name Leng Feng that coming closer and closer to the truth only made me more reluctant to face the tragedy my subconscious confirmed must have occurred?" (ACB, p. 172). The question remains unanswered, and it becomes clear that no single observer has a hold on the past. The whodunit structure disintegrates as the multiple and incomplete texts undermine Hu's attempts to get to the bottom of the historical riddle. The various voices contained in "Azaleas" not only fail to be complementary but often delimit one another. The testimonies are partial and indecisive, and the story ends with the narrator's unresolved doubts.

Far from providing the solution found in most detective novels, "Azaleas" leaves the collected evidence open to interpretation. The key evidence to Leng Feng's cannibalism is provided when she finally speaks, shouting at Hu, "Eat it up, eat it up while it's hot, hurry and eat it up, hurry and eat it up!" (ACB, p. 183). The remainder of the *Report* article, which Hu eventually retrieves in Hong Kong, quotes the same words as Leng Feng's exhortation to the troops to eat Luo Cheng's entrails. Yet even the identity between Leng Feng's words to Hu and the phrase quoted in the *Report* may be explained in a less incriminating light, as a delirious repetition of the words the Red Guards accused her of uttering and to which they made her confess. The story ends without reconciling the different versions. As David Wang remarks, Liu Daren uses the detective story structure to highlight the impossibility of attaining an answer. Liu's fiction gains its force from the gap between our desire to solve the riddle and the senselessness of historical contingency. In Wang's words, for Liu "history is . . . a rupture in meaning, an enigma to rationality."[16] The incomplete sentence, leaving open to interpretation what it is that should be eaten up, becomes in itself emblematic of the inadequacy of testimony and of later readers' tendency to read excessive meanings into it. The "it" in "eat it up" (the Chinese phrase does without the direct object altogether) remains a sign of absence of meaning that invites increasingly parabolic readings.

THE CRY OF BLOOD

As a parable about the rupture of memory, "Azaleas" especially addresses the difficulties faced by the author who wishes to reclaim historical memory. Even the story's title alludes to the inability to bear witness to trauma. Liu Daren gives new meaning to the phrase in Bo Juyi's (772–846) *Pipa xing* (Song of the lute), "What do I hear from dawn to dusk / Cuckoos cry out blood and monkeys howl mournfully."[17] The idiom has given rise to many explanations.[18] The fifth-century *Yi yuan* (Garden of oddities) is particularly relevant: "A man walked in the mountains and saw a flock [of cuckoos]. He imitated them for a while, then coughed blood and died. It is said that this bird cries ceaselessly until it emits blood, which is the reason for this case of coughing blood."[19] This interpretation underscores how the bird's call lures the listener to self-immolation. It is also an apt metaphor for the confessions extracted during the Cultural Revolution—the more one spoke, the more one would implicate oneself and others. Even imitating Maospeak often landed the Chairman's avid followers in situations that cost them their lives.

Liu's text takes advantage of the fact that the azalea flower and the cuckoo share the same name in Chinese (*dujuan*) to transfer the attributes of the bird to the azalea flower and create a complex metaphor. Like the singing cuckoos, the azaleas also await the self-destructive actions of their beholders. Hu describes the azaleas watered by Leng Feng: "These glittering and moist azaleas, by their hundreds and thousands, truly looked as if each of them contained a mouthful of fresh blood, thick and rancid, which crawled out of these many throats, gushing forth slowly but uncontained" (ACB, pp. 161–62).[20] The flowers stand for the mouths of bloodthirsty cannibals, but they also show the self-inflicted wounds of those who open their mouths.

The azalea becomes a metaphor for the pain involved in speaking out one's memories, whether of the Cultural Revolution or of the White Terror. Liu Daren returns in this text to an image already presented in Chen Ying-zhen's "Qican de wuyan de zui" (Poor poor dumb mouths, 1964). Chen's title borrows Shakespeare's words, "sweet Caesar's wounds, poor poor dumb mouths," to associate bloody wounds with speechless mouths.[21] In Liu Daren's text, it is rather mouths that are equated with wounds, evoking not only the silence imposed by mental trauma but also the potential violence committed by speech.

EXILE FROM HISTORY

The literary allusion to Bo Juyi's poem in the title of "Azaleas Cry Out Blood" also indicates the narrator's temporal and spatial dislocation. The cuckoo is said to replicate King Du Yu's lament in exile, an association preserved in Bo Juyi's *The Song of the Lute*. "Azaleas" follows the allusion, weaving together Hu's inability to solve the mystery with his abortive homecoming. Hu is a doubly exiled man, an overseas Chinese living in the United States, and attempts in vain to find roots and familiar recognition in mainland China. Professor Hu and Leng Feng fashion their respective journeys to the mainland as homecomings, yet they end up reenacting a more profound dislocation. Leng Feng tries to leave her mark on the nation's history, and Hu aims at understanding the past. Yet Leng Feng repeats her exile over and over again, fleeing from home, from reality, and from speech. Hu goes to China assuming that he can rely on his outsider's objectivity, only to find himself unable to distance himself from events. Although he tries to bridge the silence created by violence and madness, he cannot provide conclusive testimony. Neither Leng Feng's mad utterances nor Hu's rational inquiry can clarify the past beyond doubt. When attempting to trace their identity to a homeland or an originary traumatic moment, they give the lie to the possibility of return.

That events cannot be pinned down in history is further stressed by the name of the location where the plot takes place—Luzhou. History repeats itself as the characters keep returning to the town. Luzhou is the home place of Leng Feng's and Hu's family. It is to Luzhou, also Luo Cheng's ancestral home, that the latter is sent on a mission, and where he is caught. In Luzhou, Leng Feng faces Luo Cheng again and eats his heart. The incriminating evidence against Leng Feng is printed in *The Luzhou Battle Report*, and presumably it is also in Luzhou that she is "struggled against" and loses her sanity. It is back in Luzhou that Hu meets his aunt. "My blood too," says Hu, "should be traced to that place" (ACB, p. 163)—a phrasing that draws attention to the affinity between lineage and violence. Luzhou—which Liu Daren loosely associates with China[22]—is the scene of crime, of trauma, and of compulsive repetition. History advances only to return to the same place. Hu's journey to Luzhou is an attempt, doomed from the start, to penetrate the space from where no witness can escape and, in Shoshana Felman's phrasing, "testify from inside."[23]

The place where all events are anchored is elusive and unfixed. Although Luzhou is recorded as an ancient geographical region, the name has long been out of use. Literally, it means "reed islet." Like floating, disconnected and shifting ground, Luzhou is a place on which no one can set foot. Luzhou is the place of ideological utopia and historical dystopia, the blank space that signals the eternal displacement of traumatic experience. Hu's origins as an overseas Chinese, the allusion to King Du's tragic exile, and the undefined place-name all point to the fact that no one can speak from a stable point in time or space to reclaim the past, or even a more abstract "Chinese identity." As a parable about Liu Daren's own position as a Taiwan-educated writer of Chinese origin and a U.N. passport holder, the references to exile and displacement point to the limitations of writing in establishing common memories with a national community of readers.

MAY FOURTH AND TAIWANESE IDENTITY

Through reference to the Cultural Revolution, an event that shook left-wing Taiwanese intellectuals and forced them to reevaluate their relationship to the Chinese mainland and to May Fourth, Liu Daren's text reflects not only on the traumas of Mao's regime but also on the crisis of memory and identity in post-Chiang Taiwan. Ultimately, it is not only Hu's narration but also Liu's writing itself that suffers from historical dislocation. "Azaleas" may be read as the author's examination of his and his generation and as a reassessment of the relevance of the legacy of May Fourth to contemporary Taiwan. The novella's focus on the fragmented and demented text pays tribute to Lu Xun's "Diary of a Madman." As I argue in Chapter 1, Lu Xun's short story is an "ifdunit," asking if a crime has ever taken place. Both Lu Xun's and Liu Daren's texts are structured as unsolvable riddles, since the respective characters are insane and incapable of giving coherent testimony. By claiming to have eaten his own sister, Lu Xun's ranting Madman discredits his diary. Professor Hu's two sources, Leng Feng and the *Report*, have both played an active role in the violence and are therefore tendentious and suspect. Witnesses and victims alike turn out to be possible accomplices in the crime. As in "Diary of a Madman," the truth is hard to judge, too, because the horrifying experience around which the plot revolves implicates the main characters. Liu Daren explains, with some unease about crass analogies, that he associates Professor Hu with the moderate May Fourth reformer Hu Shi, on the one hand, and Leng Feng with the uncompromising Lu Xun, on the other.[24] Leng Feng's name (literally, "cold peak") may also allude to Feng Xuefeng ("snow peak"), Lu Xun's close disciple and editor, who became the target of several PRC literary purges. Lu Xun's presence is felt throughout the story, both as a source of inspiration and as an icon that needs to be taken down from the pedestal on which he was put by Mao. "Azaleas" satirizes Lu Xun's distorted reception by letting the *Report* quote the writer crudely and out of context: "Lu Xun said there's only one way to treat a dog that fell into the water—hit it! Teach it not to bite again!" (ACB, p. 188).[25] Lu Xun's legacy remains highly relevant to Liu Daren.

Yet the position of Chinese intellectuals in the 1980s was, of course, very different from the situation to which May Fourth thinkers reacted. Whereas Lu Xun located himself at the point of departure into modernity and debated future courses of action, Liu Daren observes the persistence and exacerbation of the social problems described by the earlier writer. Leng Feng's fate exemplifies the return, in increasingly horrifying forms, of the paradoxes pointed out by Lu Xun. Leng Feng could have signaled personal liberation through love and joining the revolutionary camp. Her elopement avoids the destitution that Lu Xun describes in "And What After Nora Leaves Home?" yet she meets an even more appalling end, as she is driven mad and becomes a cannibal. During the Cultural Revolution, the revolutionary generation took Lu Xun's reference to cannibalism literally, and "counterrevolutionaries" were sometimes disemboweled and devoured.[26] In telling Professor Hu, "Eat it up while it's hot," as if she were presenting her nephew with a bleeding heart, Leng Feng points to the residual cannibalism of May Fourth. The act symbolically carries the unfinished project of the Chinese Enlightenment into the 1980s and hands over the task of bearing witness to Liu Daren's generation. Yet Chen Yingzhen, Liu Daren, and other writers in post-Chiang Taiwan can only testify to a history known through silences, madness, and disrupted writing.

Liu Daren has said that he wrote "Azaleas" believing that the time had come to reclaim historical agency and counter the demand of the May Fourth generation that one sacrifice oneself for the collective. The mission in the 1980s, in Liu's view, was to differentiate oneself as an individual and "free oneself from Big Brother."[27] As a result of liberating themselves from the grand narratives and collective memory of Mao's and Chiang's dictatorships, writers turned to creating personal memories. Against the rhetoric of speaking in the name of the masses, the nation, and the revolution, writers introduced into public discourse silences that have long remained unacknowledged. Post-Chiang literature turned to mystery to free itself from dominant narratives. History would be known as many stories, enriched by the unspoken words that link them together.

8 The Aesthetics and Anesthetics of Memory

PRC Avant-Garde Fiction

With the new generation of writers that emerged in the mid-1980s, the literary scene in the PRC underwent a transformation. Young authors born in the early 1960s had few personal stakes in Maoist ideology and the May Fourth legacy. The result was a literature open to experimentation and whose debt to early twentieth-century Chinese writers was elusive and often unacknowledged. Especially conspicuous was the young authors' attitude toward bearing witness, since those who had grown up during the Cultural Revolution could not produce firsthand testimonies similar to the texts discussed in Chapter 6. Instead, the poetry, drama, and fiction of the late 1980s turned from straightforward testimony to allegory, generating absurd and shocking parables on the past. The experimental forms collectively known as "avant-garde fiction" (*xianfeng xiaoshuo*) came to dominate PRC literature until the early 1990s.

This chapter focuses on Yu Hua's (b. 1960) "Wangshi yu xingfa" (Past and punishment, 1987, first published 1989).[1] The plot involves a person who gives his consent to being hurled into the past, cut in two and left to die after his bleeding torso is placed on a glass table. I read the surreal and disturbing image as an allegory of the dangers of returning to the past in search of a transforming experience. The parable speaks to the need of Yu Hua's generation to transcend the memories of the Cultural Revolution and to the simultaneous realization that it is impossible to erase the collective memory. "Past and Punishment" resonates with concrete descriptions of the Maoist era—recall Zhang Xianliang's depiction of his experience in the labor camps: "a sharp knife had severed me at the waist."[2] Yu Hua places his protagonist in a similar situation but in a fantastic setting, not simply transposing the brutality of the Cultural Revolution to the metaphorical level, as Zhang does, but rather constructing an entirely allegorical tale. The uncomfortable juxtaposition of violence and aesthetics in "Past and Punishment" calls upon the reader to question both the realism in accounts such as those presented in scar literature and the parabolic excesses of Yu Hua's own style. The story can also be read as a parable about the limits of testimony, caught between the consciousness of the unanesthetized man witnessing his own death and the sterile conditions of the transparent glass table.

"Past and Punishment" is representative of Yu Hua's writings, which played a central role in the meteoric ascendance of Chinese avant-garde fiction, a prolific and critically acclaimed genre. The film director Zhang Yimou, among others, chose scripts associated with the trend for some of his successful movies: *Hong gaoliang* (Red sorghum, 1987), *Da hong denglong gaogao gua* (Raise the red lantern, 1991) (based on Mo Yan's and Su Tong's novellas respectively), and *Huozhe* (To live, 1992) (which the author of the originary novel, Yu Hua, disowned), yet the texts were often more daring than the films they inspired. For a short while, avant-garde fiction came to represent the essence of postsocialist literature. Subsequently, writers took their own individual paths. Perhaps owing to disenchantment with politics after the June Fourth incident of 1989 and the growing consumerism of the 1990s, Yu Hua has adopted a less belligerent style and taken up more compassionate themes in *To Live* and *Xu Sanguan mai xue ji* (translated as *Chronicles of a Blood Merchant,* 1996).[3] In retrospect, the pluralistic literary scene of the 1990s demonstrates the uniqueness of the heyday of avant-garde fiction, when "Past and Punishment" was written.

Yu Hua's story addresses issues familiar from other post–Cultural Revolution writings in novel ways. How can one revisit the past and bear witness to a cataclysm of historical magnitude? How does literature engage with personal experience and represent collective memory at the same time? In dealing with philosophical constructions of history, Yu Hua shows the influence of contemporary intellectual debates. As Xudong Zhang and Jing Wang point out, avant-garde fiction must be understood in the context of the challenges to conservative Marxism sparked by the 1983 centennial of Marx's death. During what became known as "the Culture Fever," thinkers such as Li Zehou, Liu Zaifu, and Gan Yang challenged Maoist ideology by introducing Western academic discussion of Jacques Derrida's deconstruction, Jürgen Habermas's formulation of the public sphere, and Walter Benjamin's philosophy of history.[4] Yu Hua's paradoxical representation of history reflects a similar distrust of Maoist formulations—"Past and Punishment" does not present a coherent and linear progression of time, but rather a labyrinth of subjective temporalities. Through the absurd, Yu Hua conveys a consistent view of the stories told of history. Where there is no division be-

tween past, present, and future, there can be no history; and where there is
no history, there can be no memory. By implication, testimony is no longer—in fact, has never been—able to contain past experience.

Any claim to have deciphered Yu Hua in full would, however, be reduc-
tive. His unstable texts exclude the possibility of inferring direct answers and
encourage subjective readings. Hand in hand with offering a reading of "Past
and Punishment," I examine the interpretative practices that it anticipates,
elicits, and challenges. The short story is not only a treatise on the uses of
history but also a parable about readers' response to Yu Hua's text itself. The
opaque text, I argue, demonstrates the inability of the writer to bear witness
and communicate his or her past experience in full.

THE SCANDAL

"Past and Punishment" begins in 1990, when a character known simply as
"the Stranger" opens a telegram that reads: "Return quickly." Four possible
destinations present themselves to the Stranger's mind; they are not places
but dates in the past. The Stranger decides to head for March 5, 1965. On his
way, he meets the Punition Expert, who invites him over to his apartment to
discuss several "punishments" or, rather, forms of execution. When the Punition Expert describes in a matter-of-fact manner how he is going to kill the
Stranger, the latter offers no resistance. Instead, the Stranger sees in the punishment a privileged chance to unite with his past. After the Punition Expert
turns out to be too feeble to administer the punishment, a fact that causes
both characters disappointment and distress, he prepares his own execution,
and the Stranger finds the Punition Expert's lifeless body, with a note giving
the date: March 5, 1965.

The story begs to scandalize its readers. It is a logical outrage: how can a
narrative sustain a surreal journey in time? The plot is morally shocking:
where is the responsibility of a work of fiction that depicts with detachment
the destruction of a human body and the taking of human life? The text does
not contain even an implicit denunciation of the Punition Expert's preference for aesthetics over ethics. The Stranger's cooperation with and compassion for the Punition Expert are just as unreasonable. Is one not supposed to
feel fear and revolt in face of such violence? Furthermore, the violence is
scandalously senseless—it serves no end. The "punishments" are unworthy
of the name, since they do not expiate for any crime, or even any unspecified

offense, and the Stranger is a willing participant. The textual violence is so astonishing that it literally becomes a "scandal," a stumbling block, to intellection.

This view has determined the way in which Yu Hua's text has been read, and the unaffected narrative has been assumed to assault the reader. Andrew Jones remarks that when translating Yu Hua's stories, he has often pondered, "[I]s it right to loose these sorts of representations on an unsuspecting world? . . . If we find ourselves enjoying Yu Hua's fiction, are we somehow guilty of complicity with his aestheticization of violence?"[5] Yet Yu Hua's text seems to anticipate precisely this reaction. Just as "we," the imagined readership, should not consider ourselves too blasé to be affected by the violence, neither should we fall prey to ethical posturing and assume an outraged position. Instead, I ask why it is that one supposes one's fellow readers to be scandalized. Rather than play into assumptions about the author's intent and the readers' reaction,[6] one should bear in mind that authors from Lu Xun to Yu Hua have expected the scandalized reaction and employed it consciously to distance readers from the text and thereby foreground its significance as a parable. For example, the surreal dimensions of the violence in Yu Hua's fiction discredit the text's reference to specific dates. As Jones notes about another short story by the same author, the textual violence resists reading according to the conventions of either realism or premodern Chinese fiction, so that "the depiction of violence . . . tends to . . . self-reflexively foreground its own textuality."[7] "Past and Punishment" raises the question of how to interpret a text that from the outset proclaims itself to be a parable about its own uninterpretability.

The rapidly growing critical corpus on Yu Hua has celebrated the breakdown of meaning and specifically of temporal reference. Dai Jinhua remarks that in Yu Hua's texts, history is an "empty signifier," a "transcendental sign," a "Lacanian phallic symbol."[8] Wendy Larson notes that "Yu Hua manipulates a tension between goal-oriented action and the meaninglessness that results from disassociating behavior with interpretation or a social signifier from a conventional social meaning."[9] Andrew Jones sums up: "Yu Hua's work . . . represents a *crisis of representation* . . . where history has become unintelligible."[10] Yet these descriptions do not address the fact that the text points to itself as a sign of the crisis of meaning because it aims at scandalizing the reader. As the previous chapters demonstrate, Yu Hua introduces little novelty to twentieth-century Chinese literature in claiming the breakdown of "history." What is new is the narrator's willingness to qualify all testimony. Whereas previous witness against history had, at least implicitly, claimed a stake in challenging the testimony *for* history, Yu Hua's fiction shows no pathos in defying the figure of history. The scandal revealed in "Past and Punishment" is that the storyteller has long reconciled himself to the fact that memory is aestheticized and that the witness to history is anesthetized.

MARXIST HISTORY AND THE ABSURD

What distinguishes "Past and Punishment" from the other works discussed in this book is that in the absence of history, there is no place for the witness and all testimony is invalidated. The short story is based on the temporal absurdity that the Stranger and the Punition Expert conceive of time as moving toward a "reunion" with the past rather than toward a predetermined point in the future. When the Stranger receives the telegram commanding, "Return quickly," he immediately understands the message as a demand that he travel back in time. In his nonlinear time, many realities coexist simultaneously: "the Stranger reviewed the misty events of past decades. Millions of intricate roads emerged; in their midst, he smiled faintly at one" (P&P, p. 43). The maze of temporalities is akin to the vision of Jorge Luis Borges, one of Yu Hua's major sources of inspiration. In Borges's "La muerte y la brújula" (Death and the compass, 1942), four murders trace a "symmetry in time."[11] "El jardín de sendéros que se bifurcan" (The garden of forking paths, 1941) describes a labyrinth of "convergent and parallel times" where "time forks perpetually toward innumerable futures."[12] As in Borges's stories, the Stranger is presented with multiple paths, each of which signals a different plot and a different death. Time is not out of humans' control but rather a chartable and navigable territory.

Yet unlike Borges's protagonists, who have command over their choice of paths, the Stranger has little leverage on his fate. He reaches a town called Mist—an allusion to the Chinese adage "Human life [fades] like mist" (*shishi ruyan*, also the title of another short story by Yu Hua)—and realizes that because of a "sequential error," he will be unable to arrive at either the date of his choice or at any other of the four dates he has considered (P&P, p. 43). The Stranger stands helpless, "besieged by layer upon layer of the past" (P&P, p. 44), and cannot proceed to his destination. At this point, the Punition Expert appears and offers himself as a guide to the labyrinth of time. As the Stranger searches in bewilderment for "a necessary link" that will explain

his present situation, the Punition Expert explains: "I think we all understand that the arbitrary is one of those dull, drab things . . . it can only go
witlessly forward. The random is a grand thing—wherever you throw it in, a
brand-new history will appear" (P&P, pp. 48–49). In an otherwise mystifying
plot, this retort clearly states the story's ideological ramifications. The Punition Expert engages the issue of historical determinism and celebrates the
possibility of a history based on sheer accident. Such a history would not "go
witlessly forward" or, for that matter, in any specific direction or toward any
goal.

The Stranger's traveling back in time, compounded with his patent failure
to arrive at the destination of his surreal journey, refutes the historical determinism that had been part of Maoist ideology. History in an orthodox
Marxist key is the story of progress toward the betterment of society and the
redemption of mankind. Calling for history to be given to free play, where
"brand-new histories" can be invented at random, runs counter to the tenets
of historical materialism and carries seditious undertones. Moreover,
whereas Marx proposes his theory as an antithesis to regarding "violence,
war, pillage, murder and robbery . . . as the driving force of history,"[13] in
"Past and Punishment" the Punition Expert and his punishments motivate
time. History is no longer viewed, as Hegel claims, as "the progress of the
consciousness of Freedom"[14]—unless one is willing to redefine liberty in
terms of negation and death. From a Marxist viewpoint, history as presented
by Yu Hua is, as Zhao Yiheng dubs it, "antihistory."[15]

Yu Hua's story parallels Wang Shuo's more overtly irreverent treatment
of revolutionary phrasing (see Chapter 9). In post–Cultural Revolution
China, where collective memory has retained familiarity with Maoist formulations, readers recognize the Marxist historical narrative and are sensitive to
its modification. Against the progressive view of history, "Past and Punishment" presents an alternative, in the form of the Punition Expert's reduction
of time to a single temporal dimension. He explains to the Stranger: "'In fact,
we always live in the past. The present and the future are just little tricks the
past plays on us'" (P&P, p. 46). The Punition Expert disentangles the maze of
alternative narratives and collapses all times into one road that leads everywhere. In so doing, he echoes the words of his kin, the executioner in
Borges's "Death and the Compass": "The next time I kill you . . . I promise
you that labyrinth, consisting of a single line that is invisible and unceas-
ing."[16] The promise of reducing all time to a single moment also resonates
with the idea of a messianic time that would take over history. The concept

of a messianic time that annihilates history, known now mostly from Walter Benjamin's philosophy, was already suggested by Kant, who differentiated between historic and messianic time and explained that at the apocalypse, "a moment will make its appearance when all change—and with it time itself—will cease."[17] The Punition Expert presents a similar alternative to history: when the flow of time is not confined by narratives that extend into a future goal, and when one does not expect time to present the unfolding of an immanent historical force, then one can represent all temporalities as uniting into a single dimension. "Past and Punishment" envisions time brought to a standstill and distilled into a singular instant, where it no longer expands into a history.

REVERSE NOSTALGIA

It might be argued that if the characters in "Past and Punishment" do not live in a linear time, they may represent the burden of the past, which holds back the forces of progress. Yet Yu Hua's challenge to the Maoist view of history does not imply that, as some critics would have it, "Past and Punishment" condemns the past as the source of violence. Yu Hua's strategy for obliterating the figure of history entails showing how the past has been used as a mere excuse for the failure of progress.

At first glance it is tempting to identify the Punition Expert with the past. A white-haired old man, the Punition Expert guides the Stranger into the past and even tells him, "I am your past" (P&P, p. 48). The Punition Expert wishes to administer a series of cruel executions, including dismembering the victim by castration and drawing his body apart with five carts, procedures associated with the premodern Chinese legal system.[18] He collects the laws of all times and places: "'My job is to put together all the wisdom of humankind; the most remarkable part of humankind's entire wisdom is punition'" (P&P, p. 49). He derives pleasure from dredging up figures of violence from the past.

The Punition Expert, as the gatekeeper of time, represents an authoritative and arbitrary voice, beginning with the terse and unexplained command: "Return quickly," which he has presumably sent. Without exerting any physical force, the Punition Expert's short command creates, ex nihilo, a temporal and spatial dynamics. Like every imperative, the telegram's message combines two commands, the first of which is "Obey!"—and the Stranger complies unquestioningly. He immediately acknowledges the Punition Expert's "persuasive force" (P&P, p. 46) and follows him without hesitation. The summons of the Punition Expert, who may be the telegram's sender, bears neither place nor time of issue; it is "of unclear provenance" and "without the sender's return address or name" (P&P, p. 43). The Stranger's provenance too is unknown—it is as if the Stranger himself has been called into existence by the telegram. Dai Jinhua has gone as far as to claim that the Punition Expert embodies "the name of the father," the ultimate prohibitive authority in Jacques Lacan's psychoanalytic system.[19] The Punition Expert's speech becomes the law at the moment in which he utters it. His authority is further supported by his statement that the commands do not emanate from him: "'It is not I who demand this from you, it is my punishments that call upon you in this way'" (P&P, p. 55). The Punition Expert claims his power to be immanent, beyond considerations of time, reason, or language.

Yet it would be rash to conclude that the Punition Expert stands simply for the overbearing force of tradition. Instead, he hides behind the name of the past, but his summons derives its power precisely from arguing for the urgency of the present. In fact, the Punition Expert emphasizes the tyranny of the now and the brutality of modernity. In his manifestolike essay "Xuwei de zuopin" (Hypocritical writings, 1989), Yu Hua emphasizes that violence cannot be relegated to bygone times. In response to the accusation that "Yu Hua seems to have lost his mind to violence," the author writes:

Modern civilization has banished to history scenes in which the slaves are allowed to massacre one another while their master looks on. However, I always feel that this pattern of things is the tragedy of modernism. . . . It has [merely] been substituted for by boxing matches. We can see that on the sly, civilization has given way to barbarism. . . . In the face of violence, civilization is but an empty slogan and order becomes ornamentation.[20]

In light of this statement, the Punition Expert's violence demonstrates the affinity between modernity and barbarism. Hand in hand with denouncing linear history, "Past and Punishment" refutes the progress of humanity toward a more civilized state. The Punition Expert's actions show humanity's progress to be no more than the accumulation of atrocities.[21] "History," as "Hypocritical Writing" suggests, is merely the rhetorical repository where humanity has stashed its repressed violence. The claim that history progresses toward "civilization" covers up for the failure of modernity as the age of Reason.

To claim, as does Dai Jinhua, that the Punition Expert embodies "the castrating force of history" ignores the dialectics of redemption in "Past and

Punishment."[22] The poignancy of the Punition Expert's tyranny lies precisely in the fact that he is identified, not with the past, but with an ever-present now. Reading Yu Hua's text as a condemnation of the past exhibits what may be called reverse nostalgia—conveniently falling back on the "bad old days" to explain the failure of promises made in the name of history rather than questioning the present's claim to be different from and better than the past. In this respect, "Past and Punishment" shares the fate of Lu Xun's "Diary of a Madman," a poignant critique of modernity that was nevertheless reappropriated to condemn "feudal" values (see Chapter 1). Yu Hua tempts the reader to imagine a way out of the maze of history, only to refute all possibility of deliverance.

Yu Hua goes beyond Lu Xun's critique of history, however, and negates all temporal experience. In fact, the Punition Expert is unable to make his punishments work on any temporal plane; his violence is coupled with incompetence at procuring any form of experience for the Stranger. His shortcomings are foregrounded when the Stranger discovers that the Punition Expert cannot produce even his own death—the latter neglects to include in his plans the bullet with which he is to be shot. The Punition Expert disavows any historical continuum and would like to reduce all experience to death, yet in so doing, he also excludes the material conditions necessary for putting into effect his elaborate temporal matrix.

Far from being an omnipotent, "castrating" figure, the Punition Expert is caricaturized as a charlatan, and specifically as an unsuccessful imitator of Buddhist masters who teach that enlightenment is attained by transcending time. The Punition Expert tells the Stranger: "In your last moment you will see the first dewdrop on the morning of January 9, 1958" (P&P, p. 54). The dewdrop is used in Buddhist writings to symbolize the ephemerality of worldly existence and to describe a moment of beatitude, of oneness with time and nature, often associated with the moment of death.[23] The Punition Expert's introduction of the five dates of death is reminiscent of Chan Buddhism's description of death as transcending past, present, and future.[24] Yet the Punition Expert sounds more like a parody of Buddhist teaching when he tells the Stranger, "Actually from beginning to end, you were mired in the past. At times you might feel as if you were getting away from the past, but this is a delusion: apart in form, at one in mind. This indicates that you have drawn closer to the past" (P&P, p. 47). All the Punition Expert can offer is images of tearing apart, separation, and severance, followed by no inner experience. When he tries to refute historical narratives and reject the phe-

nomenal world, the Punition Expert stands for the incompetence and pretense of those who testify to humanity's deliverance to an ahistorical utopia.

MEMORY CRYSTAL-CLEAR

The Punition Expert's failure to arrive at the moment of redemption by de-
historicizing time is complemented by the Stranger's inability to process
time into experience. The Stranger cannot turn events to which he was witness into testifiable experience to which he can bear witness (in terms of
Walter Benjamin's famous distinction, his past remains in the form of *Erlebnis* rather than *Erfahrung*).[25]

The missing link in "Past and Punishment" is memory. Yu Hua's text refers only to the past and never to memory, as if the past cannot be contained
in the characters' memory. One is reminded of the remark in Borges's
aforementioned story: "*The Garden of Forking Paths* is an enormous riddle,
or parable, whose theme is time; this recondite cause prohibits its mention.
To omit a word, to resort to inept metaphors and obvious periphrases, is
perhaps the most emphatic way of stressing it."[26] In "Past and Punishment,"
a parable on searching for one's memories of the past, the word "memory"
appears only three times, never in direct relation to past events, and the
content of memories is never specified.[27] Neither of the two characters can
access his memories; instead, they command the past through acts of violence. The past always remains deferred and mutilated. If, as Ban Wang suggests, Yu Hua's stories are allegories for the resurgence of traumatic memories of the Cultural Revolution,[28] the memories keep reappearing in unassimilated form, forever displaced. The Stranger never achieves the moment
of testimony, when he would rescue his repressed memories and repossess
the past. "*Antihistory*" *is also antitestimony.*

"Past and Punishment" provides a vivid illustration of the gap between
what one goes through and what one can express of that experience in the
image of the transparent glass surface. For the final punishment, the Punition Expert intends to place the Stranger's severed torso on a glass table.
There is noticeable dissonance, and not only between the aesthetic preten-
sions of the punishments and the presumed pain of the executed man. It
may be worth noting that Yu Hua was trained as a dentist and would be
acutely aware of the implications of the neglect of anesthetics. Furthermore,
a contradiction exists between administering the punishment to a man who
remains conscious throughout the prolonged process and conducting the

procedure on a close-to-invisible surface. While the Punition Expert emphasizes the Stranger's experience and gives an elaborate account of what the
Stranger would see while slowly bleeding to death, it is also made obvious
that the glass table only gives the semblance of full visibility. The Punition
Expert tells that if he failed to place the Stranger's torso squarely on the table,
the latter would see up close earthworms "and worse." The table is made of
glass precisely to conceal the fact that the Stranger will not be able to look
through it. The glass surface, although part of the Punition Expert's aesthetics of awakening, in fact has an anesthetizing effect.

The glass table evokes an aesthetics of transparency that has its precedents
in modernist literature and art. One may gain insight into the significance of
this specific punishment by comparing it with three other glass contraptions,
imaginary and real. The first is found in Walter Benjamin's parable that likens historical determinism to a chess game played on a seemingly transparent table. An automaton seems to win invariably, but the game is manipulated by a little hunchback who hunches under the table, hidden by a clever
maze of mirrors. Only wishful thinking allows the spectators to imagine that
a machinelike determinism can generate a redemptive narrative from the
heap of random events called history.[29] The phantasmagoria of historical narratives relies on the make-believe of the diaphanous surface. Like Benjamin's
parable, "Past and Punishment" describes history as a rigged game. Benjamin
implies that the aesthetics of transparency not only hides the true agent but
also distracts the observers by the magic of placing the chess pieces as if
hanging in midair. History, it might seem, can be played without a board and
float in thin air. Yet whereas Benjamin embraces an alternative history that
relies on "dialectics at a standstill," Yu Hua refutes the transparency of the
instant. The Punition Expert, who dismisses historical determinism, also engages in sleight of hand and visual illusions.

Another glass object to which the final punishment may be compared is
Marcel Duchamp's sculpture *La Mariée mise à nu par ses célibataires, même*
(The bride stripped bare by her bachelors, even), also known as *The Large
Glass,* considered to be a key work of modern art (1915–23, now in the Philadelphia Museum of Art), which consists of an upright glass pane in which are
embedded objects made mostly of lead wire and foil. The glass-table punishment, too, is considered art: the Punition Expert refers to it as his
"creation" and "masterpiece" (P&P, p. 58) and presents it as an artwork. In
many respects, the glass-table punishment adheres to aesthetic principles
similar to those of *The Large Glass.* The Punition Expert uses techniques and

approaches well-known to modernist art. He seeks to redefine art, looks for new forms, and mocks accepted perceptions. Whereas *The Large Glass* encases objects in glass and claims that they represent the human form of "the bride," the Punition Expert's art goes a step further and like many performance art pieces includes a human body as part of the work. He juxtaposes the flesh-and-blood body with the table, a ready-made consumption product. When put together, the materials parody the genre of the sculptured bust, the effigy of a historical figure put on a pedestal. The artwork's message would be that for a certain price, namely, sacrificing commodities and human life, history can be made accessible here and now. The Punition Expert's work literally places the reality of life and the lifeless artifact on a temporal continuum, as the living body would turn into an inanimate corpse. *The Large Glass* and the Punition Expert's artwork both make use of the glass pane because it is a medium emblematic of modern aesthetics. The glass table stands for more than design chic: it points to how conceptions bleed into one another. The see-through surface functions as an invisible boundary that delimits the subject and at the same time connects it seamlessly to the room's space. It makes a clean cut, hiding in transparency the violence to the severed body. It gives the illusion that the torso can stand all by itself, that it has never been cut, that it does not hark back to a different state of being. The claim to an origin disappears, together with the lower part of the body, which is never mentioned again.

Moreover, *The Large Glass* denotes the confluence of space into time. Duchamp remarks how the glass is a plane that "emancipates" objects into "a four-dimensional perspective." The fourth dimension is associated with time, symbolized by embedded clockwork parts. The work captures time: "picture on glass becomes delay in glass," writes Duchamp.[30] Similarly, the glass-table punishment demonstrates in visual form the arrest of time. It is an artwork that literally proclaims its own death, a work limited to the instant of dying. The Punition Expert seeks to capture an instant that negates time. He shows an affinity with Western avant-garde artists who seek to represent the unrepresentable. Compare, for example, Jean-François Lyotard's description of Barnett Newman's sculpture *Broken Obelisk* (1961): "The work rises up in an instant, but the flash of the instant strikes it like a minimal command: *Be*."[31] The Punition Expert's artwork enunciates the command: *Cease*. As a death-work, it introduces an ethical challenge. The glass table foregrounds the tension between the aesthetics of immediacy and the ethics of negating experience.

Finally, the glass table in "Past and Punishment" bears a resemblance to—and is possibly inspired by—the punishment described in Franz Kafka's *In der Strafkolonie* (In the penal colony, 1916). In Kafka's story, a man is executed by means of a torture machine that slowly stabs the victim to death. The man is executed without trial, and the very verdict is proclaimed to him only through an inscription that the torture machine traces on his own body. Just before his death, the victim will decipher, "with his wounds," the sentence meted to him.[32] The torture machine is made of glass "[s]o that the actual progress of the sentence can be watched." "Past and Punishment" resonates with *In the Penal Colony,* not only in that Kafka's executioner takes pride in the aesthetics of his work, but also in his remark that the machine's "one drawback is that it gets so messy." Eventually, the apparatus breaks down, slipping from "exquisite torture" to "plain murder."[33] Disorder catches up with the aesthetics of death and proves that the executioner's claim to civilized punishment is a sham. Yu Hua seizes the theme of transparence in *In the Penal Colony* to stress the position of the witness who gains self-consciousness at the price of dying immediately afterwards. In Kafka's story, the executed reaches "enlightenment," but he will never be able to convey his newfound knowledge to those who watch him through the glass machinery. Likewise, the glass-table punishment in "Past and Punishment" is designed to benefit only the Stranger. Despite its clarity, the glass surface signals that the executed man's experience is limited to his own consciousness. The Punition Expert's artwork triggers various aesthetic visions in the Stranger's mind, but they are reserved for him alone. The spectacle turns absurd when the Stranger is both the object of the execution spectacle and its only audience. The punishments capture in parabolic form the paradox of all testimony to disaster: no one can testify to an event from which there are no survivors, to a cataclysm that kills its own witnesses.

RESIDUES OF REDEMPTION

Yu Hua twists the Hegelian model that places historical consciousness as a step in the narrative of humanity's self-realization. "Past and Punishment" portrays a bleak situation in which an understanding of one's place in time cannot, paradoxically, be attested to. The short story presents a variation on Lu Xun's parable of the iron chamber. As discussed in Chapter 1, Lu Xun's text describes a witness who can only speak to an audience that will die upon hearing his words. Yu Hua's parable is equally pointed—the only firsthand witness is also the victim of a slow and lonely death. Experience is hermetically enclosed in the paralyzed body and confined within the walls of a dying brain. The punishment raises a barrier to testimony made not of iron walls but of glass, the transparency of which emphasizes the illusory nature of communication between the witness and his subsumed audience.

The similarities between Yu Hua and Lu Xun—fellow natives of Shaoxing in Zhejiang Province—are striking. Both provide compact, paradoxical parables that challenge the promise of modernity and doubt the efficacy of public discourse. The resonance between the two writers has been duly noted—Li Tuo compares Yu Hua's revolution of literary language to Lu Xun's explosion of the Chinese idiom, and Zhao Yiheng points out the similarity between the two authors' construction of signification systems bursting with inner tension.[34] Yu Hua has recently acknowledged his debt to Lu Xun,[35] and Ban Wang regards Yu Hua as the antithesis of Lu Xun's redemptive vision.[36] Yu Hua is doubtless a worthy heir to the vision of the author shouting himself breathless. Reluctantly as Yu Hua may find common ground with May Fourth literature, his fiction takes up major themes in earlier twentieth-century Chinese literature. Inasmuch as Lu Xun turned out to be prophetic of the failure of literary testimony, Yu Hua's fiction looks back on twentieth-century Chinese literature and presents a parable about the writer's inadequacy at bearing witness to history.

If Yu Hua hesitates to acknowledge his affinity with May Fourth writers, it is mostly because the May Fourth critique of public discourse has been understated. Andrew Jones notes that "May Fourth discourses ... contain within them an inherent potential for social and political violence. ... Yu Hua's aestheticized brutality is ... a strategic response to this crisis of representation that seeks to render the inherent violence of representation manifest to the reader."[37] Yu Hua emphasizes the "crisis of representation"—which amounts, as I have argued, to a crisis of testimony—that was left inexplicit in May Fourth texts. The unabashed descriptions of violence, the failure to suggest any hope for an individual awakening or collective redemption—all these resonate with earlier dystopian visions of public discourse.

Yet dystopia also signals the hope that a different course of action might succeed, and in the end, "Past and Punishment" allows the Stranger to arrive at his destination. The Punition Expert hangs himself, a form of death he had previously considered "defiled" (P&P, p. 50), but he leaves behind a note saying, "I have redeemed this punishment" (P&P, p. 64). At least from his own viewpoint, the Punition Expert's death is meaningful and worthwhile.

At first, when the Stranger finds the Punition Expert's corpse, he feels that his past is lost forever: "for him to look at the Punition Expert was just like looking at his own past having hanged itself" (P&P, p. 63). The ending (as in *Oedipus Rex*) leaves the key to the story's meaning literally suspended. Yet soon afterwards, the Stranger finds the Punition Expert's suicide note, dated March 5, 1965, the same date to which the Stranger has been trying unsuccessfully to get throughout the story. What is the significance of the Punition Expert's death on the day reserved for the Stranger's return? How can one reconcile the Punition Expert's self-incurred death with the fact that it could not be a suicide (otherwise, according to his logic, it would not be "redeemed")? Is it that in dying and dating his death, the Punition Expert was able to redirect the course of time in the way desired by the Stranger, and that the death would therefore be "redeemed" as a sacrifice for the Stranger's sake? The story leaves space for a possible redemption, not only for the characters but for time itself, which is allowed to flow in concert with human will.

Moreover, the suicide note, as a text that attests to one's death and gives it meaning beyond the moment of its occurrence, introduces the possible redemption of historical consciousness and of testimony. To understand the importance of dating as a means of giving credibility to witnessing, one may recall Lu Xun's "Diary of a Madman." As discussed in Chapter 1, the Madman does not date his "diary," and his voice is reappropriated by the self-proclaimed friend, who adds a dated prologue. In "Past and Punishment" written messages—first the telegram, then the suicide note—attempt to redirect time and affect a return to historical experience. Where the telegram patently fails, the suicide note gives at least a glimmer of hope that the task might be accomplished.

"Past and Punishment" presents in stark terms a crisis of testimony rooted in the aftermath of the Cultural Revolution, while establishing a textual experience based on the absurd. By pointing out the flaws of both historical grand narratives and messianic time, Yu Hua makes a case for a literary discourse that does not directly reflect material events. Yet avant-garde fiction's radical break with realism sustained itself for less than a decade. As the next chapter shows, the postsocialist discourse would continue to be haunted by memories of the Maoist era.

9 Memory at a Standstill

From Maohistory to Hooligan History

The crisis of testimony seemed to abate in the market economy of the 1990s. In the postsocialist era, realistic memoirs, Wang Shuo's witty stories, and Qiong Yao's romance fiction shared bookshelves. To many survivors of the Cultural Revolution, the commercialization of literature and film signaled the bankruptcy of public debate, inasmuch as the younger generation was unwilling to shoulder the "sense of responsibility" that had dominated intellectual discourse since May Fourth. The film *Yangguang canlan de rizi* (known in English as *In the Heat of the Sun*, 1995) is a case in point. Set during the Cultural Revolution, the film depicts the bittersweet experience of a young boy growing up. Skirting the harsher aspects of the Cultural Revolution earned the film condemnation as indiscriminate nostalgia. The writer Feng Jicai, a veteran of "scar literature," has recently deplored the movie, saying, "I regret that the Cultural Revolution it represents has nothing in common with mine. Until now no film has truly represented the Cultural Revolution."[1] The film, based on Wang Shuo's (b. 1958) novella and directed by Jiang Wen (b. 1963), marks a rift between the generation of its creators and May Fourth ideals. The hugely popular Wang Shuo struck at the heart of the May Fourth legacy by criticizing Lu Xun, taking his prose to task for never developing beyond short stories and essays.[2] Yet the irreverent attitude displayed by Wang Shuo and his generation, and in particular their parody of Maoist rhetoric conveyed in fiction, rock music, performance art, and other media, provides a poignant, if humorous, social commentary.

In this chapter, I focus on *In the Heat of the Sun* and argue that its value lies precisely in skirting both nostalgic invocation and traumatic enactment in favor of regarding memory as a form of mythmaking. Cinematic fiction compensates for the failure of memory, as evidenced by Jiang's many allusions to earlier Chinese movies. Despite its seeming disinterest in offering historical testimony, *In the Heat of the Sun* provides a concise history of PRC cinema and demonstrates the power of films to reconfigure the past.

In the Heat of the Sun starts with the narrator disclaiming the reliability of his memory: "Beijing has changed so fast. In twenty years, it has changed into a modern city, and I can find almost nothing the way I remember it. Actually, the change has already wrecked my memories, so that I can't tell the imagined from the real."[3] From the very beginning, the film blurs the distinction between history and fiction. While the narrator tells of his experience during the Cultural Revolution, *In the Heat of the Sun* touches neither on that momentous political upheaval nor on the social turmoil of the period. Instead, the film disregards official history and weaves together memory and fantasy. Through its idiosyncratic form of narration, *In the Heat of the Sun* addresses the marks left by the Cultural Revolution on contemporary China and asks poignant questions. What has persisted not in collective memory but rather in individuals' recollections of the period? Can a true picture of the past be reconstituted, and should one allow fabulation to compensate for the shortcomings of memory? How should cultural production in late twentieth-century China wrestle with the lingering presence of earlier texts and images?

Jiang's attitude is to a large extent representative of his generation, which was too young to take part in the Cultural Revolution. He explores the collective memory from the vantage point of a man who came of age in post-Mao China. Jiang's career as an actor and a director is emblematic of the generational transition. For his (unsuccessful) audition at the Film Academy in 1980, he chose a scene from the film *Liehuo zhong yongsheng* (Living forever in the blazing fire, adapted from the revolutionary novel *Hong yan* [Red crag], 1965).[4] Soon after graduating from the Central Academy of Drama in 1984, Jiang played the male lead in groundbreaking films, notably Xie Jin's *Furong zhen* (Hibiscus town, 1986) and Zhang Yimou's *Red Sorghum*. Like Mo Yan's original novel of the same title, *Red Sorghum* debunks many of the heroic Maoist myths extolled in films such as *Living Forever in the Blazing Fire*. Jiang's choice of the novella *Dongwu xiongmeng* (Wild beasts, 1992) as the inspiration for the script of *In the Heat of the Sun* takes the film even farther away from earlier heroic models. *Wild Beasts,* written by Wang Shuo, is typical of Wang's playful depictions of disillusioned youth, a literary form that has been derogatorily tagged "hooligan literature" (*pizi wenxue*).[5] The irreverent treatment of historically significant moments in *In the Heat of the Sun* is a filmic equivalent of Wang Shuo's approach.

Although in retrospect *In the Heat of the Sun* is emblematic of artistic production in mid 1990s China, it at first took audiences by surprise. Jiang's directorial debut won immediate success in China and abroad, and *In the*

Heat of the Sun was acclaimed by major critics as the most important work in Chinese cinema since *Red Sorghum*.[6] Not only do the two films use innovative cinematic language, but, more important, both *In the Heat of the Sun* and *Red Sorghum* have changed the way key moments in China's history have been recounted. Whereas Zhang Yimou's piece counters earlier heroic portrayals of the war against Japan,[7] Jiang revisits the Cultural Revolution through the nostalgic eyes of a man who remembers the period as a time of thrilling street fights and sexual initiation. It is also noteworthy that *In the Heat of the Sun* alludes to the imagery of *Red Sorghum*,[8] and that Jiang's second film as director, *Guizi laile* (known in English as *Devils on the Doorstep*, 1999) was another controversial rendering of the war against Japan, in which he plays the anti-hero protagonist.

Despite its ostensible indifference to the human suffering associated with the Cultural Revolution, *In the Heat of the Sun* contains an eloquent criticism of Maoist rhetoric, or what Geremie Barmé calls "Maospeak."[9] *In the Heat of the Sun* readily rehashes phrases, tunes, gestures, and icons from the Cultural Revolution. Maospeak, having once made tragic history, reappears as farce, and as such gains a critical edge. *In the Heat of the Sun* is at its most scathing on the subject of the Maoist view of history precisely when the film resists the temptation to bear witness to the atrocities of the "ten years of turmoil." Accounts such as Ji Xianlin's and Zhang Xianliang's (see Chapter 6) share Mao's view of the writer's debt to history, whereas Jiang's film refutes the correlation between history and memory from the outset.

In the Heat of the Sun brings a sense of closure to the May Fourth project of formulating history through grand narratives. Writers from Lu Xun to Zhang Xianliang and filmmakers from Ma-Xu Weibang to Yang Yanjin have tried to relieve fiction of the need to act as objective testimony. Jiang Wen continues that task but further challenges the role of witnessing by questioning one's ability to tell truth from fiction. Whereas earlier texts and films, such as those examined in previous chapters, have largely entertained the readers' faith in the written word and the cinematic image as truthful records—if only to work against the grain of realism—*In the Heat of the Sun* assumes the audience to be as blasé as the narrator about one's ability to reclaim the past as real. When testimony breaks down, Jiang's narrator unapologetically picks up the broken pieces of evidence in front of the camera and nonchalantly strides on.

FROZEN MEMORY

In the Heat of the Sun is set in Beijing around 1970 and follows the fifteen-year-old Ma Xiaojun's adolescence. The protagonist's age is of major significance, since beginning with founding the Red Guards in May 1966, Mao called upon China's youth to carry out the Cultural Revolution. After the Red Guards spun out of Mao's control and engaged in armed fighting among themselves, as well as against military units, they were disbanded in the summer of 1967. Yet the experience of high school and university students continued to be an essential part of the Cultural Revolution after the Red Guards had been dissolved. Millions of youths were sent to the countryside, either to punitive camps or to "study from the peasants." Those who were too young remained in the cities—many of them separated from their Party cadre parents who had fallen out of favor, others secure in their position as the children of army officers—and were left to their own devices. Children, some underage, formed gangs, fought brutally, smoked, stole, and resisted all authority, even Mao's.[10] Ma Xiaojun (played by Xia Yu), the son of a high-ranking officer, leads just such a delinquent life on the fringes of the Cultural Revolution. He and his friends rarely see their parents, and their schooling is entirely devoted to a "revolutionary" curriculum, such as making wine. On the surface, at least, their adolescence is experienced as "sunny days," the literal meaning of the film's Chinese title.

Yet as the opening passage warns, those sunny days are as much a figment of the narrator's imagination as they are rooted in reality. Nothing is as the narrator remembers it, nor can he tell the imagined from the real. The present projects itself onto his memory and renders him incapable of knowing the past. This is best illustrated in the film's most striking sequence, which takes place at the Moscow Restaurant. Ma Xiaojun sits next to Mi Lan (played by Ning Jing), a girl whom he has befriended and introduced to his gang. Across from Ma Xiaojun sits Mi Lan's boyfriend, the gang leader, Liu Yiku (Geng Yue). Xiaojun and Yiku are celebrating their birthdays, which fall on the same day. Irritated by the bond between Liu Yiku and Mi Lan, Xiaojun takes out his anger on the young woman, then picks a fight with Yiku. Breaking a wine bottle, he uses the jagged edge to stab Yiku repeatedly.

Up until this point, some 100 minutes into the film, the story has been told in a straightforward manner and the camera work has supported a realistic feeling. Viewers may already have forgotten the reservations about memory expressed by the narrator in the introductory passage. Then realism breaks down all of a sudden. Xiaojun's stabbing motions are repeated so many times that the situation seems unreal. He continues to strike at Yiku, but the latter shows no signs of pain and looks around in amazement, as if he does not belong in the scene. The sound track is muted; it is as if Yiku has been pasted onto the set and exists on a plane where Xiaojun cannot touch him.

Next, the image freezes altogether and the voice of the narrator, the grown-up Ma Xiaojun, explains: "Ha-ha! . . . Don't believe any of it. I never was this brave or heroic. I have kept swearing to tell the story truthfully, but no matter how strong my wish to tell the truth, all kinds of things have gotten in the way, and I sadly realize that I have no way to return to reality." Memory finds itself at a standstill. The inability to capture the past—the impossibility of ever reconstructing the past as a reality—causes the narrative to grind to a halt; one is reminded of the Stranger's efforts to achieve a timeless experience in Yu Hua's "Past and Punishment" (see Chapter 8). The narrator in *In the Heat of the Sun* has tried to tell things as they were, convey history as it actually was. He must, however, beat a hasty retreat, while the past shatters into a still image, not a vision of reality but a resplendent cinematic mirage.

The editing renders the act of stabbing disaffected and even unreal. After the freeze-frame, the sequence is played backward in slow motion, and the images roll back until the spilled wine returns into the bottle. Xiaojun is shown again going through the futile motions of stabbing the unaffected Yiku twenty-five times. The viewer's initial shock turns soon into disbelief. In reverse slow motion, the languorous stabbings become more of a dance than an act of violence.

The sudden turn away from violence signals the narrator's reluctance to deal with the painful past. As already noted in connection with Ma-Xu Weibang's *Song at Midnight* and the model play *The Red Lantern* (see Chapters 3 and 4), Chinese revolutionary rhetoric has often used bodily injury to invoke a sense of reality. Violence signals the place where history hurts, and engaging in violence is tantamount to making history. In the restaurant scene, however, the bodily injury does not materialize. Filmic devices further accentuate the immateriality of the events by retracting the entire sequence. The young Ma Xiaojun is stopped, as it were, by his grown-up persona, the self-conscious narrator who cannot commit the story to the reality of violence. The freeze-frame draws attention to the surface, to the representative medium rather than the represented persons and remembered events. Once the false pretense of the first-person narrative is revealed, the narrator's voice—now skeptical and ironic—resumes.

THE POSTSUBLIME CONDITION

Significantly, the narrator fails to retrieve the past precisely as he is about to engage in a violent fight. When disclaiming his own account, he explains that he could not have been "heroic" enough to have picked a fight with Yiku. The term "heroic" (*zhuanglie*), used to describe a petty brawl, is not simply ironic. Understood in the context of Maoist rhetoric, it reveals an ambivalence toward the Cultural Revolution, during which "heroism" was used to refer to political and aesthetic ideals, especially as expounded in the model plays.

"Heroism" has often been cited as the main standard for evaluating the characters in the Cultural Revolution productions. Among the most "heroic" is Li Yuhe, the protagonist of *The Red Lantern*, who exemplifies the intransigence of the communist anti-Japanese underground. As noted in Chapter 4, *The Red Lantern* reflects Mao's requirement that revolutionary literature and art "can and must be more lofty, more intense, more concentrated, more typical, and more ideal than daily life,"[11] and Li's character reflects Jiang Qing's directive "to make this heroic image . . . more sublime."[12] When the narrator of *In the Heat of the Sun* explains that he "never was this brave or heroic," he admits his failure to take after the model plays—or the model plays' failure to become a viable model. Either way, the narrative freezes when Xiaojun tries to come to terms with the revolutionary paragon.

The narrator's inability to cope with his lack of "heroism" is especially poignant inasmuch as Xiaojun's generation of young Chinese aspired to be heroic and represented themselves as fearless fighters. Xiaojun often acts out a more heroic version of himself in front of a mirror. In one scene, he shouts into an imaginary radio: "Fire your artillery at me," imitating the hero of the war film *Yingxiong ernü* (Heroic sons and daughters, 1964). Jiang Wen's testimony about his own youth also refers to the pervasive images of heroism. Commenting on the Red Guards' response to the rhetoric of the sublime, Ban Wang argues that the youth of the Cultural Revolution found both an object of admiration and an identity for themselves in Mao and the state, which "because of their sublime qualities, were seen as an enlargement of [the Red Guards'] own selves."[13] Ma Xiaojun bears strong resemblance to Jiang Wen and Wang Shuo. Xiaojun's family, like Jiang Wen's, is from the city of Taishan; the novella's author and the film's director are of the same age as the fictional Xiaojun, and like him they grew up in Beijing, in the idiosyncratic environment of military family housing.[14] Jiang Wen says of his youth, "I don't know if I believed in Marxism, but struggle, or competition, stimulated and attracted me. . . . At the time, we believed what the 'Internationale' sings about: there has been no savior, and we cannot rely on gods or emperors. And I admired heroism and romanticism."[15]

Although the narrator, like Jiang Wen himself, looks back on the Cultural Revolution as his heroic days, he does so from the viewpoint of post-Maoist China, in which the revolutionary idiom has been discredited. The narrative breaks down, not only because of Xiaojun's failure to live up to heroic standards, but also because the remembering subject, speaking from his position in the mid 1990s, can no longer identify with the jargon and ideals of the Cultural Revolution. The attempt to explain his actions in terms of Maoist heroism aptly coincides with the moment when the realistic narrative stops in its tracks.

UNSPEAK, MEMORY

After the restaurant scene rewinds, Xiaojun's story is taken in another direction. The narrator acknowledges that the failure of his memory and his inability to record reality call for changing the story line. During the freeze-frame, the narrator continues to say:

My emotions changed my memories, which have in turn played with me and betrayed me. It got me all mixed up to the point where I can't distinguish between true and false. Now I suspect that the first time I met Mi Lan was fabricated. Actually, I never met her on the road. . . . I was never that familiar with Mi Lan. I never got familiar with Mi Lan. . . .

I simply don't dare think any further. I started telling the story wishing to be sincere, yet my determined efforts have turned into lying. I can't give up at this point, can I? No, no, I certainly can't. Are you going to be so heartless as to do this to me? Now I understand the plight of those people who make promises so well. It's simply impossible to be sincere.

Memory serves, not to recapture the events, but rather to obfuscate them and to silence the past that must be taken up by the storyteller. The narrator looks for objective history, but he must submit to fiction as the only way to retrieve the past. The resulting narrative is revised while being told. It is altered to the point where the viewers, like all readers of fiction, must suspend their disbelief when the alternative plotline resumes.

The restaurant scene informs the question posed at the beginning of this chapter, namely, what kind of history is yielded by the tainted recollections of the Cultural Revolution? What comes out of that frozen frame, the moment in which history and fiction are fused, confused, dissolved, and then supposedly resolved through a reinvention of memory? The sequence of freezing time, reversing it, and restarting the plot, I shall show, presents an image emblematic of the film's resistance to the Maoist vision of history.

Parodying the Maoist rhetoric of heroism and other dislocated Maospeak is part of an insidious way to counter Maoist formulations of the past, namely, by skirting official history altogether. Jiang's film stands in stark contrast to other accounts of the Cultural Revolution, which have focused mainly on the torture administered by the Red Guards and the painful experiences of sent-down youth. Such accounts provide important documentation and were written in hope of preventing the recurrence of similar disasters.[16] Yet these chronicles run the danger of achieving undesirable results. As Xiaomei Chen notes, survivor accounts published in English have curried favor with American nationalism and converged into a corpus of "China-bashing memoirs."[17] Within China, memoirs that identify personal experience with the collective upheaval might also end up perpetuating the Maoist discourse that subsumes individual will under the state, the same rhetoric that they set out to repudiate. In other words, firsthand chronicles of the Cultural Revolution are arguably the most conspicuous contemporary genre that ascribes to the pathos of what I call bearing witness *for* history.

In the Heat of the Sun refrains from such pathos and depicts an adolescence graced by dreamlike beauty. The political events stay at the fringes of the plot and do not seem to touch the adolescent protagonists (references in Wang Shuo's novella to incidents such as Mao's viewing of the Red Guards are excised from the film). The underage protagonists go through the Cultural Revolution spending their time like many of their counterparts in other places and times—bumming around, masturbating,[18] and beating each other up. The director explains the film's title at face value: "When one is seventeen or eighteen—that's the most beautiful time in one's life. One feels a fervor then, as in bright sunny days."[19] Jiang Wen does not, however, simply skirt the atrocities of the Cultural Revolution. By describing the period through Xiaojun's first love, the film avoids what Kundera calls the "Orwellizing" of life,[20] that is, viewing the Cultural Revolution through the single prism of political oppression. In this sense, Jiang's script follows Wang Shuo's fiction, infamous for foregrounding, instead of the heroic characters of "serious" literature, punks (*liumang*), hooligans (*pizi*), and smooth operators (*wanzhu*)[21]—hence its derogatory designation as "hooligan literature." Jiang, for his part, had portrayed Beijing punks in films such as *Benmingnian* (Black snow, 1988; dir. Xie Fei) and *You hua haohao shuo* (English title *Keep Cool*, 1994; dir. Zhang Yimou). Presenting simple quotidian events, *In the Heat of the Sun* reclaims the experience of the street-smart hooligans and resists the History of grand narratives. Jiang Wen's depiction of Xiaojun and his generation may, by analogy to Wang Shuo's "hooligan literature," be dubbed "hooligan history."

Critics have often dwelled on the pitfalls of referring to the time when many people were incarcerated, exiled to the countryside, and beaten to death as "sunny days." Huang Shixian, professor at the Beijing Film Academy, writes: "For many many Chinese, the summers of the 1970s were the darkest years of their lives, but for these pure youngsters, they were a bright, sunny vacation."[22] Huang observes that the Cultural Revolution provided youngsters with a rush of heroism and a sense of freedom from school and other institutional control, and that seen from twenty years' distance, the narrator's imagination might delude him into seeing only the bright side of the Cultural Revolution. The Taiwanese film critic Jiao Xiongping (Peggy Chiao) calls the plot "a spring utopia."[23] Geremie Barmé draws an insightful analogy between recent eastern European "totalitarian nostalgia" and what he calls the Chinese "CultRev nostalgia" and "retro Cultural Revolution" of the 1990s, in which context he puts *In the Heat of the Sun*.[24]

Unlike Barmé, however, I do not see the plot as expressing "real and vital nostalgia" and reaffirming a "sense of lost innocence."[25] Jiang's film presents a complex version of memory, one that shows nostalgia to be tainted by one's inability to remember things as they were. In so doing, Jiang follows the pattern established by Wang Shuo's novels. It is useful to compare *In the Heat of the Sun* to another film based on a Wang Shuo plot, namely, *Qingchun wuhui* (No regrets about youth, 1992), which portrays the new construction and demolition projects in Beijing as emblematic of the destruction of memory in contemporary China. By the late 1980s, the city has been transformed into a space quickly losing its spatial memory, an apt metaphor for the displacement of collective memories of the Maoist era. A similar sense of forgetting is invoked at the end of *In the Heat of the Sun*, where the grown-up Ma Xiaojun (played by Jiang Wen himself) is shown as a yuppie riding in a luxurious limousine through a new traffic junction in present-day Beijing. He tries in vain to invoke the past by exchanging words with the neighborhood idiot, who does not recognize him, and the film ends with the idiot's yelling an expletive at the nostalgic Xiaojun.[26] Against a present irreverent of the past, Wang Shuo and Jiang Wen present an equally nonchalant hooligans' version of history. Where memory is brought to a standstill, the historian is a smooth operator, sliding between fact and fiction and playing them one against the other.

THE ICONOLOGY OF MAOHISTORY

In the Heat of the Sun calls collective memory into question by presenting an account that comports neither with the authoritative lingo of Maospeak nor with the official chronicles of what may be called Maohistory. Yet what is at stake is not political dissidence that questions the hegemony of the CCP. Instead, Jiang Wen presents an alternative order of things and redefines the linguistic and historical frames of reference that supported Mao's authority.

The film contrasts the sanctioned rhetoric with the unseen side of the Cultural Revolution, for example, in one of the street-fight scenes. In this long sequence, Xiaojun's gang ride their bikes to retaliate against another gang. As one of the attackers, Ma Xiaojun hits a boy repeatedly on the head with a brick until he is wallowing in his own blood. Later a gang member admits that he cannot remember whether it was the right person. The senseless violence acquires an additional meaning in that the scene is accompanied by the music of the "Internationale." Played at official events (and in this case, at the end of the daily radio broadcast), the tune came to symbolize ideological rectitude. As I have already mentioned, Jiang Wen associated the song with heroism; in fact, the "Internationale" has long been a filmic trope for revolutionary martyrdom. Possibly taking their clue from Ding Ling's "Mou ye" (One certain night, 1932), in which revolutionaries sing the "Internationale" until they are mowed down by a firing squad,[27] films such as *Qingchun zhi ge* (Song of youth, 1959) and *Living Forever in the Blazing Fire* (which Jiang would use for his college audition) accompany the martyrs to the execution ground with the Communist anthem. In the musical productions *The Long March Chorus* and *Dongfang hong* (The east is red, 1965), as well as in the model plays *The Red Lantern* and *Hongse niangzi jun* (Red detachment of women), the heroes choreograph their steps in unison with the "Internationale." The boy's near death at Xiaojun's hands, by contrast, is far from the martyrdom at the execution grounds depicted in the Maoist productions. Whereas *The Red Lantern* is said to have followed the "Internationale" closely, and to have embodied its words,[28] the dissonance in *In the Heat of the Sun* is startling and in fact incensed censors, who demanded that the music be toned down.[29]

The fight scene illustrates the difference between Jiang's film and less critical nostalgic pieces. The model plays have enjoyed revivals since the late 1980s that offered little criticism of Maoist aesthetics.[30] *In the Heat of the Sun* irreverently reappropriates icons of the Maoist period. Among other charged symbols, it engages Soviet cinema in many spoofs staged by Xiaojun and his friends. Just as the street fight ridicules the "Internationale" and Xiaojun's fantasy mocks *Heroic Sons and Daughters*, the boys' reenactment of Vasili's death in Mikhail Romm's *Lenin v 1918 godu* (Lenin in 1918, 1939) fails to carry the original heroic tone. In the Soviet movie, Vasili risks his life and jumps from the second floor to thwart a counterrevolutionary conspiracy. When Ma Xiaojun and his friend act out the film stunt, they make a dangerous jump with no more of a heroic purpose in mind than to impress Mi Lan. As the critic Dai Jinhua points out, such references rely on the audience's familiarity with the cinema of the "Socialist Camp."[31] Jiang Wen uses the collective memory of spectators who have seen numerous replays of the Soviet film in a dubbed version to recast the audacious escape as a thoughtless prank.

In the Heat of the Sun joins the counterculture that has reread Marxist symbols, such as Cui Jian's "red rock music," which introduced sarcasm even into revolutionary songs. Instead of seeing the Cultural Revolution in black and white, the film partakes of the social critique that Barmé terms "the graying of Chinese culture."[32] Inspired by Wang Shuo's resistance through parody, the film undoes Maohistory by presenting alternative images to Maoist filmic iconology.

The first salvo against Maoist rhetoric is already fired in the introductory passage, right after the narrator admits that he cannot distinguish reality from fiction. He continues:

My stories always take place in summer. People expose more of themselves in the heat and find it harder to conceal their desires. It seems like it was an eternal summer then. The sun always had time to come out and accompany us. There was plenty of sunlight, too bright, washing our eyes in waves of blackness.

As already mentioned, the director stands by this description and equates adolescence with "bright sunny days," thereby rejecting the subjection of personal experience to the national narrative of suffering during the Cultural

Revolution. Yet the description of the period as flooded in eternal sunlight cannot avoid being interpreted in the light of the cult of Mao as the "Bright Red Sun." The unofficial anthem during the Cultural Revolution went: "The East is red; the sun has arisen; a Mao Zedong has appeared in China." Or, as the song in the beginning of *In the Heat of the Sun* says: "In the raging storm of revolution / The soldiers' hearts turn toward the sun / O Chairman Mao! Chairman Mao! . . . / Your brilliant thoughts have nurtured us like the dew and sunlight."[33] The adulating texts were known and sung by all. The title and opening passage of *In the Heat of the Sun* recontextualize Mao's personality cult in terms of raw emotions and reinterpret Mao's relentless light as the scorching of memory. Moreover, the depiction of the Cultural Revolution as a period of brightness becomes ironic when one recalls that the Red Guards would at times order incarcerated "counterrevolutionaries" to look straight at the sun, hours on end.[34] The consequent permanent damage to eyesight entailed that victims would carry the memory of their torture in the form of ever-visible blurs and black spots. Mao's sun was literally too bright, and the opening passage foreshadows the breakdown of memory.

A SKELETON KEY TO HISTORY

The "hooligan history" of *In the Heat of the Sun*, replete with tongue-in-cheek Maoist references that are nostalgic and scathingly critical at the same time, frustrates any attempt to pass final judgment on the Cultural Revolution. The very resistance to one-sided interpretation runs counter to Maoist rhetoric. As noted in Chapter 4, the revolutionary operas buttressed an aesthetics that left all authority over interpretation in the hands of a small number of ideologues and stressed the validity of their coding system alone. *In the Heat of the Sun*, on the other hand, reads Maohistory in multiple keys. It is no coincidence that Xiaojun often breaks into other people's apartments using a skeleton key. Wang Shuo's novella stresses the point: "This activity gave me strong evidence to refute a folk saying that verges on a truism: every lock has its key. In fact, with a few keys, one can open many locks, and with some patience and skill, countless locks—this is the case with the skeleton key."[35]

Xiaojun's habit is typical of the Cultural Revolution, a period when Red Guards invaded homes and disregarded their privacy, but significantly different in that the boy comes and leaves surreptitiously. His character resonates not so much with Mao's "small soldiers" as with juvenile pranksters such as Faye in Wong Kar-wai's *Chongqing senlin* (*Chunking Express*, 1993). He does not reappropriate the spaces outright but rather dislocates their usage to another key. While his narrative displaces Maoist metaphors, his skeleton key replaces social patterns and interpretative schemes within the film. Like the totalitarian state, Xiaojun lays claim to people's private spaces, but as the above passage accentuates, the key that opens every door is also the key that refutes truisms and that no figure of speech can withstand.

The skeleton key opens the doors to an alternative fantasy world for Xiaojun, to a place that is paradoxically truly his own. Yet the key brings him face to face with more mysteries he cannot sort out and more memories suspended between fiction and reality. Significantly, the most conspicuous of these memories involves another still image. Xiaojun breaks into an apartment (this time picking a Yuejin, or "[Great] Leap Forward" brand lock), where he finds a photo of a young woman wearing a red swimsuit. When he first sees Mi Lan, he immediately recognizes her as the woman in the photo. Yet when she invites him to the apartment, he sees a similar but different photograph, a black-and-white shot of Mi Lan in a white shirt, in the same spot. When Ma Xiaojun questions her, the young woman says that she never had herself photographed in a swimsuit.[36] Memories cancel out one another, inasmuch as Mi Lan is later seen wearing such a swimsuit. Moreover, in the restaurant scene that Xiaojun hurries to rescind, it is Mi Lan who presents Xiaojun with red swimming trunks. When the image freezes, the narrator also wonders: "Goodness! Is Mi Lan the girl in the photo? . . . I never really knew Mi Lan." Memories are unstable and given to interpretation in different keys. The frustrated Xiaojun yanks away Mi Lan's key from her ankle toward the end of the film, trying in vain to regain control over the narrative.

Even more than the freeze-frame at the Moscow Restaurant, Xiaojun's fickle recollection of the swimsuit photo signals the breakdown of memory and shows how the narrator compensates for his mnemonic deficiency through fabulation. In Wang Shuo's novella, the narrator describes his reaction right after seeing the photo: "In my imagination I couldn't help enlarging that standard-size photo to [the size] of a billboard. . . . By dusk I had already lost normal reactions to the outside world. Her image grew as large as my entire field of vision, and her expression intimated as much as my imagination could hold."[37] While the image looms large in Xiaojun's imagination, he envisions the actual woman as smaller than he finds Mi Lan to be when he first meets her in person: "her warm, voluptuous figure hung all over me, like the sunlight in which everything shows its colors."[38]

The distorted reconstruction of memories from absent or partial evidence resonates with earlier texts, from Lu Xun's preface to *Outcry* to Zhang Xian-liang's *My Bodhi Tree*. Yet the photograph scenes in *In the Heat of the Sun* demonstrate how experience has been remolded and memory reencoded through Maoist rhetoric. The infatuated Xiaojun shapes Mi Lan as a sensuous version of Mao, the object of adoration at the time. Like Mao, she is equated with sunlight, associated with red, and bigger than life. Wang Shuo's narrator as good as admits that his imagination was conditioned by the Mao cult. He explains that the photo made a striking impression on him, since "this was the first time in my life that I saw a color photograph of such realistic effect, other than those of the Great Leader Chairman Mao and his close comrades-in-arms."[39] Even in postsocialist China, memory is tinted in red and tainted by residual images of Maoist iconology.

In the Heat of the Sun offers itself as a way of reworking the past, of transforming the standstill of memory into moving pictures reanimated by present insight. To judge by Wang Shuo's comment on the film, the preproduction research had precisely that effect on the writer:

My impression had been that we were all pretty, pure, and healthy then [during the Cultural Revolution]. . . . Only when I saw the [period] photos did I realize that we had not been pretty, but rather swarthy and emaciated, our eyes dull and dogged, if not outright witless. I thought we had been pure, yet when were we pure? I couldn't find us as I had envisioned us.[40]

If Wang Shuo and Jiang Wen are nostalgic, it is because they cannot free the collective memory from the spell of past images but are aware of their compromised position, unable to create an idiom free of Maospeak and Mao-history.

In the film's last sequence, Ma Xiaojun and his friends ride a limousine in 1990s Beijing. The scene is shot in black and white, suggesting that the present too is only a faded memory, as flat as an old photograph. It is in fact the past, embellished by fantasy, which is brighter and more real. The grown-up Xiaojun, like Jiang Wen and his generation, cannot reassert collective memory. Together with the rest of China's economy, their memory has been privatized. "Hooligan history" openly gives up relying on reminiscence and reinvents the past as it goes. *In the Heat of the Sun* redefines all experience as confabulated, the result of a biased witness's unstable memory, fixed and frozen for a short while, only to be swept away by the flow of events and the oncoming flood of new images.

Epilogue

I have prefaced this book by noting that although the texts and films examined here fall into the category of "modern Chinese literature," they nevertheless challenge the definitions of modernity, Chineseness, and literariness. The present study may serve as a point of departure for remapping the twentieth-century narrative arts in China and reevaluating the critical practices associated with them.

The texts discussed rely on a resistance to grand narratives and even to narrative itself. The works portray modernity as a state of crisis that bars them from bearing witness to temporal continuity or historical progress. They also defy being identified with the Chinese nation-state, which is complicit in the Enlightenment narrative of humanity's self-realization. Finally, they call for an understanding of literariness based on acknowledging the author's inability to bear witness. Paradoxically, the belated, displaced, and fractured accounts signal the resilience of modern Chinese literature as a critical discourse.

There have been convincing reasons for focusing critical debate on defining modern Chinese literature as a distinct field of study. Until recently, academic research into twentieth-century texts needed to be defended. As Rey Chow notes, only a decade ago, hostility to poststructuralist theory prevailed in China studies.[1] Establishing modern Chinese literature as an object of study in U.S., Taiwan, and PRC colleges has gradually legitimated scholarly discussion, facilitated interdisciplinary approaches, and allowed a distance from crass political concerns.[2] Yet unlike eight years ago, when I conceived this book, few would now regard twentieth-century texts in Chinese as no more than a window to understanding historical events. It may be time to emphasize that historical and geographical parameters are not only reflected in literature and film but also tropes used deliberately by the authors to fashion—and often undermine—the literary discourse.

More attention should be paid to the unstable relation between texts and historical testimony. The current study could only give preliminary answers to questions that call for further inquiry. Given the parabolic strategy of authors from Lu Xun to Yu Hua, how does fiction resist historical interpretation that would reduce all texts to evidence of unambivalent truth? Allowing for the self-incriminating witness in Ouyang Yuqian's drama, Zhang Xianliang's diary, and Liu Daren's story, does testimony thwart grand historical narratives, or might it become complicit in mythmaking? In light of *The Red Lantern*'s purloined codes, can semiotic structures preempt ambiguous and purportedly subversive interpretations? Considering the turn to subjective visions in the films of the early 1980s, what role do inner landscapes of the mind play in preserving a distance between hermeneutic systems and the real? Bearing in mind the tension between concealment and revelation in Ma-Xu Weibang's *Song at Midnight*, what are the respective advantages of verbal and visual testimonies? Following the breakdown of narrative in *In the Heat of the Sun*, how do images and words compete for access to memory and undermine each other? In sum, what is it that makes literature and film bear witness against history?

REFERENCE MATTER

Notes

PREFACE

1. Lu Xun, "Zenme xie" (How to write), in *Lu Xun zuopin quanji* (henceforth LXZPQJ), 11: 13.

2. Su Xiaokang and Wang Luxiang. Xiaomei Chen, *Occidentalism*, pp. 27–48, discusses the ideological implications of the TV program.

3. Liu Binyan, "Renxie bushi yanzhi."

4. Anagnost, pp. 17–44. See also Charles Laughlin's discussion of the aesthetics of reportage writing.

5. Li Oufan, "Mantan Zhongguo xiandai wenxue zhong de tuifei"; David Der-wei Wang, *Fin-de-Siècle Splendor*.

6. Habermas, *Structural Transformation of the Public Sphere*.

7. Discussion of the public sphere is exemplified by articles in the Hong Kong-based journal *Ershiyi shiji* (Twenty-first century): see, e.g., Wang Shaoguang, "Guan-yu 'shimin shehui' de jidian sikao"; Yang Nianqun; see also Gan. For American scholarship, see Chamberlain; Gold; Rankin; Rowe.

INTRODUCTION: CRITICAL DISCOURSE IN
TWENTIETH-CENTURY CHINA

1. Chen Kaige, pp. 125–26.

2. Judith Zeitlin, for example, discusses how although Pu Songling's *Liaozhai zhiyi* (Strange tales from Liaozhai Studio) comprises accounts of the supernatural, his posturing as "the Historian of the Strange" was defensible by contemporary conceptions (pp. 17–34).

3. Plato, pp. 167–71.

4. Chen Kaige, p. 120.

5. Kundera describes "Kafkology" as privileging "the microcontext of biography" over "the large context of literary history," "[dislodging] Kafka from the domain of aesthetics" and turning literary criticism into an exegetical exercise (pp. 42–44).

6. Arendt, p. 3.

7. See Anagnost, p. 19.

8. Lévinas.

9. Freud, *Beyond the Pleasure Principle*.

10. Caruth, *Unclaimed Experience*, p. 18.

11. Freud, "Thoughts for the Times on War and Death," in *Standard Edition*, 14: 279.

12. Adorno, p. 362.

13. Lyotard, p. 364.

14. Xiaobin Yang.

15. Caruth, *Unclaimed Experience*, pp. 91–112.

16. My argument here, and much throughout the book, is indebted to Felman and Laub's exploration of testimony.

17. Kant, "What Is Enlightenment?" in *On History*.

18. Foucault, "What Is Revolution?" in *The Politics of Truth*, p. 84 (original emphasis).

19. White, p. 11.

20. Horkheimer and Adorno, p. 6.

21. Foucault, "What is Critique?" in *Politics of Truth*, p. 32.

22. Habermas, *Theory of Communicative Action*, 2: 208.

23. Foucault, "The Ethics of the Concern of the Self as a Practice of Freedom," in *Ethics: Subjectivity and Truth*, p. 298.

24. Foucault, *Archaeology of Knowledge*, p. 55.

25. Chen Kaige, p. 126.

26. Kant, for example, deplored that "the whole Oriental nonsense … set a stumbling block for reason," and Max Weber claimed that modernity could not have taken place without "Occidental rationalism" (quoted in Zammito, p. 39); see also Habermas, *Philosophical Discourse of Modernity*, p. 1.

27. Duara, pp. 17–50.

28. I follow the encompassing definition of May Fourth offered by Tse-tsung Chow, pp. 1–6.

29. Kant, "What Is Enlightenment?" in *On History*, p. 5.

30. Judge.

31. The analogy to the Emancipation is made clear in a 1919 essay by Jiang Menglin, quoted in Tse-tsung Chow, p. 338.

32. Luo, p. 231.

33. Habermas, *Structural Transformation of the Public Sphere*, pp. 31–43.

34. Quoted in Wang Yao, pp. 25–26.

35. Wang Hui, *Wudi panghuang—wusi ji qi huisheng*, pp. 21–50.

36. Hsia, p. 536.

37. Kant, *Critique of Judgment*, pp. 82–85.

38. For a discussion of the term "belated modernity" and its implications for Chinese literature, see David Der-wei Wang, *Fin-de-Siècle Splendor*, pp. 6–17.

39. LXZPQJ, 7: 26. See also Leo Ou-fan Lee's account of Lu Xun's aversion to the crowd (*Voices from the Iron House*, pp. 69–88).

40. Camus, p. 124.

41. Weber, p. 181.

42. Li Dazhao, "'Jin' yu 'gu'" ("Now" and "antiquity") (1923), in *Li Dazhao xuanji*, p. 446.

43. Lu Xun, "Lun 'di sanzhong ren'" (On "the third category"), in LXZPQJ, 14: 25–32.

44. Mao Zedong, *Mao Zedong zhuzuo xuandu*, 2: 553–554.

45. Link, esp. pp. 56–103.

46. Zhang Xianliang, "Lao zhaopian."

47. Quoted in Xudong Zhang, p. 46.

48. Gan.

49. Xudong Zhang, p. 4.

50. Liu Suola, p. 122.

51. Jones, "Violence of the Text," p. 574.

CHAPTER 1. DREAMING A CURE FOR HISTORY

1. Lu Xun, "Ting shuo meng" (Listening to dreams), in LXZPQJ, 14: 72.

2. For an overview of Lu Xun studies, see the hefty compilation *1919–1983 Lu Xun yanjiu xueshu lunzhu ziliao huibian* (ed. Zhongguo shehui kexueyuan wenxue yanjiu-suo Lu Xun yanjiu shi); issues of the journal *Lu Xun yanjiu yuekan* (Lu Xun studies monthly); and the more recent *Shei tiaozhan Lu Xun* (ed. Chen Shuyu).

3. Mao endorses Lu Xun in his "Yan'an Talks" (*Mao Zedong zhuzuo xuandu*, 2: 555). For a summary of Maoist rhetoric on Lu Xun, see Pusey, pp. 140–48. The sources for the Hsia–Průšek debate are reproduced in Průšek, pp. 195–266. See also Paul Foster's survey of Lu Xun's fluctuating reputation in response to his rumored candidacy for the Nobel Prize.

4. David Der-wei Wang, "Lu Xun, Shen Congwen and Decapitation."

5. For sensitive literary analysis of Lu Xun's writing, see Feuerwerker; Huters; Larson, *Literary Authority and the Modern Chinese Writer*; Ban Wang; Yue. Lu Xun studies also benefited from Fredric Jameson's concern with the nomenclature of "modernism," taken up by his student, Xiaobing Tang (pp. 49–73). On the other hand, some PRC writers were inspired to claim that Lu Xun was self-Orientalizing; a debate was stirred by such a claim made by prominent author Feng Jicai in his essay of 2000, "Lu Xun de gong he 'guo'" (Lu Xun's achievements and "mistakes"), re-printed in Chen Shuyu, pp. 403–29.

6. For sources on the "de-deification" of Lu Xun, see the articles reprinted in Chen Shuyu, pp. 93–137.

7. Liu Zaifu.

8. Wang Hui, *Fankang juewang*; Wang Hui, *Wudi panghuang*.

9. See Pusey, pp. 148–52.

10. Wang Xiaoming, for example, states that "the beliefs of an Enlightenment thinker are always based on his confidence in his role as an Enlightenment person. As soon as this confidence is shaken, he starts doubting the ideal of the Enlightenment altogether. Thus, Lu Xun's despair of himself . . . aroused unconscious doubts about China's progress toward Enlightenment": Wang Xiaoming, "Shuangjia mache de qingfu," p. 3. See also Qian's reference to Lu Xun's "emotional complexes" (p. 116).

11. Li Tuo, "Haiwai Zhongguo zuojia taolun hui jiyao." For a discussion of Li's article, see Xudong Zhang, pp. 113–20.

12. Lee, *Voices from the Iron House*, p. 65.

13. Lu Xun's canonized fiction begins with "Kuangren riji" (Diary of a madman, 1918). His noteworthy publications prior to this short story include four essays, later reprinted in *Fen* (Grave, 1925), and one short story, "Huaijiu" (Nostalgia, 1913). His literary publications in fact date as far back as to 1898, long before his studies in Ja-

pan. For a detailed bibliography, see Shen. On Lu Xun's intellectual development during the decade after leaving Sendai, see Gálik.

14. Foucault, *Discipline and Punish*, p. 33.

15. David Der-wei Wang, "Lu Xun, Shen Congwen and Decapitation."

16. The formulation of nationhood as arising at the expense of the individual subject was not foreign to Lu Xun, who already in "Moluo shi li shuo" (On the power of Mara poetry, 1908) referred to Byron, Nietzsche, and Darwin to support the claim that civilization emerges from resistance, struggle, and blood (LXZPQJ, 6: 63–121). It is also in "On the Power of Mara Poetry" that Lu Xun claims that he wants to shock readers out of their complacency (LXZPQJ, 6: 72).

17. Sontag, p. 86.

18. Barthes, *Camera Lucida*, p. 32.

19. Lu Xun, "Lun zhaoxiang zhi lei" (On kinds of photography), in LXZPQJ, 6: 206.

20. These details appear in an 1860 photograph, reproduced in Chen Shen et al. (p. 55) and in a photograph discovered by Ōta Susumu and reproduced in Lydia Liu, p. 62.

21. My reading owes to Roland Barthes's discussion of the *punctum* in *Camera Lucida*, which has led Gang Yue to similar conclusions. In his recent book *The Mouth That Begs*, Yue offers an important reading of the spectacle in Lu Xun's work and argues that the narrators often work out an oral anxiety through visual regimes. Thus in the slide scene, "the real center of the 'show'—the murder—is obscured; the historical experience lays itself into a battle between the wounded self and his fellow viewers" (p. 83).

22. Rey Chow, *Primitive Passions*, p. 7.

23. When associating colonialism with the spectacle, Lu Xun comes surprisingly close to Fanon's observation that "I cannot go to a film without seeing myself" (p. 140). Lu Xun recounts how going to the movie theaters in Shanghai, teeming with elegant foreigners, he becomes a "lowly Chinaman" (LXZPQJ, 15: 150). For further readings of the slide scene, see also Larson, *Literary Authority and the Modern Chinese Writer*, p. 99.

24. Canetti, p. 30.

25. See Lydia Liu, p. 62. Identifying the slide has become a major pastime for Lu Xun scholars. PRC scholars have collected pictures from the Russian-Japanese war (reproduced in Li Helin, 1: 168–70), but their heroic imagery is incongruent with Lu Xun's description. Jay Leyda offers stills from a film shot during the war (p. 13 and plate 3a). Yang Ze, in an unpublished paper, presents a photograph that comports with Lu Xun's description in every detail except for the date, 1860, and refers also to the pictures of the assassination of the Manchu prince that became well-known in the West after Georges Bataille reproduced them in his *Les larmes d'Éros* (1961).

26. Rey Chow, *Primitive Passions*, p. 11 (original emphases).

27. Sontag, p. 149.

28. Ibid., p. 19.

29. On Lu Xun's writing habits, see Xu Guangping, pp. 76–79.

30. The affinity between the parable of the iron chamber and "father's illness" has curiously been little commented on, with the exception of Spence (p. 145).

31. On Lu Xun's portrayal as a realist, see Tang, p. 51.

32. Qian, pp. 141–42. For an example of Lu Xun's use of Petöfi's line, see LXZPQJ, 3: 25–28.

33. Dostoevsky writes: "So, perhaps, a man who has been buried alive in his coffin and who has woken up in it hammers on its lid and struggles to throw it open, although of course his reason tells him that all his efforts will be in vain. But this is not a matter of reason; rather it is one of convulsions" (p. 110).

34. In another variation on the parable, the narrator in Lu Xun's "Si hou" (After dying) can observe things while being nailed in a coffin: "Too bad it's been a long time since I had paper and brush; even if I had them, I wouldn't be able to write; and even if I wrote, I would have no place to publish" (LXZPQJ, 3: 72).

35. Lu Xun returns to the same gesture in other stories as well. In "Chang ming deng" (The ever-burning lamp, 1925), Lu Xun tells of a madman who, irritated by his fellow villagers' veneration of it, seeks to put out a lamp that is kept burning continuously in the local temple. When he is shut out of the temple, he proposes to burn it down, and the villagers lock him up in its wing. Like the Madman, the protagonist fashions himself as the would-be instrument of a redemptive secularism. Like the Madman, too, he is locked up in the structure he has set out to destroy (LXZPQJ, 2: 67–81).

36. Karl Marx, quoted in Benjamin, *Gesammelten Schriften*, 5: 570.

37. Carolyn T. Brown, p. 76.

38. See Sontag, pp. 167–68.

39. Karl Marx, "Contribution to the Critique of Hegel's Philosophy of Law," in Marx and Engels, 3: 175.

40. Wang Hui, *Fankang juewang*, p. 40.

41. See, e.g., Gang Yue's observation, in an otherwise perceptive and insightful book, that the Madman's narrative "culminates in his seeing through the book of 'Confucian Virtue and Morality'" (p. 78).

42. Gogol, p. 24. In fact, although Gogol's text employs diarylike dating, the title should be properly translated as "Notes of a Madman."

43. Patrick Hanan, for example, claims that "[t]he relationship is important in terms of form … but that is all … any comparison of the two stories is likely to dwell on the differences rather than the similarities" (p. 66).

44. Holquist, *Dostoevsky and the Novel*, pp. 22, 27.

45. Tang.

46. Gogol, p. 22.

47. Ibid., p. 21.

48. Holquist, *Dostoevsky and the Novel*, p. 25.

49. Gogol, p. 21.

50. In the Taiwanese edition on which my references are based, the prologue comes after the text of the diary; this deviates from the original versions of 1918 and 1923.

51. Gogol, p. 21.

52. Huters, p. 281.

53. As Xiaobing Tang notes, the Madman's insanity is denoted by the word *kuang*, identifying his insanity with a Nietzschean self-affirmation (p. 58). However, Tang's claim that Lu Xun chose *kuang* deliberately over the more common term *feng* ignores the fact that Lu Xun's title uses the same characters as Futabatei Shimei's Japanese translation of Gogol's story, *Kyōjin nikki* (1907). In Japanese, the word *kyōjin* is the normative term for "madman."

54. Lu Xun, "'Mou' zi de disi yi" (The fourth meaning of "so-and-so"), in LXZPQJ, 24: 81. Ironically, Lu Xun himself often employs the designation "so-and-so."

55. Dostoevsky, p. 26.

56. Kuriyagawa Hakuson, *Kumon no shōchō*, pp. 150–51, 155–56.

57. Andreyev, p. 27.

58. Lu Xun, in a letter to Xu Qinwen, quoted in Xue, p. 569. Lu Xun started translating Andreyev's story in 1909: see Shen, p. 14. On Andreyev's influence, see Hanan, p. 55.

59. Huters, pp. 276, 278.

60. Wu Yu, p. 580.

61. See Yan.

62. Perhaps more than any other work in modern Chinese literature, "Diary of a Madman" can serve as a gauge of the change in scholarly approaches. The first challenge to the dogmatic paradigm was presented in the famous debate between C. T. Hsia and Jaroslav Průšek, in which Hsia rejected Průšek's argument for Lu Xun's clear social position and argues for the ambivalence in "Diary of a Madman" (Průšek, pp. 195–266). David Wang implicitly continues Hsia's line and claims that "Diary of a Madman" introduces a model of paradox and heteroglossia to modern Chinese fiction: Wang Dewei, "Chongshi 'Kuangren riji'" (Reviewing "Diary of a Madman"), in *Zhongsheng xuanhua*, pp. 31–43. Fredric Jameson observes that Lu Xun's story "is profoundly discontinuous, a matter of breaks and heterogeneities, of the multiple polysemia of the dream rather than the homogeneous representation of the symbol" (p. 73). Xiaobing Tang has emphasized how the story "constructs a reality that it refers to and at the same time belies" (p. 61). For a list of recent Chinese publications on "Diary of a Madman," see Tang, pp. 62–63.

63. Pusey, pp. 152–60.

64. The remarks should be understood in the context of Lu Xun's intricate relations with the camp of "left-wing literature and arts." Lu Xun introduces his own work among others' in an anthology and refers to himself in the third person, thereby distancing this interpretation from his earlier work.

65. Ji, *Niupeng zayi* p. 85.

CHAPTER 2. REWRITING TRADITION,
MISREADING HISTORY

1. The concern with "national character" (*guominxing*, and in the 1940s *minzu xingshi*) may be traced to the more conservative "national essence" (*guocui*) movement, which introduced the issue of the transmission of culture in the 1910s (see Furth, pp. 30–32).

2. Shi and Luo.

3. Ouyang Yuqian, *Pan Jinlian*, in *Ouyang Yuqian quanji*, 1: 55–91.

4. Wei Minglun, *Pan Jinlian—Yige nüren de chenlun shi*, in *Pan Jinlian—Yige nüren de chenlun shi*, pp. 1–66.

5. For example, *Guben Shuihu zhuan* (The ancient text of *The Water Margin*) by Mei Jihe (1891–1969) circulated in the mid-1930s. This version rewrites the novel to stress egalitarianism and democracy. The playwright Tian Han wrote a dramatic version, *Wu Song* (1942), and Lu Qun's short novel *Pan Jinlian* (1987) stresses the psychological background and portrays her as the victim of a molesting father.

6. Borges, *Seven Nights*, p. 74.

7. Jin, pp. 390, 391.

8. See Rolston, p. 25.

9. Hu Shi, "Zhongxue guowen de jiaoshou" (High school instruction of Chinese literature), in *Hu Shi zuopin ji*, 3: 143–44.

10. Hu Shi, "Da Qian Xuantong shu" (Response to letter from Qian Xuantong), in *Hu Shi zuopin ji*, 3: 42.

11. See Ge, pp. 47–48.

12. See Hu Xingliang, *Zhongguo huaju yu Zhongguo xiqu*, pp. 76–95.

13. Ouyang Yuqian, "Wo zipai ziyan de jingju" (The Beijing operas that I directed and played in), in *Ouyang Yuqian quanji*, 6: 278. On Ouyang Yuqian's career, see McDougall and Louie, pp. 161–64.

14. Ouyang Yuqian, "*Pan Jinlian* Zixu" (Author's preface to *Pan Jinlian*), in *Ouyang Yuqian quanji*, 1: 93.

15. LXZPQJ, 6: 125. Lu Xun goes as far as to equate the oppression of women with cannibalism: "In ancient society women often counted as men's property; men could kill them, eat them—nothing was beyond men's power" (ibid., 128).

16. Ouyang, "*Pan Jinlian* Zixu," 1: 93.

17. For a discussion of the New Woman plays, see Zhou Huiling.

18. A similar phrase is used by the *Jin Ping Mei*; see *Xinke xiuxiang piping Jin Ping Mei—huijiao ben*, p. 1247.

19. Cixous, p. 43 (original emphasis).

20. In the Buddhist context, *ai* means "avarice" (see Lin and Gao, 4: 185). For a discussion of *ai* in premodern novels, see Tonglin Lu, pp. 11–13. Lu notes that despite the absence of a linguistic distinction, the novel *Dream of the Red Chamber* was the first to introduce the notion of non-carnal love. Neither was the distinction clear in Western literary traditions. St. Augustine, for example, eroticized the love of God, whereas troubadour songs spiritualized erotic love. It seems that the first consistent

attempt to divorce eroticism from love was made in the eighteenth-century novels of libertinage, which parody the allegorical use of lust.

21. *Xinke xiuxiang piping Jin Ping Mei*, p. 61. By the late Ming, vernacular fiction introduced "affection" (*qing*) as a more positive force that allows lovers to transcend the boundary between life and death and reunite. Evidence is found in Pu Songling's commentary to his "Xiangyu" (p. 1555). Yet unlike Ouyang's heroine's *ai*, *qing* upholds Confucian values.

22. Ibsen, p. 570.

23. When Ouyang was attacked in the 1950s for his "bourgeois views," the playwright Tian Han found fault with the play for vindicating a murderous adulteress (Tian, p. 138).

24. Ouyang Yuqian, "*Zhongwang Li Xiucheng* xuyan" (Preface to *Li Xiucheng, Loyal Prince*), in *Ouyang Yuqian quanji*, 2: 124. Ouyang's remark, written in 1941, should be read in the context of the war against Japan.

25. Wu Song is a *dutou*, or military troop commandant, and here assumes the judicial function of a civilian sheriff. This is in fact the only legal transgression he commits during Pan's trial. Wu Song's usurpation of authority may reflect the contested division of labor between the civil (*wen*) and military (*wu*) branches of government. On the status of the military branch in the period depicted in *The Water Margin*, see McKnight, pp. 191–93, 198–201. Wu Song's defiance of the law eventually leads him to join the outlaws at the Liangshan marsh.

26. Ibid., pp. 100–103, 453, 159; Ch'ü, p. 125 (although Ch'ü describes Qing court procedure, the law remained practically unaltered through dynastic changes).

27. The Pan Jinlian episode is finely wrought, featuring dialogues that stand out as some of the most lively in the novel. My impression is that Pan Jinlian's story stems from a now-lost drama independent of the outlaw plot. This observation is supported by Liu Jingzhi's study of Yuan sources of *The Water Margin*. The outlaws' story is told in many earlier plays, yet relatively few sources mention Wu Song. Even in those cases, Wu Song is considered one of the "tigers," i.e., outlaw leaders, and no source noted by Liu mentions Pan Jinlian.

28. See Kao.

29. The commentator of the popular Chongzhen edition of *Jin Ping Mei* emphasizes that Wu Song's righteousness is manifested in his act of revenge (*Xinke xiuxiang piping Jin Ping Mei*, p. 1244).

30. Ouyang's Pan Jinlian uses the phrase to defy Zhang Dahu's messenger (HWD, p. 352). Wei's Pan Jinlian sings it, too, when she defends her husband from bullies (HWD, p. 24). The original performance of Ouyang's play, in which the author himself impersonated Pan Jinlian, may have further emphasized Pan Jinlian's manliness.

31. Jin, pp. 391–92.

32. Wang Guowei, p. 17.

33. Ouyang Yuqian, "Xiju gaige zhi lilun yu shiji" (Theory and practice of drama reform), in *Ouyang Yuqian quanji*, 4: 63. Ouyang refers to Max Reinhardt's *Oedipus Rex*, the 1910 staging of which constitutes a milestone in twentieth-century revival of Greek tragedy, as well as to Barry Jackson's 1925 production of *Hamlet*, noted for its use of modern dress.

34. The first and last chapters of the novel, functioning as a frame narrative, clearly set up the plot as a retribution narrative and claim that the downfall of the Jia household stems from an unsettled debt between two immortals reincarnated as the protagonists Lin Daiyu and Jia Baoyu. Wang Guowei plays down the karmic motivation and emphasizes that the plot would not have taken place but for Jia Baoyu's tragic hubris, his primal desire to reincarnate.

35. Ouyang Yuqian, "Wo zipai ziyan de jingju." *Wheat-Cake Priory* is one of nine episodes from the novel that Ouyang rewrote into drama.

36. Quoted in Wei Shaochang, p. 145.

37. Wu Jianren, pp. 221, 57.

38. Ibid., p. 14.

39. Ibid., p. 41.

40. See Jin Shengtan, "Xu san" (Third preface), in Jin, p. 25. The debate about Song Jiang's "true character" was facilitated by the fact that Song Jiang was a flesh-and-blood man, mentioned in court documents, yet Jin Shengtan also devoted considerable attention to fictional characters, notably according special favor to Wu Song (Rolston, p. 36).

41. Rolston, pp. 191–225. Jin justified his editorial choices by writing a preface, which he attributed to Shi Nai'an, thereby construing an authorial intent. Rolston also suggests that "creating implied authors and readers" gives weight to the period in which a work is written and to the historical context of original reception (p. 105).

42. Ibid., 180.

43. David Wang, *Fin-de-Siècle Splendor*, p. 257.

44. Ouyang Yuqian, *"Taohuashan xuyan"* (Preface to *Peach Blossom Fan*), in *Ouyang Yuqian quanji*, 2: 439.

45. Ouyang Yuqian, *"Zhongwang Li Xiucheng xuyan,"* 2: 122–23.

46. Lu Xun, "Nala zou hou zenyang?" (And what after Nora leaves home?), in LXZPQJ, 6: 176.

47. Wei keeps referring to Ouyang's modification of Pan Jinlian's role. See, e.g., Wei Minglun, "Guanyu 'huangdan chuanju' chengwei yifeng xin" (About the letter entitled "Sichuan-style opera of the absurd"), in Wei Minglun, *Kuyin chengxi*, p. 355.

48. Ibid., pp. 354–55.

49. See Yuhuai He, pp. 30–37.

50. Wei Minglun, "Wo zuozhe feichang 'huangdan' de meng" (I am dreaming a very "absurd" dream), in *Pan Jinlian*, p. 68.

51. Quoted in Xudong Zhang, p. 46.

52. Xiaomei Chen, *Acting the Right Part*, p. 298.

53. A sampling among college students in the mid-1980s showed that only 2 percent of the respondents included Sichuan drama among their favorite operas (Deng, p. 504). The same period witnessed an overall decline of interest in Chinese opera (Hu Shijun, "Lun Wei Minglun de juzuo" [On Wei Minglun's drama], in Wei Minglun, *Kuyin chengxi*, p. 361).

54. Wei's playfulness may in some ways be closer to the experimental drama in Hong Kong and Taiwan. In fact, Wei's play was very successful in these countries, and plays such as Taiwan's Pingfeng Theater's *Taiping tianguo* (The Taiping rebel-

lion, 1994) betray his influence. The latter play displays a strikingly similar device of freezing history on stage and reassessing its ideological implications, only to acknowledge the inevitability of history.

55. The play, which follows the plotline of Akira Kurosawa's *Kumonosu jō* (Throne of blood, 1957), was staged at the First Chinese Shakespeare Festival in Beijing and Shanghai (see Ye Changhai, pp. 43–45).

56. Ouyang Yuqian makes a similar statement in his *"Pan Jinlian Zixu,"* 1: 92.

57. Wei Minglun, "Wo zuozhe feichang 'huangdan' de meng," p. 68.

58. Tony Tanner argues that in nineteenth-century European novels the theme of adultery foregrounds the force of social and legal norms (p. 14).

59. The epigraph of Tolstoy's novel, "Vengeance is mine; I will repay," foregrounds the question of who can be responsible for Karenina's death. *Anna Karenina* has also been read as a variation on the Buddhist retribution scheme: Harry Walsh discusses the possibility that Tolstoy was influenced by Schopenhauer and fashioned Karenina's suicide as a form of nirvana.

60. Green.

61. Wei Minglun, "Wo zuozhe feichang 'huangdan' de meng," p. 77.

62. Ibid.

63. Schopenhauer, 1: 322.

64. Ximen Qing's death as a result of being thrown out of a window in fact resonates not with *Jin Ping Mei* but rather with the plot of *The Water Margin*.

65. The retribution narrative is especially foregrounded in the first chapter of the Chongzhen versions; see *Xinke xiuxiang piping Jin Ping Mei*, pp. 1–4.

66. *Jin Ping Mei* tells how Ximen Qing dies after he takes an aphrodisiac overdose and Pan Jinlian fellates him dry of life essence. According to the retribution scheme's rule of correspondence in categories, Ximen Qing dies like his victim. Wu Song's brother dies of poisoning, and Ximen Qing too dies of substance intake; moreover, the description of Pan Jinlian crouching on top of Ximen Qing and sucking blood from his penis is reminiscent of the episode in which she sits astride her husband and stifles his last cries (*Xinke xiuxiang piping Jin Ping Mei*, pp. 1142–43).

67. Shan Yulian's tragedy may also be attributed to the repression of desire by CCP ideology. She and Wu Long are required to show allegiance to the Party by renouncing their love. As Yulian is "fought against," she is told, "Marxism-Leninism does not allow for any personal feelings!" Yulian is left with no choice other than to demonstrate her love by the act of dying.

68. Perhaps the most famous literary reference to enlightenment through remembering a former reincarnation is found in chapter 117 of *The Dream of the Red Chamber*, in which Baoyu starts seeing through "the veil of earthly vanity and illusion" when asked about his karmic provenance (Cao, 5: 302).

69. Abbas.

70. Cavell, pp. 327–28.

CHAPTER 3. REVOLUTION AND REVULSION

1. On Tian Han's change of name, see Luguang xiyuan, p. 3.

2. See Wang Yao, 1: 173.

3. Ye Di, "Yeban gesheng."

4. Cheng Jihua, *Zhongguo dianying fazhan shi*, p. 490.

5. Lee, *Shanghai Modern*, p. 114.

6. The quote is from Ye Shengtao's short story of 1926, "Yibao dongxi" (The package), in *Ye Shengtao wenji*, p. 147.

7. Yingjin Zhang, "Introduction," in *Cinema and Urban Culture in Shanghai*, p. 9.

8. Pickowicz, "The 'May Fourth' Tradition of Chinese Cinema," p. 301.

9. Luguang xiyuan, p. 8.

10. An establishing shot shows a poster, dated May 1926, calling for the reopening of the old opera house; the script also makes clear that the theater had been closed for ten years. If the poster were hung soon after the opera house was closed down, it would set the narrated time close to the date of the film's release.

11. The film refers to Danping's struggle against "feudalism," but identifies the hero as a member of the Revolutionary Party (Geming dang). The Revolutionary Party was an alias of the Tongmenghui (in full, Zhongguo geming tongmenghui), precursor to the KMT. This entails both an anachronism—the Tongmenghui changed its name in 1912, well before the time of the plot—and a logical contradiction, since Danping's ideology is clearly of a left-wing bent. Ma-Xu probably wished to appease KMT censors and perhaps also to appeal to the leftist sentiments of a larger audience than CCP supporters.

12. See Marston Anderson, pp. 18–19.

13. *Yingxi shenghuo* 1, no. 1; 1, no. 4; Ti Xiu, p. 8.

14. Chen Huiyang, "Ziwo zhi shanghen," p. 28; Du, pp. 97–98.

15. *Song at Midnight* and its sequel were remade several times in Hong Kong: Li Ying's *Song at Midnight* came in 1956, followed by *Song at Midnight* and *Song at Midnight, Part II* by Ma-Xu's protégé Yuan Qiufeng (1962, 1963); lately both parts were combined in Ronny Yu's *The Phantom Lover*. A PRC version also entitled *Song at Midnight* (dir. Yang Yanjin) was released in 1986. Other films inspired by *Song at Midnight* include Ma-Xu Weibang's own films, discussed in the main text, as well as *Qiu Haitang* and *The Haunted House*, Yang Gongliang's *Wanli xingshi* (The corpse that walked ten thousand miles, 1954) and *Guixia* (Ghost warrior, 1956), and the Taiwanese production *Gesheng meiying* (The phantom of singing; English title *Family Love*, 1970). More recently, John Woo's *Face/Off* (1997) shows the influence of Ma-Xu's film.

16. On the production of *Monster in Love*, see Gongsun, pp. 205–9. For a complete filmography of Ma-Xu Weibang, see Teo, p. 277. On Ma-Xu's late career, see also Chen Huiyang, "Chuanqi de moluo," pp. 58–63.

17. Ma-Xu attributed much of the film's success to the unique prewar circumstances that allowed him access to "ideal production facilities" (Chen Wei).

18. See Marston Anderson, pp. 27–60.

19. Hu and Zhang, pp. 110–14.

20. Chen Wu (Wang Chenwu), "Qingsuan Liu Na'ou de lilun" (Exposing and criticizing Liu Na'ou's theory), reprinted in *Wang Chenwu dianying pinglun xuanji*, p. 174.

21. See Brooks, p. 39.

22. Curiously, the same words would be used by Ma-Xu in a 1945 interview to describe his own undying commitment to filmmaking: "But my ambition to take part more directly in producing a film did not die" (Chen Wei). The fact that Song Danping has already been presumed dead twice also resonates with the Soviet literary model, which often depicts the hero as having risen miraculously from the ashes (see Katerina Clark, p. 74).

23. Curiously, *Song at Midnight* anticipates the 1943 Hollywood remake of *Phantom of the Opera* (dir. Arthur Lubin), where the phantom is a musician scarred by acid.

24. The voice on the soundtrack does not, in fact, belong to the actor Jin Shan but to the singer Sheng Jialun (see Lin Jinlan, "'Yeban gesheng' de gezhe," in *Yueye youyu*, pp. 166–68).

25. The dialogue also introduces homoerotic undertones, a theme outside the scope of my present study.

26. In *Haunted House* one also recognizes the master plot of *Song at Midnight*: Lingjuan's music teacher and lover Fang Qiufan bears a large scar across his cheek, a reminder of how he was brutally beaten by the young landlord, Chen. The double, Yuqin, begins by comforting a person gone mad and ends up avenging an exposed crime. The lover is duped by the double's song, as Yuqin imitates Lingjuan's singing, and Qiufan, thinking it is the voice of his dead beloved, comes in. The film concludes with a fire that burns down the mansion, while old Gao returns to his senses. At the end, Yuqin and Qiufan, standing shoulder to shoulder, look at the meadows on which Qiufan intends to build a music school for the benefit of China's children. The erasure of the scar is also the focus of the KMT-commissioned *Family Love*, set in the 1960s. A communist spy comes to Taiwan pretending to be Fenggu, the lost daughter of the Zhus. Unlike the true Fenggu, she has no birthmark on her nape, but after an accident a large scar forms on her cheek. Eventually, the spy dies and the true Fenggu returns to her parents; the brand of truth replaces the ugly scar associated with deception and ideological evil.

27. Leroux's Phantom, Erik, shares many traits with Dracula: he sleeps in a coffin, for years at a time; he is ageless and seems to be an animate corpse; he comes from the East but wanders across borders as he pleases (Leroux, pp. 123–24). Other important Gothic influences on *Phantom* include E. A. Poe's stories and the tradition of portraying the beautiful voice, especially of castrati, as evil and ultimately repulsive. Whale's film version of *Frankenstein* was influenced by Julian's *The Phantom of the Opera* and was conceived by the producer, Carl Laemmle Jr., as a follow-up to *Dracula* (dir. Tod Browning, 1931), released a year earlier. The Creature was to be played by Bela Lugosi, who performed the title role in *Dracula* (eventually, the role was given to Boris Karloff) (see Forry, p. 92; Blake, p. 244).

28. Shelley, p. 97; Leroux, p. 224. Julian's film takes up the theme in Erik's retort to Christine: "If I am the phantom, it is because man's hatred has made me so."

29. Some clarification was probably necessary, and in *Song at Midnight, Part II,* Xiaoxia explains: "I still love only one man, Danping."

30. Ma-Xu's grafting of Julian's and Whale's films illustrates the difficulty of determining the genealogy of Ma-Xu's film. The Hollywood scriptwriters also took liberties in rendering the original novels. The film version of *Phantom* changes Leroux's novel and portrays Erik as a heartless assailant who dies when Raoul rescues Christine. Whale's film changes the pessimistic ending of Shelley's novel and adopts Leroux's original ending, where the monster frees the couple and dies.

31. Curiously, when *Song at Midnight* is weighed down by its precedents, it ends up illustrating the implicit conclusion of Shelley's *Frankenstein*, namely, that modern literature cannot escape the path dictated by premodern texts. Michael Holquist notes how the reference to Prometheus confines Shelley's *Frankenstein* to the failure and suffering with which the Greek myth ends as well. Shelley's plot is subjected to its literary precedent: "Frankenstein is not only the modern Prometheus, he is only a modern Prometheus: his story is known before he acts it, his fate has been thought before" (Holquist, *Dialogism*, p. 94).

32. Quoted in Gatiss, p. 82.

33. After viewing *The Cabinet of Dr. Caligari*'s (1919) first American screening, the art critic Willard Huntington Wright claimed that the film "represents the inevitable line along which the cinema must evolve" (quoted in Skal, p. 38). On the role of horror in early cinema, see also Neale, pp. 50–55; Gunning, "Aesthetic of Astonishment."

34. Men.

35. See Skal, pp. 125, 137–38, 186–91.

36. Chen Wei.

37. *Xinhua huabao* 2, no. 2 (Mar. 1937).

38. "Kongbupian daoyan Ma-Xu Weibang shi xinli biantaizhe," p. 6.

39. Feifei.

40. Zhao Shihui, p. 270.

41. "*Yeban gesheng* guanggao niangcheng renming."

42. Zhao Shihui, pp. 270–71.

43. The Creature in *The Bride of Frankenstein* sees his image in the water and disturbs the water in dismay; in Browning's *Dracula*, the title character violently throws away a mirror held up to him.

44. A clearer example of how reaction shots establish horror film dynamics is found in Ma-Xu's later film *Haunted House*. When the nurse Lin Yuqin arrives at the Gao mansion, steps out of the car and enters the house, the camera follows her from behind and captures the faces of those who welcome her. Everyone she meets recedes, terrified by the sight; by the time the camera turns to show Yuqin's face—which is in fact beautiful and unblemished, but bears uncanny resemblance to that of the dead daughter—an atmosphere of horror has already been established.

45. *The Invisible Man* continues a major theme in horror fiction, namely, the fear that there might be nothing behind the mask. Leroux portrays the phantom's face as an abyss: "His eyes are so deep that . . . all you can see is two big black holes . . . and *the absence* of that nose is a horrible thing *to look at*" (p. 8). The original emphases are significant—the phantom's face is nonexistent yet visible at the same time. The

phantom's face is described as "Red Death's mask suddenly coming to life" (p. 125), referring to Erik's appearance at a dance ball in the guise of Red Death. The scene is taken straight out of Edgar Allan Poe's "The Masque of the Red Death." In Poe's short story, the prince who hosts the masked ball falls dead in front of Red Death, and when the guests try to seize the latter "[they gasp] in unutterable horror at finding the grave cerements and corpse-like mask . . . untenanted by any tangible form" (p. 273).

46. The coincidence of the spectators' and the protagonist's views of the scar follows Whale's convention and differs significantly from the exposure of Erik's face in Julian's *Phantom*, where Christine sees the face only after the film spectators can see it. Ma-Xu's editing conforms with Linda Williams's observation that in horror films, the camera identifies with the male characters. Julian's sequence deprivileges Christine and prepares the audience to watch the reaction of the female face (Williams, pp. 564–67).

47. Gunning, *D. W. Griffith*, p. 41.

48. The Soviet master plot ends with a funeral or visiting the graves of the fallen heroes (see Katerina Clark, p. 259).

49. Shelley (p. 57) and Leroux (p. 125) also describe the monster's face as an animate skull.

50. On the controversies around the Shanghai Painting Academy, see Zhu and Chen, pp. 50–62.

51. See Wu Hao, p. 72.

52. The connection between the scar's horror and the love story is emphasized in Ronny Yu's recent *The Phantom Lover*. Keeping to the conventions of Hong Kong cinema, Yu's film further privileges the romance over the political plot by depicting the revolutionary opera *Warm Blood* as a box-office failure soon replaced by *Romeo and Juliet*, which becomes a hit. Yu's choice of *Romeo and Juliet* as Song Danping's trademark performance enhances the plot of Ma-Xu's *Part II*, which—like Shakespeare's play—is a tale about lovers who are hindered from seeing each other in living effigy and are united only in death (see also references to *Romeo and Juliet* in Leroux, p. 95). In *The Phantom Lover*, the lovers reunite to live happily ever after. Yu's film unreservedly states the power of theater to nourish love, ignoring the obstacles to transmitting ideology as presented in Ma-Xu's film.

53. Chen Huiyang, "Ziwo zhi shanghen—lun Ma-Xu Weibang" (The scar of the id—on Ma-Xu Weibang), in *Mengying ji*, pp. 25–40.

54. Berman, p. 110.

55. Žižek, pp. 63–64.

56. See Sterrenburg; Paulson; Botting.

57. Žižek, p. 62. Whale's horror films, which were produced after he had directed a number of war films, also allude to historical trauma. In *The Old Dark House*, for example, one of the characters is asked whether he was "knocked about a bit by the war" and answers: "War generation, slightly soiled. A study in the bittersweet, the man with the twisted smile."

58. Whale took the torch chase from Julian's *Phantom* and employed it consistently in his films. In *Frankenstein*, the mob follows the Creature to a hilltop wind-

mill and sets it on fire; in *The Invisible Man*, the invisible mad scientist is burned out of his hiding place; in *The Old Dark House*, visitors to an old house are warned of a pyromaniac locked in the attic.

59. Canetti, p. 22.

60. Marx and Engels, 6: 481.

61. Ibid., 35: 83. Translation modified according to Buck-Morss, p. 399.

62. See Crary, p. 136.

CHAPTER 4. THE PURLOINED LANTERN

1. Ban Wang.

2. See esp. Dai Jiafang.

3. See McDougall and Louie, pp. 205–6; Dai Jiafang, p. 27.

4. According to Dai Jiafang, the conference was originally intended to curb Mao's and Jiang Qing's influence on the arts, although it soon backfired on its organizers (p. 14).

5. See Dai Jiafang, pp. 28–30.

6. See Mowry, pp. 14–20.

7. Ban Wang, p. 214.

8. See Mowry, pp. 60, 113; Dai Jiafang, p. 42.

9. See Dai Jiafang, pp. 11–14.

10. See ibid., pp. 48–49.

11. See ibid., pp. 23–25.

12. For a synopsis of the various sources in Chinese, see Xiaomei Chen, *Acting the Right Part*, pp. 134–36.

13. Zhongguo jingjutuan *hongdeng ji juzu*, p. 17.

14. See Dai Jiafang, pp. 46–47, 266–68.

15. See Mowry, p. 21; Dai Jiafang, p. 152.

16. Ling and Xia, p. 86. For Chinese viewers, the film's title would invoke the full phrase (*qianpu houji, zi you hou lairen*).

17. All casting details refer to the 1970 film. At Jiang Qing's suggestion, Qian changed his name to Hao Liang and is credited by this name (see Dai Jiafang, p. 267).

18. On political criminal fiction in Maoist China, see Kinkley, pp. 243–56.

19. See Xiaomei Chen, *Acting the Right Part*, p. 135.

20. *The Invisible Battlefront* clearly aimed at raising proletarian awareness (or fanning a popular panic). Yin Xiquan, a Shanghai railway worker who participated in a special discussion session, is quoted as saying: "At the time . . . I thought that the [KMT] intelligence couldn't get in, but after listening to everybody talk today, I believe that it's extremely dangerous" (Gao, p. 24). The film also facilitates the task of the Public Security Bureau by portraying its workers as the new brand of fighters. As a contemporary review suggests, "This film also tells us how the workers for the public safety of the people are doing a selfless job" (Yang Fan, p. 2).

21. Yin and Xie, p. 117.

22. Niu, p. 104.

23. Nan, p. 50; Fudan daxue "wu-qi" wenliao xiezuo zu, p. 154.

24. Zhong Shan, p. 14.

25. Tong Ping, p. 121.

26. Quoted in Lan Yang, p. 29. The theory of the Three Prominences was first expounded in May 1968 by Yu Huiyong, then minister of culture, and later standardized by Yao Wenyuan.

27. Niu, p. 106.

28. Yin and Xie, p. 113.

29. The scene had also been integrated, in shorter form, into the revolutionary musical *Dongfang hong* (The east is red, 1965).

30. Qian Haoliang, "Suzao gaoda de wuchanjieji yingxiong xingxiang" (Creating images of sublime proletarian heroes), quoted in Lan Yang, p. 29.

31. Kant, *Critique of Judgment*, pp. 109–34.

32. Hong Feng, pp. 35–36.

33. Ban Wang.

34. Hong Xin, p. 175.

35. For a discussion of the Yan'an Talks, see McDougall and Louie, pp. 194–96.

36. *Mao Zedong zhuzuo xuandu*, pp. 550, 547.

37. See Mowry, p. 29.

38. Quoted in ibid., p. 21.

39. Zhongguo jingjutuan *Hongdeng ji jutuan*, p. 5.

40. Yin and Xie, p. 110. See also Tong Ping.

41. Ban Wang, p. 204.

42. Zhongshan daxue geming weiyuanhui xiezuo zu, p. 70.

43. Yin and Xie, pp. 113, 115.

44. Fudan daxue "wu-qi" wenliao xiezuo zu, p. 151.

45. *The Urgent Letter*, the second children's film produced in the PRC, won the Culture Ministry's third prize for films from 1949 to 1955 and a prize at the Edinburgh Festival of 1955 (see Cheng Shu'an, pp. 150–53).

46. Jiang and Cheng.

47. The plot is purportedly based on the true story of Li Bai; for a short hagiography of Li, see the account of Sun Daolin (p. 13), the actor who played Li Xia.

48. Criticism of the film also expressed unease about the premarital relationship between Li Xia and his partner ("Lishi liang dami, aiqing yi gushi"; "Zhenshi, qinqie, ganren"). The film enjoyed a revival in 1978.

49. Niu, p. 108.

50. Li Qun, "Lun yishu jiagong" (On the creation of art), quoted in Galikowski, p. 165.

51. Ding Xuelei, p. 19.

52. Hong Xin, p. 170.

53. Yin and Xie, p. 110.

54. Hong Feng, p. 37.

55. Jiang Yibing, p. 148.

56. Ding Xuelei, p. 24.

57. Jiang Yibing, p. 148.

58. Ibid.

59. Niu, pp. 104, 105.

60. Ren, pp. 39–40.

61. Ling and Xia, p. 76.

62. Ding Xuelei, p. 27; see also Tong Yun's claim that the theme of the three generations in *The Red Lantern* exemplifies the communist call for the proletariat to unite (pp. 97–105).

63. Xiaomei Chen, *Acting the Right Part*, pp. 128–37.

64. Ling and Xia, p. 69.

65. Ibid., p. 61.

66. Niu, p. 107.

67. Ling and Xia, pp. 83–84.

68. For interpretations of Poe's short story, see Muller and Richardson.

69. Chu, p. 130.

CHAPTER 5. A BLINDING RED LIGHT

1. Lu Xun, "Li lun" (Establishing an opinion), in LXZPQJ, 3: 67–68.

2. Berry, p. 2.

3. See Pickowicz, "Popular Cinema and Political Thought in Post-Mao China," p. 40.

4. Films focusing on the theme of love included, among others, *Tamen zai xiang'ai* (They're in love, 1980; dir. Qian Jiang and Zhao Yuan), *Bushi weile aiqing* (Not for love's sake, 1980; dir. Yin Xianglin) and *Bei aiqing yiwang de jiaoluo* (The corner forsaken by love, 1981; dir. Zhang Qi and Li Yalin). For a perceptive survey of the genre, see Louie.

5. The film may also sound a subversive chord by placing the lovers' romantic encounter in Lushan, a place associated with recent political events—as the location of party plenums, Lushan witnessed Mao's denunciation of Peng Dehuai in 1959 (largely considered the prelude to the Cultural Revolution) and Lin Biao's ascension to power in 1970.

6. See Paul Clark, pp. 167–72. For the script and related documents, see the bilingual edition, *Unrequited Love*.

7. Zhang and Li.

8. Ibid., pp. 10–11.

9. For extensive surveys of Chinese cinema in the early 1980s, see Berry; Xi, pp. 353–446; Shu, pp. 158–228.

10. On the Lu Xun revival of 1979, see Spence, pp. 406–7. The cinematic interest in Lu Xun's story foreshadows the productions of 1981, when in celebration of his 100th anniversary, three of his stories were made into films: *A Q zhenzhuan* (Story of Ah Q; dir. Cen Cang), *Yao* (Medicine; dir. Lu Shaolian), and *Shangshi* (Mourning the dead; dir. Shui Hua). They received mixed reviews in a debate that took place on the pages of the journal *Dianying yishu* (see *Zai Chuangzuo*, pp. 80–180).

11. *Mao Zedong zhuzuo xuandu*, p. 555.

12. Zhang and Li, p. 19; translation modified.

13. Yang Yanjin and Xue Jing, "Dianying meixue suixiang" (Random thoughts on film aesthetics), quoted in Ma Debo, p. 173.

14. Ma Ning.

15. Bai Jingsheng, "Guanying zagan" (Some reactions to watching a film), quoted in Ma Debo, p. 174.

16. Chen Huangmei, "Wo ai *Bashan yeyu*," p. 281.

17. Ye Nan, p. 166.

18. Bulgakov, p. 245.

19. Wu Yigong, p. 214.

20. Lu Mei, p. 36.

21. Among the first works in mainland China to deal with facing the memories of the Cultural Revolution was Dai Houying's *Ren a ren* (Oh! Humankind, 1980; translated as *Stones of the Wall*), which also employs a multiple-narrator narrative. Examples of the *Rashōmon* structure in Taiwanese fiction are discussed in Chapter 7.

22. Yu Qian.

23. For the film's reception, see Tianyunshan chuanqi—*cong xiaoshuo dao dianying*.

24. Berry, p. 241.

25. Zhang Mingtang, p. 101.

26. See Zhang Zhongnan, "Shilun *Xiao jie* de yishu tansuo" (On the artistic quest in *The Alley*), reprinted in Wang and Wang, 2: 165.

27. Ibid., 2: 165, 166 (original emphasis).

28. Zhang Junxiang, p. 144.

29. Yang and Wu, pp. 140, 142.

CHAPTER 6. DISJOINTED TIME, SPLIT VOICES

1. See, e.g., Xu Zidong.

2. Xiaomei Chen, "Growing Up with Posters in the Maoist Era," p. 103.

3. The first half was published in 1992 as *Fannao jiushi zhihui* (Worry is wisdom), and the entire text was published in 1994 as *Wo de putishu* (My bodhi tree), henceforth cited as MBT.

4. Ji, *Niupeng zayi*, pp. 1–8.

5. Ibid., p. 216.

6. Ji also fails to mention that his account of the Cultural Revolution was written immediately after he wrote a full autobiography. The other project puts the memoirs in another context, that of a man acknowledging that "my life's journey is soon going to reach its end" (*Ji Xianlin zizhuan*, p. 268).

7. Ji, *Niupeng zayi*, frontispiece and p. 218.

8. Ibid., pp. 139–40.

9. Reportage literature on the Cultural Revolution was launched with Liu Binyan's "Ren yao zhi jian" (Between humans and monsters), published in the Beijing journal *Renmin wenxue* in 1979 (Liu Binyan, *People or Monsters*, pp. 11–68). One

of the more controversial pieces of reportage was Zheng Yi's account of cannibalism during that period, *Scarlet Memorial*, published in English in 1996. An example of Pu Ning's work may be found in *Hong sha* (Red shark, 1989; known in English as *Red in Tooth and Claw: Twenty-Six Years in Communist Chinese Prisons*). Ah Cheng became known for the novella *Qi wang* (The chess king, 1984), a fictional account of the Cultural Revolution, and his later writings, such as the collection of essays *Xianhua xianshuo* (Vacuous talk, 1997), continue to explore the topic.

10. Book reviews in *Literary Review, Independent*, and *New York Review of Books*, reprinted on the back cover of Zhang Xianliang, *Grass Soup*.

11. Zhang Xianliang, *Fannao jiushi zhihui*, frontispiece.

12. *Soul and Flesh* won the national prize for short stories in 1980. Zhang's popularity is also evidenced by the fact that *Mumaren* (The herdsman), a film based on the story and directed by Xie Jin, won the Hundred Flowers Film Award in 1982.

13. Lawrence.

14. See Caruth, "Trauma and Experience," p. 3. Important criticism was launched against the understanding of "usual human experience" on the grounds that it might ignore the ubiquity of PTSD by large numbers of people, during war and indeed in the daily life of especially vulnerable groups such as women in Western society (see Brown, "Not Outside the Range," pp. 100–112).

15. State of Israel, 3: 1237.

16. Zhang Xianliang, *Nanren de yiban shi nüren*, p. 1.

17. In fact, Zhang extends his mission to retrieving both "history and human life," as if guarding not only the past but History in the Hegelian sense of a force that governs human action through a metahistorical pattern (MBT, p. 3).

18. See Caruth, "Trauma and Experience," p. 4.

19. Quoted in Zhang Zianliang, "Wo de qingsu—*Nanren de yiban shi nüren* zixu (I pour my heart out: preface to *Half of Man is Woman*), in *Nanren de yiban shi nüren*, pp. 1–7.

20. See, e.g., Zhang's "Shenru shenghuo yu xuexi lilun" (Delving into life and theories of study), in *Xie xiaoshou de bianzhengfa*, pp. 99–100.

CHAPTER 7. RETELLING TAIWAN

1. Chen Yingzhen, "Shanlu" (Mountain path), in *Chen Yingzhen zuopin ji*, 5: 37–66.

2. Liu Daren's "Azaleas Cry Out Blood" was first serialized in *Zhongguo shibao* (China Times), Mar. 31–Apr. 3, 1984; reprinted in Liu Daren, *Dujuan ti xue*, pp. 153–92.

3. See Benedict Anderson, p. 35.

4. See Yvonne Chang, p. 164. On Chen Yingzhen's critique of modernity as permeated with absurdity and violence, see Chen Yingzhen, "Xiandai zhuyi de zai kaifa—yanchu *Dengdai Guotuo* de suixiang" (Reinitiating modernism: Random thoughts on the performance of *Waiting for Godot*), in *Chen Yingzhen zuopin ji*, 8: 1–8. See also Chen Yingzhen, "Bianzi he tideng—*Zhishiren de pianzhi* zixu" (The whip

and the lantern: Author's preface to *The Intellectuals' Bigotry*), in *Chen Yingzhen zuopin ji*, 9: 15–21. Lü Zhenghui makes an interesting comparison between "Zhao Nandong" and Lu Xun's parable of the iron chamber: see Lü.

5. Chen Yingzhen, "Zhao Nandong," in *Chen Yingzhen zuopin ji*, 5: 67–149.

6. For versions of the legend, see *Nihon koten bungaku daijiten*, 1: 317–18.

7. On survivors' "postliberation trauma" and "failure to thrive," see Krystal.

8. Wang Dewei, "Lichengbei xia de chensi—dangdai Taiwan xiaoshuo de shenhuaxing yu lishigan" (Lost in thought under the milestone: Myth and history in contemporary Taiwanese fiction), in *Zhongsheng xuanhua*, p. 276.

9. Liu Daren, personal interview.

10. Larson, "Writing and the Writer: Liu Daren," p. 62.

11. Liu Daren, "Fengjing jiu ceng an" (Scenery once familiar), reprinted in Liu Daren, *Dujuan ti xue*, p. 90.

12. Liu Daren, "Guguo shenyou" (Magical journey home), reprinted in Liu Daren, *Dujuan ti xue*, pp. 111–51.

13. For references to the Cultural Revolution as madness, see Shaoguang Wang, *Failure of Charisma*, p. 16.

14. Ibid., p. 4; see also pp. 56, 277.

15. The fictitious article resembles existing Red Guards pamphlets; one, for example, published an article entitled "Zhanduan Liu Shaoqi shenxiang waimao bumen de heishou!" (Chop off the evil hands sent by Liu Shaoqi to the Department of Foreign Commerce!). A copy of the pamphlet is on file at the Center for Chinese Studies at UC–Berkeley, where Liu studied.

16. Wang Dewei, "Zhuixun 'lishi' de yuwang—ping Liu Daren de 'Dujuan ti xue' he 'Qiuyang si jiu'" (The desire for "history": Comments on Liu Daren's "Azaleas cry out bood" and "Autumn sun like wine"), in *Yuedu dangdai xiaoshuo*, p. 195.

17. Bo Juyi, *Pipa xing* (Song of the lute), lines 73–74, in *Bo Juyi ji jianjiao*, 2: 685–86.

18. The belief seems to have originated in the description of the cuckoo's cry in *Jing Chu suishi ji* (Annals of Chu-in-Jing, sixth century): "When one first hears the cuckoo's cry, it evokes separation. Trying to imitate the sound causes one to cough blood" (quoted in Lin and Gao, 4: 1671).

19. Ibid. See also Yu Shi et al., p. 463; Field, pp. 230–31.

20. The red azalea and the violence of the Cultural Revolution were also linked in Liu Daren's mind through the life of Zhou Shoujuan (1895–1968), a writer famous for his gardening skills. In a book published posthumously, Zhou describes the azalea and tells how he planted it as bonsai. In 1968, Zhou was murdered by Red Guards (Liu Daren, personal interview; see also Zhou Shoujuan, pp. 29–31).

21. Shakespeare, *Julius Caesar* 3.2.234. Chen Yingzhen, "Qican de wuyan de zui" (Poor poor dumb mouths), in *Chen Yingzhen zuopin ji*, 1: 153–66.

22. Liu Daren, personal interview.

23. Shoshana Felman, "The Return of the Voice: Claude Lanzmann's *Shoah*," in Felman and Laub, p. 255.

24. Liu Daren, personal interview. Liu's image of Lu Xun as asking for "total self-sacrifice" follows interpretations of the author that I question in Chapter 1.

25. The reference is to Lu Xun's essay "Lu 'feiwei bolai' yinggai huanxing" (On having to defer 'fair play'"), in LXZPQJ, 6: 309–22.

26. Liu Daren was first motivated to write "Azaleas" after reading a newspaper report about a man who confessed to having eaten the heart of a "traitor" to the communist cause (Liu Daren, personal interview). Zheng Yi has recently shown how Party members who took part in the crime were exonerated because of their records as revolutionary activists in the 1930s and 1940s (Zheng Yi).

27. Liu Daren, personal interview.

CHAPTER 8. THE AESTHETICS AND
ANESTHETICS OF MEMORY

1. Yu Hua, "Wangshi yu xingfa" (Past and punishment) in *Xiaji taifeng*, pp. 41–64.

2. MBT, p. 3.

3. For a discussion on whether Yu Hua's later novels "betray" his earlier writings, see Liu Kang, "Short-Lived Avant-Garde."

4. Xudong Zhang, pp. 35–99; Jing Wang, pp. 195–232.

5. Jones, "Translator's Postscript," p. 270.

6. Jones, for example, infers that "Yu Hua asks us to watch as he gleefully cuts apart human bodies" ("Violence of the Text," p. 574).

7. Ibid., pp. 582, 591.

8. Dai Jinhua, "Liegu de ling yice pan," pp. 29, 30.

9. Larson, "Literary Modernism and Nationalism in Post-Mao China," p. 187.

10. Jones, "Violence of the Text," pp. 574–75 (original emphasis).

11. Borges, "Death and the Compass," in *Labyrinths*, p. 82. "Death and the Compass" and "The Garden of Forking Paths" appeared in Chinese translation in 1983, as "Siwang he luopan" and "Jiaocha xiaojing de huayuan" respectively, in *Boerhesi duanpian xiaoshuo ji*, pp. 69–83, 92–107.

12. Borges, "Garden of Forking Paths," in *Labyrinths*, p. 28.

13. Marx and Engels, 5: 84.

14. Hegel, p. 19.

15. Y. H. Zhao, p. 418.

16. Borges, "Death and the Compass," p. 87.

17. Kant, "The End of All Things," in *On History*, p. 78.

18. These forms of punishments were codified during the early dynasties and are mentioned in canonical books such as the *Liji* (Book of rites, ca. fifth c. B.C.) and the *Shiji* (Records of the historian, first c. B.C.) (see *Zhongwen dacidian*, 3: 507–8, 8: 1663). Yu Hua mentions the historical context of these punishments in his short story "1986" (Yu Hua, "1986," in *Shiba sui chumen yuanxing*, p. 46).

19. Dai Jinhua, "Liegu de ling yice pan," p. 30. "It is in the name of the father that we must recognize the support of the symbolic function which, from the dawn of history, has identified his person with the figure of the law," Lacan explains ("The Function and Field of Speech and Language in Psychoanalysis," in *Écrits*, p. 67). Dai neglects to note, however, that Lacan (paying homage to Lévi-Strauss) also argues

that the father's prohibitive voice performs a legislative function, and as such constitutes a law that contributes to the socializing process by regulating the structure of communication.

20. Yu Hua, "Xuwei de zuopin," p. 10.

21. In using penal law as an index of civilization's tenuous claim to progress, Yu Hua follows a long line of critics. Punishment, and especially the death sentence, are the supreme symbol of the regimentation of power in the name of civilization. Arguably the most pertinent to "Past and Punishment" is Walter Benjamin's explanation that through penal law violence becomes its own end and that therefore "in the exercise of violence over life and death more than in any other legal act, law reaffirms itself" ("Critique of Violence," in *Reflections*, p. 286).

22. Dai Jinhua, "Liegu de ling yice pan: chudu Yu Hua," p. 30.

23. Compare Yu Hua's imagery to that of Li Yannian's (second–first c. B.C.) dirge: "The morning dew on the leeks dries so easily, / Yet the morning after the dew moistens again; / When a man dies, once departed, when will he return?" (quoted in Demiéville, p. 102). See also the words of monk Eihei Dōgen (1200–1253): "Enlightenment is like the moon reflected on the water. The moon does not get wet, nor is the water broken. . . . The whole moon and the entire sky are reflected in dewdrops on the grass. . . . The depth of the drop is the height of the moon. Each reflection, however long or short of duration, manifests the vastness of the dewdrop, and realizes the limitlessness of the moonlight in the sky" (p. 71).

24. See Faure, p. 180.

25. Benjamin distinguishes between two kinds of experience: *Erlebnis* is the result of fending off stimuli by stashing them away in the retreating past, fixing them in a specific point in time, a distant place in memory. *Erfahrung* on the other hand resists the danger of translating all stimuli into numbed *Erlebnis* (see "Some Motifs in Baudelaire," in *Illuminations*, pp. 155–200).

26. Borges, "Garden of Forking Paths," p. 27.

27. The most direct reference occurs at the very beginning of the story, as the stranger "awakened these distant memories" (P&P, p. 43). Later, "a crow-flock of memories flew across his (the Punition Expert's) face" (P&P, p. 51). The only time in which the Stranger "recalls" a specific event, it is merely the telegram (P&P, p. 53). This aspect of the text is not conveyed by Jones's translation, where "the past" is often translated as "memory."

28. Ban Wang refers to Yu Hua's "1986," a story that shares much in common with "Past and Punishment" (p. 243).

29. Benjamin, "Theses on the Philosophy of History," in *Illuminations*, p. 253. In the late 1980s, Benjamin's essays such as "Theses on the Philosophy of History" and the Baudelaire anthology became available in Chinese translation, mostly through the work of Zhang Xudong, a personal acquaintance of Yu Hua's. My thanks to Zhang Xudong for this information. On the contraption that inspired Benjamin, see Standage.

30. Duchamp, "The Green Box" and "Cast Shadows," in *Writings of Marcel Duchamp*, pp. 57, 72, 26. Incidentally, Duchamp's work and Yu Hua's story also share the concern with the issues of dismemberment and historical chance.

31. Jean-François Lyotard, "Newman: The Instant," in *Lyotard Reader*, p. 249. See also Lyotard's "The Sublime and the Avant-Garde," in ibid., pp. 196–211.

32. Kafka, "In the Penal Colony," in *Complete Stories*, p. 150.

33. Ibid., pp. 147, 149, 165. In both stories, the executioners end up directing the punishments at themselves.

34. Li Tuo, "Xuebeng hechu?" pp. 5–6; Y. H. Zhao, "Fiction as Subversion," p. 415.

35. In a personal interview (Aug. 1, 1995), Yu Hua acknowledged the pervasive influence of Lu Xun on any modern Chinese reader, yet seemed eager to emphasize the opposition between his work and the May Fourth generation and to emphasize his debt to Western modernist writers. More recently, however, Yu Hua has published Lu Xun's "Kong Yiji" in a collection of ten works that inspired him (Yu Hua, *Wennuan de lücheng*).

36. Ban Wang, p. 257.

37. Jones, "Violence of the Text," p. 596.

CHAPTER 9. MEMORY AT A STANDSTILL

1. Braester and Zhang.

2. Wang Shuo, "Wo kan Lu Xun" (My view of Lu Xun); reprinted in Chen Shuyu, pp. 435–43.

3. Whenever quoting from the script, I have modified the English subtitles according to the Chinese original. Wang Shuo's originary novella has different stresses: "Everything in this city is changing fast—the buildings, the streets, what people wear and talk about have all changed completely by now to become a new, by our standards a pretty elegant, city. There are no traces, everything has been stripped clean" (*Dongwu xiongmeng*, p. 430).

4. Li Erwei, p. 11.

5. Geremie Barmé notes the origin of the term *pizi wenxue* in former Beijing Film Studio head Song Chong (*In the Red*, p. 73). Barmé also points to the allusion to the Maoist phrase *pizi geming* (*Shades of Mao*, p. 168).

6. The film was first shown at the Venice Film Festival in September 1994, where it received first prize for best male lead. It was subsequently screened in the PRC, accompanied by a large publicity campaign (Wang Shuo, "*Yangguang canlan de rizi zhuiyi*," p. 129). The film was initially a PRC–Hong Kong co-production, but it suffered from financial problems as the shooting neared its end. The last obstacles were surmounted through the involvement of European producers, culminating in Volker Schlöndorff's assistance in gaining access to the facilities at Babelsberg (Jiang Wen, "Yangguang zhong de jiyi" [Memory in the sunlight] in Jiang Wen, *Dansheng*, p. 51). On the film's importance in the history of Chinese cinema, see the critic Ni Zhen's review in Li Erwei, p. 133. Jiang's and Wang's articles appear in a volume edited by Jiang Wen, which contains the impressions of the production crew.

7. See Braester.

8. One of the later scenes in *In the Heat of the Sun* shows the young Xiaojun crying hoarsely under blue light in a rainstorm. The image resonates with the conclud-

ing shot of *Red Sorghum*, suffused with red, where the child strikes a similar pose and cries to his dead mother.

9. Barmé, *In the Red*, p. 33.

10. For accounts of gang youth, see Thurston, p. 130; Jung Chang, pp. 490–95.

11. *Mao Zedong zhuzuo xuandu*, p. 538.

12. Quoted in Lan Yang, p. 29.

13. Ban Wang, p. 204.

14. It was this resonance that brought Jiang to read Wang's novella in one night and phone Wang in the morning, waking him up to say excitedly that he wanted to film the story (Li Erwei, p. 67).

15. Ibid., pp. 78–79.

16. See, e.g., Ji, *Niupeng zayi*, p. 6.

17. Xiaomei Chen, "Growing Up with Posters in the Maoist Era," p. 103.

18. The masturbation scene was excised by censors (Jiang Wen, "Yangguang zhong de jiyi," p. 71).

19. Li Erwei, p. 75.

20. Kundera defines "Orwellizing" as "reducing [the recollection of one's life] to the political aspect alone . . . as an undifferentiated block of horrors" (pp. 225–26).

21. In *Dongwu xiongmeng*, the narrator admits that he has aspired, without success, to be "a real operator" (Wang Shuo, *Dongwu xiongmeng*, p. 460).

22. Li Erwei, p. 139; see also the similar reaction of the director Gu Rong (ibid., p. 135) and Chen Xiaoming's observations (p. 235).

23. Ibid., p. 149.

24. Barmé, *Shades of Mao*, p. 176; Barmé, *In the Red*, p. 137.

25. Barmé, *Shades of Mao*, p. 224; Barmé, *In the Red*, p. 324. Barmé notes that Wang Shuo's alternative to the CCP lingo has been rejected by the Party ideologues (Barmé, *In the Red*, p. 306).

26. The last scene was originally shot as a longer one, but as with the entire film, Jiang had to cut it much shorter (the total length of used film for the movie amounted to 250,000 feet [Jiang Wen, "Yangguang zhong de jiyi," p. 30]).

27. Ding Ling, "Mou ye," p. 318. I thank Pieter Keulemans for the reference.

28. Tong Yun, pp. 97–105.

29. Jiang Wen, "Yangguang zhong de jiyi," p. 71.

30. As early as 1987, scene 5 of *The Red Lantern* was put on again in the Beijing People's Theater (see Dai Jiafang, p. 3); on recent production of model plays, see Melvin and Cai; Liu Kang, "Popular Culture and the Culture of the Masses in Contemporary China," p. 114; Xiaomei Chen, *Acting the Right Part*, p. 74.

31. Dai Jinhua, *Yinxing shuxie*, p. 237.

32. Barmé, *In the Red*, pp. 99–101.

33. See also lyrics translated in Barmé, *Shades of Mao*, pp. 192–94.

34. Ji, *Niupeng zayi*, p. 163. The English title of Jiang's film loses the ironic twist; Liu Kang suggests that it was chosen to please Western audiences ("Popular Culture," pp. 113–14).

35. Wang Shuo, *Dongwu xiongmeng*, p. 434.

36. The photograph sequence foreshadows the restaurant scene, since already in

this sequence, Xiaojun's vision of Mi Lan blurs into the image of another young woman. In a scene that sums up the cinematic inversion of memory, Xiaojun stumbles upon Mi Lan's photograph by looking through the other end of a telescope.

37. Wang Shuo, *Dongwu xiongmeng,* p. 437.

38. Ibid., p. 455.

39. Ibid., p. 437.

40. Wang Shuo, "*Yangguang canlan de rizi* zhuiyi," p. 127.

EPILOGUE

1. Chow, "Introduction," p. 1.

2. The implications of discussing "modern Chinese literature" may be traced to a group of young scholars at National Taiwan University (including Leo Ou-fan Lee and Joseph Lau), who promoted the ideals associated with writers such as Eliot and Joyce in the journal *Xiandai wenxue* (Modern literature). In this context, the term was associated with methodological attention to literary device, an aesthetic as well as political statement in the days when literature was embroiled in the battle between the KMT and the CCP. The term also created a legitimate academic field when recent literature was kept out of university classrooms in both the ROC and the PRC and was discussed in U.S. history departments. The attribute "modern" helped situate the study of literature in Chinese within larger academic debates on the nature of "modernity." In all these guises, "the modern" served as a code word for declaring that contemporary Chinese literature had reached the same level of sophistication as Western texts.

Bibliography

Abbas, Akbar. *Hong Kong: Culture and the Politics of Disappearance.* Minneapolis: University of Minnesota Press, 1997.

Adorno, Theodor. *Negative Dialectics.* Trans. E. B. Ashton. New York: Continuum, 1992.

Anagnost, Ann. *National Past-Times: Narrative, Representation, and Power in Modern China.* Durham, N.C.: Duke University Press, 1997.

Anderson, Benedict. *Imagined Communities.* New York: Verso, 1991.

Anderson, Marston. *The Limits of Realism: Chinese Fiction in the Revolutionary Period.* Berkeley: University of California Press, 1990.

Andreyev, Leonid. *The Red Laugh.* Trans. Alexandra Lindem. Foxton: Dedalus-Hippocrene, 1989.

Arendt, Hannah. *On Violence.* New York: Harcourt, Brace & World, 1970.

Barmé, Geremie R. *In the Red: On Contemporary Chinese Culture.* New York: Columbia University Press, 1999.

———. *Shades of Mao: The Posthumous Cult of the Great Leader.* Armonk, N.Y.: M. E. Sharpe, 1996.

Barthes, Roland. *Camera Lucida.* Trans. Richard Howard. New York: Hill & Wang, 1981.

———. *Image, Music, Text.* Trans. Stephen Heath. New York: Noonday, 1988.

Bashan yeyu (Night rain in Bashan). Dir. Wu Yonggang and Wu Yigong. Shanghai: Shanghai Film Studio, 1980.

Bataille, Georges. *Les larmes d'Éros.* Paris: J.-J. Pauvert, 1961. Trans. Peter Connor as *The Tears of Eros* (San Francisco: City Lights Books, 1989).

Bei aiqing yiwang de jiaoluo (The corner forsaken by love). Dir. Zhang Qi and Li Yalin. Chengdu: Emei Film Studio, 1980.

Benjamin, Walter. *Gesammelten Schriften.* Ed. Rolf Tiedemann and Hermann Schweppenhäuser. Frankfurt am Main: Suhrkamp, 1980–82.

———. *Illuminations.* Ed. Hannah Arendt. Trans. Harry Zohn. New York: Schocken Books, 1977.

———. *Reflections: Essays, Aphorisms, Autobiographical Writing.* Ed. Peter Demetz. Trans. Edmund Jephcott. New York: Schocken Books, 1978.

Benmingnian (Black snow). Dir. Xie Fei. Beijing: Youth Film Studio, 1988.

Berman, Marshall. *All That Is Solid Melts into Air: The Experience of Modernity.* New York: Simon & Schuster, 1982.

Berry, Chris. "Towards a Postsocialist Cinema: The Representation of the Cultural Revolution in the Cinema of the People's Republic of China, 1976–1981." Ph.D. diss., UCLA 1999.

Blake, Richard A. *Screening America: Reflections on Five Classic Films*. New York: Paulist Press, 1991.

Bo Juyi. *Bo Juyi ji jianjiao* (Annotated variorum edition of the collected works of Bo Juyi). Shanghai: Shanghai guji chubanshe, 1988.

Borges, Jorge Luis. *Boerhesi duanpian xiaoshuo ji* (Collected short stories of Borges). Trans. Wang Yangle. Shanghai: Shanghai yiwen, 1983.

————. *Labyrinths: Selected Stories and Other Writings*. Ed. Donald A. Yates and James E. Irby. New York: New Directions, 1964.

————. *Seven Nights*. Trans. Eliot Weinberger. New York: New Directions, 1984.

Botting, Fred. *Making Monstrous: Frankenstein, Criticism, Theory*. Manchester: Manchester University Press, 1991.

Braester, Yomi. "Mo Yan and *Red Sorghum*." In *The Columbia Companion to Modern East Asian Literature*, ed. Joshua Mostow. New York: Columbia University Press, 2003.

Braester, Yomi, and Enhua Zhang. "The Future of China's Memories: An Interview with Feng Jicai." *Journal of Modern Literature in Chinese* 5, no. 2 (Jan. 2002).

The Bride of Frankenstein. Dir. James Whale. Hollywood: Universal Pictures, 1935.

Brooks, Peter. *The Melodramatic Imagination: Balzac, Henry James, Melodrama, and the Mode of Excess*. New Haven: Yale University Press, 1995.

Brown, Carolyn T. "Lu Xun's Interpretation of Dreams." In *Psycho-sinology: The Universe of Dreams in Chinese Culture*, ed. Carolyn T. Brown, pp. 67–79. Washington D.C.: University Press of America, 1988.

Brown, Laura S. "Not Outside the Range: One Feminist Perspective on Psychic Trauma." In *Trauma: Explorations in Memory*, ed. Cathy Caruth, pp. 100–12. Baltimore: Johns Hopkins University Press, 1995.

Buck-Morss, Susan. *The Dialectics of Seeing: Walter Benjamin and the Arcades Project*. Cambridge, Mass.: MIT Press, 1989.

Bulgakov, Mikhail. *The Master and Margarita*. Trans. Diana Burgin and Katherine Tiernan O'Connor. Dana Point, Calif.: Ardis, 1995.

Camus, Albert. *The Fall*. Trans. Justin O'Brien. New York: Knopf, 1960.

Canetti, Elias. *Crowds and Power*. Trans. Carol Stewart. New York: Noonday, 1993.

Cao Xueqin, *The Story of the Stone*. Trans. David Hawkes and John Minford. New York: Penguin Books, 1973–86.

Caruth, Cathy. "Trauma and Experience: Introduction." In *Trauma: Explorations in Memory*, ed. Cathy Caruth, pp. 3–12. Baltimore: Johns Hopkins University Press, 1995.

————, ed. *Trauma: Explorations in Memory*. Baltimore: Johns Hopkins University Press, 1995.

————. *Unclaimed Experience: Trauma, Narrative, and History*. Baltimore: Johns Hopkins University Press, 1996.

Cavell, Stanley. *Must We Mean What We Say*. Cambridge: Cambridge University Press, 1976.

Chamberlain, Heath B. "On the Search for Civil Society in China." *Modern China* 19, no. 2 (Apr. 1993): 199–215.

Chang, Jung. *Wild Swans: Three Daughters of China*. London: Flamingo, 1993.

Chang, Yvonne Sung-sheng. *Modernism and the Nativist Resistance.* Durham, N.C.: Duke University Press, 1993.

Changzheng zuge—Zhongguo geming lishi gequ biaoyan chang (The Long March chorus: The history of the Chinese revolution in song and dance). Dir. Hua Chun, Beijing: August First Film Studio, 1963.

Chen Huangmei. "Wo ai *Bashan yeyu*" (I love *Night Rain in Bashan*). Reprinted in *Bashan yeyu: cong juben dao yingpian* (*Night Rain in Bashan*: from script to film), pp. 279–82. Beijing: Zhongguo dianying chubanshe, 1982.

Chen Huiyang. "Chuanqi de moluo: Ma-Xu Weibang Xianggang shiqi de qishi" (The fall of the strange tales genre: The rise of Ma-Xu Weibang in his Hong Kong period). In *The Fourteenth Hong Kong International Film Festival: The China Factor in Hong Kong Cinema*, pp. 58–63. Hong Kong: Urban Council, 1990.

————. *Mengying ji: Zhongguo dianying yinxiang* (Collection of dreamy shadows: Impressions of Chinese cinema). Taipei: Yunchen wenhua, 1990.

Chen Kaige. *Longxieshu* (The Dragon-blood tree). Hong Kong: Cosmos, 1992.

Chen Shen et al., eds. *Zhongguo sheying shi, 1840–1937* (History of photography in China, 1840–1937). Taipei: Sheyingjia, 1990.

Chen Shuyu, ed. *Shei tiaozhan Lu Xun—xin shiqi guanyu Lu Xun de lunzheng* (Who's challenging Lu Xun: Debates on Lu Xun in the new era). Chengdu: Sichuan wenyi chubanshe, 2002.

Chen Wei. "Fang qianqian wanwan guanzhong suo relie chongbai de Ma-Xu Weibang xiansheng" (Interview with Mr. Ma-Xu Weibang, highly admired by a large audience). *Xin Yingtan* 3, no. 5 (Jan. 1945).

Chen, Xiaomei. *Acting the Right Part: Political Theater and Popular Drama in Contemporary China.* Honolulu: University of Hawai'i Press, 2002.

————. "Growing Up with Posters in the Maoist Era." In *Picturing Power in the People's Republic of China*, ed. Harriet Evans and Stephanie Donald, pp. 101–22. Lanham, Md.: Rowman & Littlefield, 1999.

————. *Occidentalism: A Theory of Counter-Discourse in Post-Mao China.* New York: Oxford University Press, 1995.

Chen Xiaoming. "The Mysterious Other: Postpolitics in Chinese Film." *Boundary 2*, 24, no. 3 (Fall 1997): 123–41.

Chen Yingzhen. *Chen Yingzhen zuopin ji* (Collected works of Chen Yingzhen). Taipei: Renjian, 1988.

Cheng Jihua. *Zhongguo dianying fazhan shi* (History of the development of Chinese cinema). 1963. Reprint. Beijing: Zhongguo dianying chubanshe, 1980.

Cheng Shu'an, ed. *Zhongguo dianying mingpian xishang cidian* (Lexicon of famous Chinese films). Beijing: Changzheng chubanshe, 1997.

Chongqing senlin (English title *Chunking Express*). Dir. Wong Kar-wai, Hong Kong: Jet Tone Production Co., 1993.

Chow, Rey. "Introduction: On Chineseness as a Theoretical Problem." In *Modern Chinese Literary and Cultural Studies in the Age of Theory: Reimagining the Field*, ed. Rey Chow, pp. 1–25. Durham, N.C.: Duke University Press, 2000.

————. *Primitive Passions: Visuality, Sexuality, Ethnography, and Contemporary Chinese Cinema.* New York: Columbia University Press, 1995.

Chow, Tse-tsung. *The May Fourth Movement: Intellectual Revolution in Modern China.* Cambridge, Mass.: Harvard University Press, 1960.

Chu Tianshu. "Chonggao de yingxiong xingxiang, zhuangli de yishu yuyan—zan geming xiandai jingju *Hongdeng ji*" (A sublime heroic image, exalted artistic language: in praise of the revolutionary modern Beijing opera *The Red Lantern*). Reprinted in *Jingtian dongdi de weida geming zhuangju—zan geming yangban xi* (The earth-shattering great revolutionary achievement: In praise of the revolutionary model plays), pp. 122–31. Hong Kong: Xianggang sanlian shudian, 1970.

Ch'ü, T'ung-tsu. *Local Government in China Under the Ch'ing.* Cambridge, Mass.: Harvard University Press, 1962.

Cixous, Helène. "Castration or Decapitation?" Trans. Annette Kuhn. *Signs* 7 (1981): 41–55.

Clark, Katerina. *The Soviet Novel: History as Ritual.* Chicago: University of Chicago Press, 1981.

Clark, Paul. *Chinese Cinema: Culture and Politics Since 1949.* Cambridge: Cambridge University Press, 1987.

Crary, Jonathan. *Techniques of the Observer: On Vision and Modernity in the Nineteenth Century.* Cambridge, Mass.: MIT Press, 1991.

Dai Jiafang. *Yangbanxi de fengfeng yuyu—Jiang Qing,Yangban xi ji neimu* (Gossip on the model plays: Jiang Qing, the model plays and the back stage). Beijing: Zhishi chubanshe, 1995.

Dai Jinhua. "Liegu de ling yice pan: chudu Yu Hua" (The other side of the abyss: A preliminary reading of Yu Hua). *Beijing Wenxue* 1989, no. 7: 26–33.

———. *Yinxing shuxie* (Invisible writing). Nanjing: Jiangsu renmin chubanshe, 1999.

Demiéville, Paul. *Poèmes chinois d'avant la mort.* Ed. Jean-Pierre Diény. Paris: L'Asiathèque, 1984.

Deng Yunjia, ed. *Chuanju yishu gailun* (Outline of the art of Sichuan opera). Chengdu: Sichuansheng shehui kexueyuan chubanshe, 1988.

Ding Ling. "Mou ye" (A certain night). In *Ding Ling duanpian xiaoshuo xuanji* (Collected short stories by Ding Ling), pp. 313–19. Beijing: Renmin wenxue chubanshe, 1955.

Ding Xuelei. "Zhongguo wuchan jieji de guanghui dianxing—zan Li Yuhe de xingxiang suzao" (A shining paragon of the Chinese proletarian class: In praise of forming Li Yuhe's image). Reprinted in *Geming de Hongdeng—zan geming xiandai jingju* Hongdeng ji (The red lantern of the revolution: In praise of the revolutionary modern Beijing opera *The Red Lantern*), pp. 19–28. Hangzhou: Renmin chubanshe, 1970.

Dōgen, Eihei. *Moon in a Dewdrop: Writings of Zen Master Dōgen.* Ed. Kazuaki Tanahashi. Trans. Robert Aitken et al. San Francisco: North Point Press, 1985.

Dongfang hong (The east is red). Beijing: August First Film Studio, Beijing Film Studio and Central News & Documentary Film Studio co-production, 1965.

Dostoyevsky, Fyodor. *The House of the Dead.* Trans. David McDuff. New York: Penguin Books, 1985.

Dracula. Dir. Tod Browning, Hollywood: Universal Pictures, 1931.

Du Yunzhi. *Zhongguo dianying qishi nian* (Seventy years of Chinese cinema). Taipei: Zhonghua minguo dianying tushuguan chubanshe, 1986.

Duara, Prasenjit. *Rescuing History from the Nation: Questioning Narratives of Modern China*. Chicago: University of Chicago Press, 1995.

Duchamp, Marcel. *The Writings of Marcel Duchamp*. Ed. Michel Sanouillet and Elmer Peterson. New York: Da Capo, 1989.

Face/Off. Dir. John Woo, Hollywood: Paramount Pictures, 1997.

Fanon, Frantz. *Black Skin, White Masks*. New York: Grove Weidenfeld, 1968.

Faure, Bernard. *The Rhetoric of Immediacy*. Princeton: Princeton University Press, 1991.

Feifei. "Dianying guanggao shu" (Film advertisement tactics). *Yingxi shenghuo* 1 (Jan. 2, 1931): 2.

Felman, Shoshana, and Dori Laub, eds. *Testimony: Crises of Witnessing in Literature, Psychoanalysis, and History*. New York: Routledge, 1992.

Fengyun ernü (Children of troubled times). Dir. Xu Xingzhi. Shanghai: Diantong Film Co., 1935.

Feuerwerker, Yi-tsi Mei. *Ideology, Power, Text: Self-Representation and the Peasant "Other" in Modern Chinese Literature*. Stanford: Stanford University Press, 1998.

Field, Stephen L. "Injustice and Insanity in Liu Ta-jen's 'The Cuckoo Cries Tears of Blood." *Tamkang Review* 21, no. 3 (Spring 1991): 225–37.

Forry, Steven Earl. *Hideous Progenies: Dramatizations of* Frankenstein *from Mary Shelley to the Present*. Philadelphia: University of Pennsylvania Press, 1990.

Foster, Paul B. "The Ironic Inflation of Chinese National Character: Lu Xun's International Reputation, Romain Rolland's Critique of 'The True Story of Ah Q,' and the Nobel Prize." *Modern Chinese Literature and Culture* 13, no. 1 (Spring 2001): 140–68.

Foucault, Michel. *The Archaeology of Knowledge and the Discourse on Language*. Trans. A. M. Sheridan Smith. New York: Pantheon Books, 1972.

———. *Discipline and Punish: The Birth of the Prison*. Trans. Alan Sheridan. New York: Vintage Books, 1979.

———. "The Ethics of the Concern of the Self as a Practice of Freedom." In *Ethics: Subjectivity and Truth*. Ed. Paul Rabinow, pp. 281–301. New York: New Press, 1997.

———. *The Politics of Truth*. Ed. Sylvère Lotringer. New York: Semiotext(e), 1997.

Frankenstein. Dir. James Whale, Hollywood: Universal Pictures, 1931.

Freud, Sigmund. *Beyond the Pleasure Principle*. Trans. James Strachey. New York: Liveright, 1961.

———. *The Standard Edition of the Complete Psychological Works of Sigmund Freud*. Ed. James Strachey. London: Hogarth Press, 1966–74.

Fudan daxue "wu-qi" wenliao xiezuo zu (The group for writing the May Seventh documentation at Fudan University). "Wei gongren jieji de weida yingxiong zaoxiang—xuexi geming xiandai jingju *Hongdeng ji* de yishu gousi" (Creating the image of a great hero for the workers' class: Studying the artistic considerations in the revolutionary model play *The Red Lantern*). Reprinted in *Geming de Hongdeng—zan geming xiandai jingju* Hongdeng ji (The red lantern of the revo-

lution: In praise of the revolutionary modern Beijing opera *The Red Lantern*),
pp. 150–60. Hangzhou: Renmin chubanshe, 1970.

Furong zhen (Hibiscus town). Dir. Xie Jin, Shanghai: Shanghai Film Studio, 1986.

Furth, Charlotte. "Culture and Politics in Modern Chinese Conservatism." In *The Limits of Change*, ed. Charlotte Furth, pp. 22–53. Cambridge, Mass.: Harvard University Press, 1976.

Gálik, Marián. "Studies in Modern Chinese Intellectual History III: Young Lu Xun (1902–1909)." *Asian and African Studies* 21 (1985): 37–63.

Galikowski, Maria. *Art and Politics in China, 1949–1984*. Hong Kong: Chinese University Press, 1998.

Gan Yang. "Minjian shehui gainian pipan" (A critique of "Civil Society"). In *Beiju de liliang—cong minzhu yudong zhouxiang minzhu zhengzhi 1989–* (The power of tragedy: From the democracy movement toward democratic government, 1989–), ed. Lin Daoqun and Wu Zanmei, pp. 141–53. Hong Kong: Oxford University Press, 1993.

Gao Chou. "*Wuxing de zhanxian* jiaoyu le women" (*The Invisible Battle-front* has instructed us). *Dazhong dianying* 1950, no. 4.

Gatiss, Mark. *James Whale: A Biography, or, The Would-be Gentleman*. London: Cassell, 1995.

Ge Yihong. *Zhongguo huaju tongshi* (A comprehensive history of Western-style drama in China). Beijing: Wenhua yishu chubanshe, 1997.

Gesheng meiying (The phantom of singing; English title *Family Love*). Dir. Wu Hua, Taipei: Taiwan Film Studio, 1970.

Gogol, Nikolai Vasilevich. *Diary of a Madman and Other Stories*. Trans. Andrew R. MacAndrew. New York: Penguin Books, 1960.

Gold, Thomas. "The Resurgence of Civil Society in China." *Journal of Democracy* 1 (1985): 18–31.

Gongsun Lu. *Zhongguo dianying shihua* (Anecdotes on the history of Chinese film). Hong Kong: Nantian shucong, n.d. (preface dated 1961).

Green, Anne. "Time and History in Madame Bovary." *French Studies* 49, no. 3 (July 1995): 283–91.

Guling jie shaonian sha ren shijian (English title *A Brighter Summer Day*). Dir. Edward Yang. Taipei: CPMC and Edward Yang, 1991.

Gunning, Tom. "An Aesthetic of Astonishment: Early Film and the (In)Credulous Spectator." *Art & Text* 34: 31–34.

———. *D. W. Griffith and the Origins of American Narrative Film: The Early Years at Biograph*. Urbana: University of Illinois Press, 1991.

Habermas, Jürgen. *The Philosophical Discourse of Modernity*. Trans. Frederick Lawrence. Cambridge, Mass.: MIT Press, 1987.

———. *The Structural Transformation of the Public Sphere: An Inquiry into a Category of Bourgeois Society*. Trans. Thomas Burger and Frederick Lawrence. Cambridge, Mass.: MIT Press, 1989.

———. *The Theory of Communicative Action*. Trans. Thomas McCarthy. Boston: Beacon Press, 1984–87.

Haitan de yitian (*That Day on the Beach*). Dir. Edward Yang. Taipei: CPMC, 1983.

Hanan, Patrick. "The Technique of Lu Hsün's Fiction." *Harvard Journal of Asiatic Studies* 34 (1974): 53–96.

He, Yuhuai. *Cycles of Repression and Relaxation: Politico-Literary Events in China 1976–1989*. Bochum: Universitätsverlag Dr. N. Brockmeyer, 1992.

Hegel, Georg Wilhelm Friedrich. *The Philosophy of History*. Trans. J. Sibree. New York: Dover, 1956.

Holquist, Michael. *Dialogism: Bakhtin and his World*. London: Routledge, 1990.

————. *Dostoevsky and the Novel*. Princeton: Princeton University Press, 1977.

Hong Feng. "Wei you xisheng duo zhuangzhi, gan jiao riyue huan xintian—zan geming yangban xi *Hongdeng ji* zhong Li Yuhe xingxiang de suzao" (Possessing a strong will to sacrifice oneself, daring to tell the sun and moon to start a new day—in praise of forming the image of Li Yuhe in the revolutionary model play *The Red Lantern*). Reprinted in *Geming de Hongdeng—zan geming xiandai jingju Hongdeng ji* (The red lantern of the revolution: In praise of the revolutionary modern Beijing opera *The Red Lantern*), pp. 29–38. Hangzhou: Renmin chubanshe, 1970.

Hong gaoliang (Red sorghum). Dir. Zhang Yimou. Xi'an: Xi'an Film Studio, 1987.

Hong Xin. "Xiongxin zhuangzhi cong yutian—zan geming xiandai jingju *hongdeng ji* diba chang 'xingchang douzheng'" (A strong will reaches to heavens: In praise of scene 8, "At the Execution Grounds," in the revolutionary modern Beijing opera *The Red Lantern*). Reprinted in *Geming de Hongdeng—zan geming xiandai jingju Hongdeng ji* (The red lantern of the revolution: In praise of the revolutionary modern Beijing opera *The Red Lantern*), pp. 170–77. Hangzhou: Renmin chubanshe, 1970.

Hongdeng ji (The red lantern). Dir. Cheng Yin. Beijing: August First Film Studio, 1970.

Hongse niangzi jun (The red detachment of women). Dir. Pan Wenzhan and Fu Jie. Beijing: Beijing Film Studio, 1971.

Horkheimer, Max, and Theodor Adorno. *Eclipse of Reason*. New York: Continuum, 1992.

Hsia, C. T. *A History of Modern Chinese Fiction*. New Haven: Yale University Press, 1971.

Hu Shi. *Hu Shi zuopin ji* (Collected works of Hu Shi). Taipei: Yuanliu, 1986.

Hu Xingliang. *Zhongguo huaju yu Zhongguo xiqu* (Chinese modern theater and Chinese opera). Shanghai: Xuelin chubanshe, 2000.

Hu Xingliang and Zhang Ruilin, eds. *Zhongguo dianying shi* (History of Chinese cinema). Beijing: Zhongyang guangbo dianshi daxue chubanshe, 1995.

Huayuanjie wuhao (5 Huayuan St.). Dir. Jiang Shusen and Zhao Shi. Changchun: Changchun Film Studio, 1984.

Huters, Theodore. "Lives in Profile: On the Authorial Voice in Modern and Contemporary Chinese Literature." In *From May Fourth to June Fourth: Fiction and Film in Twentieth-century China*, eds. David Der-wei Wang and Ellen Widmer, pp. 269–94. Cambridge, Mass: Harvard University Press, 1993.

Ibsen, Henrik. *Nala (A Doll's House)*. Trans. Hu Shi and Luo Jialun. *Xin Qingnian* 4, no. 6 (June 15, 1918): 508–72.

The Invisible Man. Dir. James Whale. Hollywood: Universal Pictures, 1933.

Jameson, Fredric. "Third-World Literature in the Era of Multinational Capitalism." *Social Text* (Fall 1986): 65–88.

Ji Xianlin. *Ji Xianlin zizhuan* (Autobiography of Ji Xianlin). Huaiyang: Jiangsu wenyi chubanshe, 1996.

————. *Niupeng zayi* (Recollections from the cowshed). Beijing: Zhonggong zhongyang dangxiao chubanshe, 1998.

Jiang Rui and Cheng Zhi. "Ertong gushipian *Jimao xin* shezhi tongxun" (News on the shooting of the children's feature *The Urgent Letter*). *Dazhong dianying* 22, no. 22 (1953).

Jiang Wen et al. *Dansheng* (Birth). Beijing: Huayi chubanshe, 1997.

Jiang Yibing. "Guanghui de yingxiong xingxiang, zhanxin de wutai meishu—xuexi geming xiandai jingju *Hongdeng ji* wutai meishu de tihui" (A brilliant heroic image, a fresh stage art: My experience of studying the stage art of the revolutionary modern Beijing opera *The Red Lantern*). Reprinted in *Geming de Hongdeng—zan geming xiandai jingju* Hongdeng ji (The red lantern of the revolution: In praise of the revolutionary modern Beijing opera *The Red Lantern*), pp. 145–49. Hangzhou: Renmin chubanshe, 1970.

Jimao xin (The urgent letter). Dir. Shi Hui. Shanghai: Shanghai Film Studio, 1954.

Jin Shengtan, ed. *Shuihuzhuan* (The Water Margin). Taipei: Sanmin, 1993. Facsimile of the Guanhuatang edition, preface dated 1641.

Jones, Andrew F. "Translator's Postscript." In Yu Hua, *The Past and the Punishments.* Trans. Andrew F. Jones, pp. 263–73. Honolulu: University of Hawai'i Press, 1996.

————. The Violence of the Text: Reading Yu Hua and Shi Zhicun." *Positions* 2, no. 3 (Winter 1994): 570–602.

Judge, Joan. "Public Opinion and the New Politics of Contestation in the Late Qing." *Modern China* 20, no. 1 (Jan. 1994): 64–91.

Kafka, Franz. *The Complete Stories.* Ed. Nahum N. Glatzer. New York: Schocken Books, 1971.

Kant, Immanuel. *The Critique of Judgment.* Trans. James Creed Meredith. Oxford: Clarendon Press, 1991.

————. *On History.* Ed. Lewis White Beck. Trans. Lewis White Beck, Robert E. Anchor, and Emil L. Fackenheim. New York: Macmillan, 1963.

Kao, Karl S. Y. "*Bao* and *Baoying*: Narrative Causality and External Motivations in Chinese Fiction." *CLEAR* 11 (Dec. 1989): 115–38.

Kelly, Michael, ed. *Critique and Power: Recasting the Foucault/Habermas Debate.* Cambridge, Mass.: MIT Press, 1994.

Kinkley, Jeffrey C. *Chinese Justice, the Fiction: Law and Literature in Modern China.* Stanford: Stanford University Press, 2000.

"Kongbupian daoyan Ma-Xu Weibang shi xinli biantaizhe" (The horror film director Ma-Xu Weibang is a psychological pervert). *Dianying yule tuhua zhoukan* (also titled *Screen Weekly*) 91 (July 31, 1940).

Krystal, Henry. "Trauma and Aging: A Thirty-Year Follow-up." In *Trauma: Explorations in Memory*, ed. Cathy Caruth, pp. 76–99. Baltimore: Johns Hopkins University Press, 1995.

Ku'nao ren de xiao (The laughter of the man in distress, known as *Bitter Laughter*). Dir. Yang Yanjin and Deng Yimin. Shanghai: Shanghai Film Studio, 1979.

Kundera, Milan. *Testaments Betrayed*. Trans. Linda Asher. New York: HarperCollins Publishers, 1995.

Kuriyagawa Hakuson. *Kumon no shōchō* (Symptoms of anxiety). In *Kuriyagawa Hakuson zenshū* (Complete works of Kuriyagawa Hakuson). Tokyo: Kaizōsha, 1929.

Lacan, Jacques. *Écrits: A Selection*. Trans. Alan Sheridan. New York: Norton, 1977.

Larson, Wendy. *Literary Authority and the Modern Chinese Writer: Ambivalence and Autobiography*. Durham, N.C.: Duke University Press, 1991.

————. "Literary Modernism and Nationalism in Post-Mao China." In *Inside Out: Modernism and Postmodernism in Chinese Literature*, ed. Wendy Larson and Wedell-Wedellsborg, pp. 173–97. Aarhus, Denmark: Aarhus University Press, 1993.

————. "Writing and the Writer: Liu Daren." In *Proceedings of the Summer 1986 Intensive Workshop in Chinese and Russian*, ed. Martha Sherwood-Pike and Wendy Larson, pp. 59–63. Department of Russian, University of Oregon. Eugene: University of Oregon Books, 1987.

Laughlin, Charles A. *Chinese Reportage: The Aesthetics of Historical Experience*. Durham, N.C.: Duke University Press, 2002.

Lawrence, Susan V. "Voice of the Gulag." *Far Eastern Economic Review*, July 18, 2002.

Lee, Leo Ou-fan. "The Politics of Technique: Perspectives of Literary Dissidence on Contemporary Chinese Fiction." In *After Mao: Chinese Literature and Society 1978–1981*, ed. Jeffrey C. Kinkley, pp. 159–90. Cambridge, Mass.: Harvard University Press, 1985.

————. *Shanghai Modern: The Flowering of a New Urban Culture in China, 1930–1945*. Cambridge, Mass.: Harvard University Press, 1999.

————. *Voices from the Iron House: A Study of Lu Xun*. Bloomington: Indiana University Press, 1987.

Lenin v 1918 godu (Lenin in 1918). Dir. Mikhail Romm. Moscow: Mosfilm, 1939.

Leroux, Gaston. *The Phantom of the Opera*. Trans. Alexander Teixeira de Mattos. New York: Warner, 1986.

Lévinas, Emanuel. *Entre nous: On Thinking-of-the-Other*. Trans. Michael B. Smith and Barbara Harshav. New York: Columbia University Press, 1998.

Leyda, Jay. *Dianying: An Account of Films and the Film Audience in China*. Cambridge, Mass.: MIT Press, 1972.

Li Bihua. *Pan Jinlian zhi qianshi jinsheng* (Past and present incarnations of Pan Jinlian). Hong Kong: Tiandi, 1989.

Li Dazhao. *Li Dazhao xuanji* (Selected works of Li Dazhao). Beijing: Renmin chubanshe, 1959.

Li Erwei. *Hanzi Jiang Wen* (Tough guy Jiang Wen). Shenyang: Chunfeng wenyi chubanshe, 1998.

Li Helin, ed. *Lu Xun nianpu* (Lu Xun chronicles). Beijing: Xinhua, 1981.

Li Oufan [Leo Ou-fan Lee]. "Mantan Zhongguo xiandai wenxue zhong de tuifei" (On decadence in modern Chinese literature). In *Xiandai xing de zhuiqiu—Li*

Oufan wen hua ping lun jing xuan ji (In search of modernity: Li Oufan's essays in cultural criticism), pp. 191–225. Taipei: Maitian, 1996.

Li Tuo. "Haiwai Zhongguo zuojia taolun hui jiyao" (Talk at the seminar of overseas Chinese writers). *Jintian* 1990, no. 2: 96–99.

———. "Xuebeng hechu?" (Where is the avalanche?). Reprinted in Yu Hua, *Shiba sui chumen yuanxing* (At age eighteen, leave home and travel far), pp. 5–14. Taipei: Yuanliu, 1990.

Liehuo zhong yongsheng (Living forever in the blazing fire, also known as *Red crag*). Dir. Shui Hua. Beijing: Beijing Film Studio, 1965.

Lin Jinlan. *Yueye youyu.* Zhengzhou: Zhongyuan nongmin chubanshe, 1994.

Lin Yin and Gao Ming, eds. *Zhongwen dacidian* (Encyclopaedic dictionary of the Chinese language). Taipei: Zhongguo wenhua daxue, 1990.

Ling Dake and Xia Jianqing. *Hongdeng ji (huju)—Aihua hujutuan gaibian* (The red lantern—Shanghai opera: Modified by the Patriotic Shanghai Opera Troupe). Shanghai: Shanghai wenhua chubanshe, 1965.

Link, Perry. *The Uses of Literature: Life in the Socialist Chinese Literary System.* Princeton: Princeton University Press, 2000.

"Lishi liang dami, aiqing yi gushi—tan *Yongbu xiaoshi de dianbo*" (Two historical riddles, one love story: On *The Undying Transmission*). Newspaper clipping in the Beijing Film Archives, dated Jan. 21, 1978.

Liu Binyan. *People or Monsters? and Other Stories and Reportage from China After Mao.* Trans. James V. Feinerman and Perry Link. Bloomington: Indiana University Press, 1983.

———. "Renxie bushi yanzhi" (Human blood isn't rouge). In *Renxie bushi yanzhi*, pp. 218–255. Hong Kong: Guotai chubanshe, n.d.

Liu Daren. *Dujuan ti xue* (Azaleas cry out blood). Taipei: Yuanjing chubanshe, 1984.

———. Personal interview, May 29, 1997.

Liu Jingzhi. *Yuanren* Shuihu *zaju yanjiu* (Studies in Yuan drama on the *Water Margin* theme). Hong Kong: Sanlian, 1990.

Liu Kang. "Popular Culture and the Culture of the Masses in Contemporary China." *Boundary 2*, 24, no. 3 (Fall 1997): 99–122.

———. "The Short-Lived Avant-Garde: The Transformation of Yu Hua." *Modern Language Quarterly* 63, no. 1 (Mar. 2002): 89–117.

Liu, Lydia. *Translingual Practice: Literature, National Culture, and Translated Modernity—China, 1900–1937.* Stanford: Stanford University Press, 1995.

Liu Suola. "Zuihou yizhi zhizhu" (The last spider). In *Ni bie wuxuanze* (Don't tell me you can't do anything about it), pp. 119–40. Taipei: Xindi wenxue chubanshe, 1988.

Liu Zaifu. *Lu Xun meixue sixiang lungao* (Theses on the aesthetic thought of Lu Xun). Beijing: Zhongguo shehui kexue chubanshe, 1981.

Louie, Kam. "Love Stories: The Meaning of Love and Marriage in China, 1978–1981." In Kam Louie. *Between Fact and Fiction: Essays on Post-Mao Chinese Literature and Society*, pp. 49–75. Sydney: Wild Peony, 1989.

Lu Mei. "Quan shehui dou lai 'xiang yi xiang'—ping huaju *Tianshan shenchu*" (Let the entire society "think it over": An evaluation of the play *Deep in Tianshan*). *Wenyi bao* 390 (Sept. 22, 1981): 35–37.

Lu, Tonglin. *Rose and Lotus: Narrative of Desire in France and China*. Albany: State University of New York Press, 1991.

Lu Xun. *Lu Xun zuopin quanji* (The complete works of Lu Xun). Taipei: Fengyun shidai, 1992.

Lü Zhenghui. "Lishi de mengyan—shilun Chen Yingzhen de zhengzhi xiaoshuo" (The nightmare of history: On Chen Yingzhen's political fiction). In *Chen Yingzhen zuopin ji* (Collected works of Chen Yingzhen), 15: 214–224. Taipei: Renjian, 1988.

Luguang xiyuan (Capitol movie theater). Movie program for *Song at Midnight*. Chengdu, 1956.

Luo Jialun. "Jindai xiyang sixiang ziyou de jinhua" (The progress of freedom of thought in the modern West). *Xin chao* 2, no. 2 (Dec. 1919): 231–39.

Lushan lian (Love in Lushan). Dir. Huang Zumo. Shanghai: Shanghai Film Studio, 1980.

Lyotard, Jean-François. *The Lyotard Reader*. Ed. Andrew Benjamin. New York: B. Blackwell, 1989.

Ma Debo. "Zhongguo dianying xin chaoliu—jin shinian (1976–1986) woguo" (New trends in Chinese cinema: Our country in the recent ten years—1976–1986). In *Dianying yanjiu* (Film research), ed. Zhongguo dianyingjia xiehui yishu yanjiubu (Chinese Filmmaker Association Art Research Department), pp. 127–82. Beijing: Zhongguo dianying chubanshe, 1987.

Ma Ning. "Notes on the New Filmmakers." In *Chinese Film: The State of the Art in the People's Republic*, ed. George Semsel, pp. 63–73. New York: Praeger, 1987.

Mao Zedong. *Mao Zedong zhuzuo xuandu* (Selected readings in the works of Mao Zedong). Beijing: Renmin chubanshe, 1986.

———. *Selected Works*. Beijing: Peking Foreign Languages Press, 1967.

Marx, Karl, and Frederick Engels. *Karl Marx and Frederick Engels: Collected Works*. Trans. Richard Dixon et al. New York: International Publishers, 1975–97.

McDougall, Bonnie S., and Kam Louie. *The Literature of China in the Twentieth Century*. New York: Columbia University Press, 1997.

McKnight, Brian E. *Law and Order in Sung China*. Cambridge University Press, 1992.

Melvin, Sheila, and Jingdong Cai. "Nostalgia for the Fruits of Chaos in Chinese Model Operas." *New York Times*. Oct. 29, 2000.

Men Lusi. "Yeban gesheng" (Song at midnight). *Dianying huabao*, Sept. 1941, p. 45.

Mowry, Hua-yuan Li. Yang-pan hsi—*New Theater in China*. Berkeley: Center for Chinese Studies, University of California, 1973.

Muller, John P., and William J. Richardson, eds. *The Purloined Poe: Lacan, Derrida, and Psychoanalytic Reading*. Baltimore: Johns Hopkins University Press, 1988.

Nan Shao. "Yizhao wuchan jieji xianfengdui de mianmao gaizao shijie—zan geming yangban xi *Hongdeng ji* zhong Li Yuhe yingxiong xingxiang de suzao" (Changing the world according to the mien of the proletarian avant-garde: In praise of forming the heroic image of Li Yuhe in the revolutionary model play *The Red*

Lantern). Reprinted in *Geming de Hongdeng—zan geming xiandai jingju* Hongdeng ji (The red lantern of the revolution: In praise of the revolutionary modern
Beijing opera *The Red Lantern*), pp. 49–55. Hangzhou: Renmin chubanshe, 1970.

Neale, Stephen. *Cinema and Technology: Image, Sound, Colour*. Bloomington: Indiana University Press, 1985.

Nihon koten bungaku daijiten (Encyclopedia of classical Japanese literature). Tokyo:
Iwanami shoten, 1983.

Niu Jing. "Geming de hongdeng, canlan de guanghui—zan geming xiandai jingju
hongdeng ji de jingyi qiujing" (The red lantern of revolution, the shining brilliance: In praise of striving for greater excellence in the revolutionary modern
Beijing opera *The Red Lantern*). Reprinted in *Geming de Hongdeng—zan geming
xiandai jingju* Hongdeng ji (The red lantern of the revolution: In praise of the
revolutionary modern Beijing opera *The Red Lantern*), pp. 103–9. Hangzhou:
Renmin chubanshe, 1970.

The Old Dark House. Dir. James Whale. Hollywood: Universal Pictures, 1932.

Ouyang Yuqian. *Ouyang Yuqian quanji* (Complete works of Ouyang Yuqian).
Shanghai: Shanghai wenyi chubanshe, 1990.

Paulson, Ronald. *Representations of Revolution, 1789–1820*. New Haven: Yale University Press, 1983.

The Phantom of the Opera. Dir. Rupert Julian. Hollywood: Universal Pictures, 1925.

Pickowicz, Paul. "The 'May Fourth' Tradition of Chinese Cinema." In *From May
Fourth to June Fourth*, ed. David Der-wei Wang and Ellen Widmer, pp. 295–326.
Cambridge, Mass.: Harvard University Press, 1993.

————. "Popular Cinema and Political Thought in Post-Mao China: Reflections
on Official Pronouncements, Film, and the Film Audience." In *Unofficial China:
Popular Culture and Thought in the People's Republic*, ed. Perry Link, Richard
Madsen, and Paul G. Pickowicz, pp. 37–53. Boulder, Colo.: Westview Press, 1989.

Plato. *Republic*. Trans. G. M. A. Grube. Indianapolis: Hackett, 1974.

Poe, Edgar Allan. "The Masque of the Red Death." In *The Complete Tales and Poems
of Edgar Allan Poe*, pp. 269–73. New York: Modern Library, 1938.

Průšek, Jaroslav. *The Lyrical and the Epic: Studies of Modern Chinese Literature*.
Bloomington: Indiana University Press, 1980.

Pu Songling. *Liaozhai zhiyi* (Liaozhai's records of the strange). Taipei: Hanjing, 1984.

Pusey, James Reeve. *Lu Xun and Evolution*. Albany: State University of New York
Press, 1998.

Qian Liqun. *Zoujin dangdai de Lu Xun* (Lu Xun approaching the contemporary).
Beijing: Beijing daxue chubanshe, 1999.

Qingchun wuhui (No regrets about youth). Dir. Zhou Xiaowen. Xi'an: Xi'an Film
Studio, 1992.

Qingchun zhi ge (Song of youth). Dir. Cui Wei and Chen Huaiai. Beijing: Beijing
Film Studio, 1959.

Qionglou hen (Rancor at a luxuriant mansion, also known as *The Haunted House* or
A Maid's Bitter Story). Dir. Ma-Xu Weibang. Hong Kong: Great Wall Film Co.,
1949.

Qiu Haitang. Dir. Ma-Xu Weibang. Shanghai: United China Film Co. (Huaying), 1943.

Rankin, Mary Backus. "The Origins of a Chinese Public Sphere: Local Elites and Community Affairs in the Late-Imperial Period." *Études chinoises* 9, no. 2 (Fall 1990): 13–60.

Ren Dawen. "Wuchan jieji yingxiong de guanghui dianxing—zan *Hongdeng ji* zhong Li Yuhe xingxiang de suzao" (The brilliant paragon of a hero of the proletarian class: In praise of forming the image of Li Yuhe in *The Red Lantern*). Reprinted in *Geming de Hongdeng—zan geming xiandai jingju* Hongdeng ji (The red lantern of the revolution: In praise of the revolutionary modern Beijing opera *The Red Lantern*), pp. 39–48. Hangzhou: Renmin chubanshe, 1970.

Rolston, David L. *Traditional Chinese Fiction and Fiction Commentary: Reading and Writing Between the Lines*. Stanford: Stanford University Press, 1997.

Rowe, William T. "The Public Sphere in Modern China," *Modern China* 16, no. 3 (July 1990): 309–29.

Schopenhauer, Arthur. *The World as Will and Representation*. Trans. E. F. J. Payne. 2 vols. New York: Dover, 1969.

Semsel, George S., Xia Hong, and Hou Jianping, eds. *Chinese Film Theory—A Guide to the New Era*. New York: Praeger, 1990.

Shelley, Mary. *Frankenstein, or the Modern Prometheus*. 1818. London: Penguin Books, 1992.

Shen Rengfu, ed. *Lu Xun zhu yi xinian mulu* (Index of writings and translations of Lu Xun, in order of year of publication). Shanghai: Shanghai wenyi chubanshe, 1981.

Shi Nai'an and Luo Guanzhong (attributed). *Shuihu quanzhuan* (The complete Water Margin). Taipei: Wannianqing shudian, 1971.

Shidai zhi feng (*L'Air du temps*). Dir. He Fan. Taiwan Motion Pictures Corp., 1990.

Shizi jietou (Crossroads). Dir. Shen Xiling. Shanghai: Mingxing Film Co., 1937.

Shu Xiaoming. *Zhongguo dianying yishu shi jiaocheng* (Lectures on the history of Chinese film art). Beijing: Zhongguo dianying chubanshe, 1996.

Skal, David J. *The Monster Show: A Cultural History of Horror*. New York: Norton, 1993.

Songhuajiang shang (Along the Sungari river). Dir. Jin Shan. Changchun: Changchun Film Studio, 1947.

Sontag, Susan. *On Photography*. New York: Farrar, Straus & Giroux, 1977.

Spence, Jonathan D. *The Gate of Heavenly Peace: The Chinese and Their Revolution, 1895–1980*. New York: Penguin Books, 1986.

Standage, Tom. *The Turk: The Life and Times of the Famous Eighteenth-Century Chess-Playing Machine*. New York: Walker, 2002.

State of Israel. Ministry of Justice. *The Trial of Adolf Eichmann: Record of Proceedings in the District Court of Jerusalem*. Jerusalem: Keter, 1993.

Sterrenburg, Lee. "Mary Shelley's Monster: Politics and Psyche in Frankenstein." In *The Endurance of* Frankenstein, ed. George Levine and U. C. Knoepflmacher, pp. 143–71. Berkeley: University of California Press, 1979.

Su Xiaokang and Wang Luxiang. *Heshang* (River elegy). Taipei: Jinfeng chubanshe, 1988.

Sun Daolin. "Dui dang de gaodu zhongcheng he wangwo—banyan *Yongbu xiaoshi de dianbo* zhong Li Xia de tihui" (Preeminent loyalty to the Party and selflessness: My experience of playing Li Xia in *The Undying Transmission*). *Dazhong dianying* 1958, no. 19.

Tang, Xiaobing. *Chinese Modern: The Heroic and the Quotidian*. Durham, N.C.: Duke University Press, 2000.

Tang, Xiaobing, and Kang Liu, eds. *Politics, Ideology, and Literary Discourse in Modern China: Theorectical Interventions and Cultural Critique*. Durham, N.C.: Duke University Press, 1993.

Tanner, Tony. *Adultery and the Novel: Contract and Transgression*. Baltimore: Johns Hopkins University Press, 1979.

Teo, Stephen. *Hong Kong Cinema: The Extra Dimensions*. London: British Film Institute, 1997.

Thurston, Anne F. *Enemies of the People*. New York: Knopf, 1987.

Ti Xiu. "Zhongwai mingxing xiangxiang lu" (On the resemblance between Chinese and foreign film stars). *Yingxi shenghuo* 1, no. 5 (Jan. 3, 1931).

Tian Han. "Ta wei Zhongguo xiju yundong fendou le yisheng" (He struggled for the Chinese drama movement throughout his life). In *Ouyang Yuqian yanjiu ziliao* (Research material on Ouyang Yuqian), ed. Su Guanxin, pp. 130–50. Beijing: Zhongguo xichu, 1989.

Tianming (Daybreak). Dir. Sun Yu. Shanghai: Lianhua Film Co., 1932.

Tianyunshan chuanqi (The legend of Tianyunshan). Dir. Xie Jin. Shanghai: Shanghai Film Studio, 1980.

Tianyunshan chuanqi—*cong xiaoshuo dao dianying* (*The Legend of Tianyunshan*: From novel to film). Beijing: Zhongguo dianying chubanshe, 1983.

Tiedao youjidui (Railroad guerrilla). Dir. Zhao Ming. Shanghai: Shanghai Film Studio, 1956.

Tong Ping. "Zhanxin de wuchan jieji de yishu dianxing—zan geming xiandai jingju *Hongdeng ji* zhong Li Yuhe wutai yingxiong xingxiang de suzao" (A fresh artistic paragon of the proletarian class: In praise of forming on stage the heroic image of Li Yuhe in the revolutionary modern Beijing opera *The Red Lantern*). Reprinted in *Geming de Hongdeng—zan geming xiandai jingju* Hongdeng ji (The red lantern of the revolution: In praise of the revolutionary modern Beijing opera *The Red Lantern*), pp. 120–26. Hangzhou: Renmin chubanshe, 1970.

Tong Yun. "Quan shijie wuchanzhe lianhe qilai—zan geming yangban xi *hongdeng ji* zhong Li Yuhe yijia de shenhou jieji qingyi" (Unite, proletarians of the entire world: In praise of the deep class camaraderie in Li Yuhe's family, in the revolutionary model play *The Red Lantern*). Reprinted in *Jingtian dongdi de weida geming zhuangju—zan geming yangban xi* (The earth-shattering great revolutionary achievement: In praise of the revolutionary model plays), pp. 97–105. Hong Kong: Xianggang sanlian shudian, 1970.

Unrequited Love. Taipei: Institute of Current China Studies, 1981.

Walsh, Harry. "A Buddhistic Leitmotif in *Anna Karenina*." *Canadian-American Slavic Studies* 11, no. 4 (Winter 1977): 561–67.

Wang, Ban. *The Sublime Figure of History: Aesthetics and Politics in Twentieth-Century China*. Stanford: Stanford University Press, 1997.

Wang Chenwu. *Wang Chenwu dianying pinglun xuanji* (Collected film criticism of Wang Chenwu). Beijing: Zhongguo dianying chubanshe, 1994.

Wang, David Der-wei. *Fin-de-Siècle Splendor: Repressed Modernities of Late Qing Fiction, 1949–1911*. Stanford: Stanford University Press, 1997.

———. "Lu Xun, Shen Congwen and Decapitation." In *Politics, Ideology, and Literary Discourse in Modern China: Theoretical Interventions and Cultural Critique*, ed. Xiaobing Tang and Kang Liu, pp. 174–87. Durham, N.C.: Duke University Press, 1993.

Wang Dewei. *Yuedu dangdai xiaoshuo* (Reading contemporary novels). Taipei: Yuanliu, 1991.

———. *Zhongsheng xuanhua: sanshi yu bashi niandai de Zhongguo xiaoshuo* (Polyphonous clamor: Chinese fiction in the 1930s and 1980s). Taipei: Yuanliu, 1988.

Wang Guowei. *Honglou meng pinglun* (Critique of *The Dream of the Red Chamber*). Taipei: Tianhua, 1979.

Wang Hui. *Fankang juewang—Lu Xun de jingshen jiegou yu* Nahan Panghuang *yanjiu* (Resisting despair: Lu Xun's mental makeup and studies in *Outcry and Wandering*). Shanghai: Shanghai renmin chubanshe, 1991.

———. *Wudi panghuang—wusi ji qi huisheng* (No place for wandering: May Fourth and its echoes). Shangyu: Zhejiang wenxue chubanshe, 1994.

Wang, Jing. *High Culture Fever: Politics, Aesthetics, and Ideology in Deng's China*. Berkeley: University of California Press, 1996.

Wang, Shaoguang. *Failure of Charisma: The Cultural Revolution in Wuhan*. Hong Kong: Oxford University Press, 1995.

———. "Guanyu 'shimin shehui' de jidian sikao" (Some reflections on "civil society"). *Ershiyi shiji* 6 (1991): 102–14.

Wang Shuo. *Dongwu xiongmeng* (Wild beasts). In Jiang Wen et al., *Dansheng* (Birth), pp. 430–513. Beijing: Huayi chubanshe, 1997.

———. "*Yangguang canlan de rizi zhuiyi*" (Recollections of *In the Heat of the Sun*). In Jiang Wen et al., *Dansheng* (Birth), pp. 126–129. Beijing: Huayi chubanshe, 1997.

Wang Xiaoming. "Shuangjia mache de qingfu—Lu Xun de xiaoshuo chuangzuo" (The carriage capsizes: On Lu Xun's fictional work). In Wang Xiaoming, *Zixuanji* (Collection by the author), pp. 1–36. Guilin: Guangxi shifan daxue chubanshe, 1997.

Wang Yao. *Zhongguo xin wenxue shigao: zengding ben* (The history of China's new literature: Revised edition). Hong Kong: Bowen shuju, 1972.

Weber, Max. *The Protestant Ethic and the Spirit of Capitalism*. Trans. Talcott Parsons. New York: Charles Scribner's Sons, 1958.

Wei Minglun, ed. *Kuyin chengxi* (Drama wrought in cries of pain). Shanghai: Shanghai wenyi chubanshe, 1989.

————. *Pan Jinlian—Yige nüren de chenlun shi* (Pan Jinlian: History of a woman's downfall). Harbin: Beifang wenyi chubanshe, 1987.

Wei Shaochang. *Wu Jianren yanjiu ziliao* (Research materials on Wu Jianren). Shanghai: Shanghai guji chubanshe, 1980.

White, Hayden. *The Content of the Form: Narrative Discourse and Historical Representation*. Baltimore: Johns Hopkins University Press, 1990.

Williams, Linda. "When the Woman Looks." In *Film Theory and Criticism: Introductory Readings*, ed. Gerald Mast, Marshall Cohen, and Leo Braudy, pp. 561–77. 4th ed. New York: Oxford University Press, 1992.

Wu Hao. *Shidai de chuangshang—Ma-Xu Weibang* (The scars of the times—Ma-Xu Weibang). In *The Thirteenth Hong Kong International Film Festival: Phantoms of the Hong Kong Cinema*, pp. 68–74. Hong Kong: Urban Council, 1989.

Wu Jianren. *Xin Shitou ji* (New Story of the Stone). Zhengzhou: Zhongzhou guji chubanshe, 1986.

Wu Yigong. "Fengyu tongzhou, lingxi xiangtong—*Bashan yeyu* daoyan zhaji" (Weathering the storm in the same boat, achieving a meeting of the minds: Notes by the director of *Night Rain in Bashan*). Revised version reprinted in *Bashan yeyu: cong juben dao yingpian* (*Night Rain in Bashan*: From script to film), pp. 206–23. Beijing: Zhongguo dianying chubanshe, 1982.

Wu Yu. "Chiren yu lijiao" (Cannibalism and Confucianism). *Xin Qingnian* 6 (Nov. 1, 1919): 578–80.

Wuxing de zhanxian (The invisible battlefront). Dir. Yi Ming. Changchun: Changchun Film Studio, 1949.

Xi Shanshan et al., eds. *Dangdai Zhongguo dianying* (Contemporary Chinese cinema). Beijing: Zhongguo shehui kexue chubanshe, 1989.

Xiao jie (The alley). Dir. Yang Yanjin. Shanghai: Shanghai Film Studio, 1981.

Xiaohua (Little flower). Dir. Zhang Zheng. Beijing: Beijing Film Studio, 1979.

Xin nüxing (New woman). Dir. Cai Chusheng. Shanghai: Lianhua Film Co., 1934.

Xin yeban gesheng (English title *The Phantom Lover*). Dir. Ronny Yu. Hong Kong: Mandarin Films Co., 1995.

Xinhua huabao (Xinhua illustrated magazine) 2, no. 2 (Mar. 1937).

Xinke xiuxiang piping Jin Ping Mei—huijiao ben (A new illustrated and annotated *Jin Ping Mei*, variorum edition). Taipei: Xiaoyuan, 1990.

Xu Guangping. *Xinwei de ji'nian* (Comforting memories). Beijing: Renmin wenxue chubanshe, 1981.

Xu Zidong. *Dangdai xiaoshuo yu jiti jiyi—xushu wenge* (Contemporary fiction and collective memory: Narrating the Cultural Revolution). Taipei: Maitian chuban, 2000.

Xue Suizhi. *Lu Xun zawen cidian* (Lexicon of Lu Xun's essays). Jinan: Shandong jiaoyu, 1995.

Yan Jiayan. "'Kuangren riji' de sixiang he yishu" (Thought and art in "Diary of a Madman"). In *Liushi nian lai Lu Xun yanjiu lunwen xuan* (Collection of essays in Lu Xun studies from the past sixty years), ed. Li Zhongying and Zhang Mengyang, pp. 444–59. Beijing: Zhongguo shehui kexue chubanshe, 1982.

Yang Fan. "*Wuxing de zhanxian* gaosu women xie shenme?" (What does *The Invisible Battlefront* tell us?). *Dazhong dianying* 1950, no. 1.

Yang, Lan. *Chinese Fiction of the Cultural Revolution*. Hong Kong: Hong Kong University Press, 1998.

Yang Nianqun. "Jindai Zhongguo yanjiuzhong de 'shimin shehui'—fangfa ji xiandu" ("Civil society" in research on modern China—Methods and limitations). *Ershiyi shiji* 32 (1995): 29–38.

Yang, Xiaobin. "Whence and Whither the Postmodern/Post-Mao-Deng: Historical Subjectivity and Literary Subjectivity in Modern China." In *Postmodernism and China*, ed. Arif Dirlik and Xudong Zhang, pp. 379–98. Durham, N.C.: Duke University Press, 2000.

Yang Yanjin and Wu Tianren. "*Xiao jie* daoyan chanshu" (Clarifications from the directors of *The Alley*). *Dianying wenhua* 1981, no. 4: 140–47.

Yang Ze. "Bianyuan de dikang—shilun Lu Xun de xiandaixing yu foudingxing" (Resistance from the margins: On Lu Xun's modernity and its negation). Unpublished paper presented at the International Conference on Chinese Modern Literature, Academica Sinica, Taipei, Dec. 2–21, 1993.

Yangguang canlan de rizi (English title *In the Heat of the Sun*). Dir. Jiang Wen. China Film Co-production Corp (PRC) and Dragon Films (Hong Kong), 1995.

Yasui qian (New year's coin). Dir. Zhang Shichuan. Shanghai: Mingxing Film Co., 1937.

Ye Changhai. *Dangdai xiju qishi lu* (The birth of modern drama). Taipei: Luotuo chubanshe, 1991.

Ye Di. "Yeban gesheng" (Song at midnight). *Dawanbao*, Feb. 22, 1937.

Ye Nan. "Xi chuang jian zhu hua Bashan" (Clipping the candle at the western window, talking of Bashan). Reprinted in Bashan yeyu—*cong juben dao yingpian* (*Night Rain in Bashan*: From script to film), pp. 165–78. Beijing: Zhongguo dianying chubanshe, 1982.

Ye Shengtao. *Ye Shengtao wenji* (Collected works of Ye Shengtao). Beijing: Renmin wenyi chubanshe, 1958.

Yeban gesheng (Song at midnight). Dir. Ma-Xu Weibang. Shanghai: Xinhua Film Co., 1937.

"*Yeban gesheng* guanggao niangcheng renming" (Advertisement for Song at Midnight slowly takes a life). *Diansheng zhoukan* (Movie tone weekly) 6, no. 11 (Mar. 19, 1937): 521.

Yeban gesheng xuji (Song at midnight, part II). Dir. Ma-Xu Weibang. Shanghai: United Chinese Film Co., 1941.

Yin Bin and Xie Yingping. "Gongchan zhuyi de yingxiong shibian—zan geming xiandai jingju *Hongdeng ji* de juben chuangzuo" (The heroic poem of communism: In praise of the script for the revolutionary modern Beijing opera *The Red Lantern*). Reprinted in *Geming de Hongdeng—zan geming xiandai jingju Hongdeng ji* (The red lantern of the revolution: In praise of the revolutionary modern Beijing opera *The Red Lantern*), pp. 110–19. Hangzhou: Renmin chubanshe, 1970.

Yingxi shenghuo (Cinema life) 1, no. 1 (Dec. 26, 1930).

Yingxi shenghuo (Cinema life) 1, no. 4 (Jan. 16, 1931).

Yingxiong ernü (Heroic sons and daughters). Dir. Wu Zhaodi. Changchun: Changchun Film Studio, 1964.

Yong bu xiaoshi de dianbo (The undying transmission). Dir. Wang Ping. Beijing: August First Film Studio, 1958.

You hua haohao shuo (English title *Keep Cool*). Dir. Zhang Yimou. Nanning: Guangxi Film Studio, 1994.

Yu Hua. *The Past and the Punishments*. Trans. Andrew F. Jones. Honolulu: University of Hawai'i Press, 1996.

————. Personal interview, Aug. 1, 1995.

————. *Shiba sui chumen yuanxing* (At age eighteen, leave home and travel far). Taipei: Yuanliu, 1990.

————. *Wennuan de lücheng—yingxiang wo de shibu duanpian xiaoshuo* (A warm journey: Ten short stories that influenced me). Beijing: Xinshijie chubanshe, 1999.

————. *Xiaji taifeng* (Summer typhoon). Taipei: Yuanliu, 1993.

————. "Xuwei de zuopin" (Hypocritical writings). Reprinted in *Shishi ru yan* (A world of clouds), pp. 5–21. Taipei: Yuanliu, 1991.

Yu Qian. "Suzao shidai de linghun—lun yinmu shang de xinli miaoxie" (Creating the spirit of the time: On psychological description on the silver scree). *Dianying wenhua* 4 (1981): 28–40.

Yu Shi et al., eds. *Changyong diangu cidian* (Lexicon of common literary allusions). Shanghai: Shanghai cishu chubanshe, 1985.

Yue, Gang. *The Mouth That Begs: Hunger, Cannibalism, and the Politics of Eating in Modern China*. Durham, N.C.: Duke University Press, 1999.

Zai Chuangzuo: dianying gaibian wenti taolun ji (To recreate: A collection on problems in film adaptation). Beijing: Zhongguo dianying chubanshe, 1992.

Zammito, John H. *The Genesis of Kant's Critique of Judgment*. Chicago: University of Chicago Press, 1992.

Zeitlin, Judith T. *Historian of the Strange: Pu Songling and the Chinese Classical Tale*. Stanford: Stanford University Press, 1993.

"Zhanduan Liu Shaoqi shenxiang waimao bumen de heishou!" (Chop off the evil hands sent by Liu Shaoqi to the department of foreign commerce!). *Jingji pipan*, May 29, 1967.

Zhang Junxiang. "*Xiao jie* xin zai nali?" (Where is the new in *The Alley*?). Reprinted in *Yingshi suoyi* (Trivial opinions on film matters), pp. 142–45. Beijing: Zhongguo dianying chubanshe, 1985.

Zhang Mingtang. "Yong jingtou jiexie renwu de neixing shijie—*Tianyunshan chuanqi* de daoyan yishu tese" (Revealing characters' inner world of the mind through the lens: The distinct art of directing in *Legend of Tianyunshan*). Reprinted in *Dangdai Zhongguo dianying pinglun xuan* (An anthology of contemporary Chinese film criticism), ed. Wang Baoshi and Wang Wenhe, 2: 101–63. Beijing: Zhongguo guangbo dianshi chubanshe, 1987.

Zhang Nuanxin and Li Tuo. "The Modernization of Film Language." Trans. Hou

Jianping. In *Chinese Film Theory—A Guide to the New Era*, ed. George S. Semsel, Xia Hong, and Hou Jianping, pp. 10–20. New York: Praeger, 1990.

Zhang Xianliang. *Fannao jiushi zhihui* (Worry is wisdom). Hong Kong: Mingchuang, 1992.

————. *Grass Soup*. Trans. Martha Avery. Boston: D. R. Godine, 1995.

————. "Lao zhaopian" (An old photograph). In *Qingchun qi*, pp. 118–29. Beijing: Jingji ribao chubanshe and Shanxi lüyou chubanshe, 1999.

————. *Nanren de yiban shi nüren* (Half of man is woman). Taipei: Yuanjing, 1988.

————. *Wo de putishu* (My bodhi tree). Beijing: Zuojia chubanshe, 1994.

————. *Xie xiaoshou de bianzhengfa* (The dialectics of writing fiction). Shanghai: Shanghai wenyi chubanshe, 1987.

Zhang, Xudong. *Chinese Modernism in the Era of Reforms: Cultural Fever, Avant-Garde Fiction, and the New Chinese Cinema*. Durham, N.C.: Duke University Press, 1997.

Zhang, Yingjin, ed. *Cinema and Urban Culture in Shanghai, 1922–1943*. Stanford: Stanford University Press, 1999.

Zhang Zhongnan. "Shilun *Xiao jie* de yishu tansuo" (On the artistic quest in *The Alley*). Reprinted in *Dangdai Zhongguo dianying pinglun xuan* (An anthology of contemporary Chinese film criticism), ed. Wang Baoshi and Wang Wenhe, 2: 163–74. Beijing: Zhongguo guangbo dianshi chubanshe, 1987.

Zhao Shihui. *Yingtan gouchen* (Inquiring the depths of film circles). Zhengzhou: Dajia chubanshe, 1998.

Zhao, Y. H. "Fiction as Subversion." *World Literature Today* 65, no. 3 (Summer 1991): 415–20.

Zheng Yi. *Scarlet Memorial: Tales of Cannibalism in Modern China*. Trans. T. P. Sym. Boulder, Colo.: Westview Press, 1996.

"Zhenshi, qinqie, ganren—xu tan *Yongbu xiaoshi de dianbo*" (Authentic, affectionate, moving: More on *The undying transmission*). Newspaper clipping in the Beijing Film Archives, dated Jan. 21, 1978.

Zhong Shan. "Geming yangban xi suzao le wanmei gaoda de gongnongbing yingxiong xingxiang" (The revolutionary model plays formed a perfect and sublime heroic image of workers, peasants and soldiers). Reprinted in *Jingtian dongdi de weida geming zhuangju—zan geming yangban xi* (The earth-shattering great revolutionary achievement: In praise of the revolutionary model plays), pp. 14–29. Hong Kong: Xianggang sanlian shudian, 1970.

Zhongguo jingjutuan *hongdeng ji* juzu (The drama group of the troupe of the Chinese Bejing opera *The Red Lantern*). "Wei suzao wuchan jieji de yingxiong dianxing er douzheng—suzao Li Yuhe yingxiong xingxiang de tihui" (To struggle for creating a paragon of a proletarian hero—the experience of forming the heroic image of Li Yuhe). Reprinted in *Geming de Hongdeng—zan geming xiandai jingju Hongdeng ji* (The red lantern of the revolution: In praise of the revolutionary modern Beijing opera *The Red Lantern*), pp. 5–18. Hangzhou: Renmin chubanshe, 1970.

Zhongguo shehui kexueyuan wenxue yanjiusuo Lu Xun yanjiu shi (Chinese Academy of Social Sciences, Institute for Literary Studies, Lu Xun Studies Center), ed. *1919–1983 Lu Xun yanjiu xueshu lunzhu ziliao huibian* (Compiled scholarly works and sources on Lu Xun studies, 1919–1983). Beijing: Zhongguo wenlian chubanshe, 1987.

Zhongshan daxue geming weiyuanhui xiezuo zu (The writing group of The Revolutionary Committee at Sun Yat-Sen University). "Zhongguo gongchandangren geming yingxiong zhuyi de zhuangli songge—zan Li Yuhe de geming qijie" (A sublime praise-song for the revolutionary heroism of the people of the Chinese Communist Party: In praise of Li Yuhe's revolutionary rectitude). Reprinted in *Geming de Hongdeng—zan geming xiandai jingju* Hongdeng ji (The red lantern of the revolution: In praise of the revolutionary modern Beijing opera *The Red Lantern*), pp. 65–74. Hangzhou: Renmin chubanshe, 1970.

Zhongwen dacidian (Encyclopaedic dictionary of the Chinese language). Taipei: Zhongguo wenhua daxue, 1990.

Zhou Huiling. "Nü yanyuan, xieshi zhuyi, 'xin nüxing' lunshu—wanqing dao wusi shiqi zhong Zhongguo xiandai juchang zhong de xingbie biaoyan" (Female players, realism, the 'new woman' discourse—Gendered performance on the modern Chinese stage from the late Qing to May Fourth), *Jindai Zhongguo funüshi yanjiu* 4 (Aug. 1998): 87–133.

Zhou Shoujuan. *Huamu congzhong* (Amidst flowers and trees). Jiangsu: Jinling shuhuashe, 1981.

Zhu Boxiong and Chen Ruilin, eds. *Zhongguo xihua wushi nian, 1898–1949* (Fifty years of Western painting in China, 1898–1949). Beijing: Renmin meishu chubanshe, 1989.

Ziyou hou lairen (Where one falls another rises). Dir. Yu Yanfu. Changchun: Changchun Film Studio, 1963.

Žižek, Slavoj. "Grimaces of the Real, or When the Phallus Appears." *October* 58 (Fall 1991): 45–68.

Index

In this index an "f" after a number indicates a separate reference on the next page, and an "ff" indicates separate references on the next two pages. A continuous discussion over two or more pages is indicated by a span of page numbers, e.g., "57–59." *Passim* is used for a cluster of references in close but not consecutive sequence.